Napoleon's Letters
to Josephine

NAPOLEON
FROM AN ENGRAVING BY T. WRIGHT
AFTER AN ORIGINAL DRAWING

Napoleon's Letters to Josephine
Correspondence of War, Politics, Family and Love 1796-1814

Henry Foljambe Hall

LEONAUR

Napoleon's Letters
to Josephine
Correspondence of War, Politics, Family and
Love 1796-1814 by Henry Foljambe Hall

First published under the title
Napoleon's Letters
to Josephine

Leonaur is an imprint
of Oakpast Ltd

Copyright in this form © 2010 Oakpast Ltd

ISBN: 978-0-85706-062-4 (hardcover)
ISBN: 978-0-85706-061-7 (softcover)

http://www.leonaur.com

Publisher's Notes

In the interests of authenticity, the spellings, grammar and place names
used have been retained from the original editions.

The opinions of the authors represent a view of events in which he
was a participant related from his own perspective,
as such the text is relevant as an historical document.

The views expressed in this book are not necessarily
those of the publisher.

Contents

When all the lesser tumults, and lesser men of our age, shall have passed away into the darkness of oblivion, history will still inscribe one mighty era with the majestic name of Napoleon.—Lockhart (in Lang's *Life and Letters of J. G. Lockhart*, 1897, vol. 1. 170).

Preface

I have no apology to offer for the subject of this book, in view of Lord Rosebery's testimony that, until recently, we knew nothing about Napoleon, and even now "prefer to drink at any other source than the original."

"Study of Napoleon's utterances, apart from any attempt to discover the secret of his prodigious exploits, cannot be considered as lost time." It is then absolutely necessary that we should, in the words of an eminent but unsympathetic divine, know something of the "domestic side of the monster," first hand from his own correspondence, confirmed or corrected by contemporaries. There is no master mind that we can less afford to be ignorant of. To know more of the doings of Pericles and Aspasia, of the two Caesars and the Serpent of old Nile, of Mary Stuart and Rizzio, of the Green Faction and the Blue, of Orsini and Colonna, than of the Bonapartes and Beauharnais, is worthy of a student of folklore rather than of history.

Napoleon was not only a King of Kings, he was a King of Words and of Facts, which "are the sons of heaven, while words are the daughters of earth," and whose progeny, the Genii of the Code, still dominates Christendom. [1] In the hurly-burly of the French War, on the chilling morrow of its balance-sheet, in the Janus alliance of the Second Empire, we could not get rid of the nightmare of the Great Shadow. Most modern works on the Napoleonic period (Lord Rosebery's "Last Phase "being a brilliant exception) seem to be (1) too long, (2) too little confined to contemporary sources. The first fault, especially if merely discursive enthusiasm, is excusable, the latter pernicious, for, as Dr. Johnson says of Robertson, "You are sure he does not know the people whom he paints, so you cannot suppose a likeness. Characters should never be given by a historian unless he knew

---

1 See *infra*. Napoleon's Heritage, p. 14., Introduction.

the people whom he describes, *or copies from those who knew him*"

Now, if ever, we must *fix* and *crystallise* the life-work of Napoleon for posterity, for "when an opinion has once become popular, very few are willing to oppose it. Idleness is more willing to credit than inquire . . . and he that writes merely for sale is tempted to court purchasers by flattering the prejudices of the public." [2]

We have accumulated practically all the evidence, and are not yet so remote from the aspirations and springs of action of a century ago as to be out of touch with them. The Vaccination and Education questions are still before us; so is the cure of croup and the composition of electricity. We have special reasons for sympathy with the first failures of Fulton, and can appreciate Napoleon's primitive but effective expedients for modern telegraphy and transport, which were as far in advance of his era as his nephew's ignorance of railway warfare in 1870 was behind it. We must admire The Man [3] who found within the fields of France the command of the Tropics, and who needed nothing but time to prosper Corsican cotton and Solingen steel. The man's words and deeds are still vigorous and alive; in another generation many of them will be dead as Marley—*dead as a door-nail*. Let us then each to his task, and each try, as best he may, to weigh in honest scales the modern Hannibal *"our last great man,"* [4] *"the mightiest genius of two thousand years."* [5]

H. F. Hall.

---

2. Dr. Johnson (*Gentleman's Magazine*, 1760), in defence of Mary Stuart.
3. *L'Homme*, so spoken of during the Empire, outside military circles.
4. Carlyle.
5. Napier.

Introduction

Napoleon is by no means an easy writer to translate adequately. He had always a terse, concise mode of speaking, and this, with the constant habit of dictating, became accentuated. Whenever he could use a short, compact word he did so. The greatest temptation has been to render his very modern ideas by modern colloquialisms. Occasionally, where Murray's Dictionary proves that the word was in vogue a century ago, we have used a somewhat rarer word than Napoleon's equivalent, as e.g. "coolth," in Letter No. 6, Series B (*pendant le frais*), in order to preserve as far as possible the brevity and crispness of the original.

Napoleon's vocabulary was not specially wide, but always exact. In expletive it was extensive and peculiar. Judging his brother by himself, he did not consider Lucien sufficient of a purist in French literature to write epics; and the same remark would have been partly true of the Emperor, who, however, was always at considerable pains to verity any word of which he did not know the exact meaning. [1] His own appetite for literature was enormous, especially during the year's garrison life he spent at Valence, where he read and re-read the contents of a *bouquiniste's* shop, and, what is more, remembered them, so much so that, nearly a quarter of a century later, he was able to correct the dates of ecclesiastical experts at Erfurt.

Whatever he says or whatever he writes, one always finds a

---

1 Sometimes he is perhaps more to be trusted than the leading lexicographer, as for example when, the day after Wagram, he writes his Minister of War that the *coup de Jarnac* will come from the English in Spain. Now, when the Jarnac in question was slain in fair fight by La Chateignerie by a blow *au jarret,* it was an *unexpected* blow, but not surely, as Littre tells us, *manœvre perfide, déloyale*. Nothing was too disloyal for perfidious Albion, but for 30,000 English to outmanoeuvre three marshals and 100,000 French veterans would be, and was, the unexpected which happened at Talavera three weeks later.

specific gravity of stark, staring facts altogether abnormal. For generations it was the fashion to consider "as false as a bulletin" peculiar to Napoleon's despatches; but the publication of Napoleon's correspondence, by order of Napoleon III., has changed all that. In the first place, as to dates. Not only have Haydn, Woodward and Gates, and the *Encyclopaedia Britannica* made mistakes during this period, but even the *Biographie Universelle* (usually so careful) is not immaculate. Secondly, with regard to the descriptions of the battles. We have never found one that in accuracy and truthfulness would not compare to conspicuous advantage with some of those with which we were only too familiar in December 1899.

Napoleon was sometimes 1200 miles away from home; he had to gauge the effect of his bulletins from one end to the other of the largest effective empire that the world has ever seen, and, like Dr. Johnson in Fleet Street reporting Parliamentary debates (but with a hundred times more reason), he was determined not to let the other dogs have the best of it. The notes on the battles of Eylau (Series H) and Essling (Series L), the two most conspicuous examples of where it was necessary to colour the bulletins, will show what is meant. Carlyle was the first to point out that his despatches are as instinct with genius as his conquests his very words have "Austerlitz battles" in them. The reference to "General Danube," in 1809, as the best general the Austrians had, was one of those flashes of inspiration which military writers, from Napoleon to Lord Wolseley, have shown to be a determining factor in every doubtful fray.

"*Approfondissez*—go to the bottom of things," wrote Lord Chesterfield; and this might have been the life-motto of the Emperor. But to adopt this fundamental commonsense with regard to the character of Napoleon is almost impossible; it is, to use the metaphor of Lord Rosebery, like trying to span a mountain with a tape. We can but indicate a few leading features. In the first place, he had, like the great Stagirite, an eye at once telescopic and microscopic. Beyond the *mècanique cèleste*, beyond the nebulous reign of chaos and old night, his ken pierced the primal truth—the need of a Creator: "not everyone can be an atheist who wishes it."

No man saw deeper into the causes of things. The influence of sea power on history, to take one example, was never absent from his thoughts. Slowly and laboriously he built and rebuilt his fleets, only to fall into the hands of his "Punic "rival. Beaten at sea, he has but two weapons left against England—to "conquer her by land," or to stir up a maritime rival who will sooner or later avenge him. We have the Emperor Alexander's testimony from the merchants of Manchester, Birmingham, and Liverpool how nearly his Continental System *had* ruined us. The rival raised up beyond the western waves by the astute sale of Louisiana is still growing. In less than a decade Napoleon had a first crumb of comfort (when such crumbs were rare) in hearing of the victories of the *Constitution* over British frigates.

As for his microscopic eye, we know of nothing like it in all history. In focussing the facets, we seem to shadow out the main secret of his success—his ceaseless survey of all sorts and conditions of knowledge. "Never despise local information," he wrote Murat, who was at Naples, little anticipating the extremes of good and evil fortune which awaited him there. Another characteristic—one in which he surpassed alike the theory of Macchiavelli and the practice of the Medici—was his use of *la bascule*, with himself as equilibrist or average adjuster, as the only safe principle of government.

Opinions on the whole[2] lean to the idea that, up to the First Consulate, Napoleon was an active Freemason, at a time when politics were permitted, and when the Grand Orient, having initiated Voltaire almost on his deathbed, and having been submerged by the Terror, was beginning to show new life. In any case, we have in O'Meara the Emperor's statement (and this is rather against the theory of Napoleon being more than his brother Joseph, a mere patron of the craft) that he encouraged the brotherhood. Cambacérès had more Masonic degrees than probably any man before or since, and no man was so long and so consistently trusted by Napoleon, with one short and significant exception.

Then there was the *gendarmerie d'èlite*, then the ordinary police, the myrmidons of Fouché of Nantes—in fact, if we take Lord Rosebery literally, Napoleon had "half-a-dozen police agencies of his own." There was also Talleyrand and, during the Concordats, the whole priest-craft of Christendom as enlisting sergeants and spies extraordinary for the Emperor. Finally, when he wishes to attack Russia, he convokes a Sanhedrim at Paris, and wins the active sympathies of Israel. "He was his own War Office, his own Foreign Office, his own Admiralty."[3] His weak

2. Findel's *History of Freemasonry*.
3. Lord Rosebery.

spot was his neglect of woman as a political factor; this department he left to Josephine, who was a failure. She gained popularity, but no converts. The Faubourg St. Germain mistrusted a woman whose chief friend was the wife of Thermidorian Tallien—Notre Dame de Septembre. In vain Napoleon raged and stormed about the Tallien friendship, till his final mandate in 1806; and then it was too late.

Another characteristic, very marked in these Home Letters, is the desire not to give his wife anxiety. His ailments and his difficulties are always minimised.

Perhaps no man ever worked so hard physically and mentally as Napoleon from 1796 to 1814. Lord Rosebery reminds us that "he would post from Poland to Paris, summon a council at once, and preside over it with his usual vigour and acuteness." And his councils were no joke; they would last eight or ten hours. Once, at two o'clock in the morning, the councillors were all worn-out; the Minister of Marine was fast asleep. Napoleon still urged them to further deliberation: "Come, gentlemen, pull yourselves together; it is only two o'clock, we must earn the money that the nation gives us." The Commission who first sifted the *Correspondence* may well speak of the ceaseless workings of that mind, which *knew no rest save change of occupation*, and of "that universal intelligence from which nothing escaped." The chief fault in Napoleon as a statesman was intrinsically a virtue, *viz.*, his good nature.

There was, as Sir Walter Scott has said:

> gentleness and even softness in his character. It was his common and expressive phrase that the heart of a politician should be in his head; but his feelings sometimes surprised him in a gentler mood.

To be a relation of his own or his wife's, to have been a friend in his time of stress, was to have a claim on Napoleon's support which no subsequent treachery to himself could efface. From the days of his new power—political power, first the Consulate and then the Empire—he lavished gifts and favours even on the most undeserving of his early comrades. Fouché, Talleyrand, Bernadotte were forgiven once, twice, and again, to his own final ruin. Like Medea, one of whose other exploits he had evoked in a bulletin, he could say—but to his honour and not to his shame—

Si possem, sanior essem.
Sed trahit invitam nova vis; aliudque Cupido,

Mens aliud suadet. Video meliora, proboque
Deteriora sequor.

Treachery and peculation against the State was different, as Moreau, Bourrienne, and even Massena and Murat discovered.

As for his family, they were a flabby and somewhat sensual lot, with the exception of Lucien, who was sufficiently capable to be hopelessly impracticable. He was, however, infinitely more competent than the effeminate Joseph and the melancholy Louis, and seems to have had more command of parliamentary oratory than Napoleon himself.

Napoleon's influence on literary men may be gauged by what Wieland [4] and Müller [5] reported of their interview with him at Erfurt. That with Wieland took place at the ball which followed the entertainment on the field of Jena.

"I was presented," he says, "by the Duchess of Weimar, with the usual ceremonies; he then paid me some compliments in an affable tone, and looked steadfastly at me. Few men have appeared to me to possess, in the same degree, the art of reading at the first glance the thoughts of other men. He saw, in an instant, that notwithstanding my celebrity I was simple in my manners and void of pretension; and, as he seemed desirous of making a favourable impression on me, he assumed the tone most likely to attain his end. I have never beheld any one more calm, more simple, more mild, or less ostentatious in appearance; nothing about him indicated the feeling of power in a great monarch; he spoke to me as an old acquaintance would speak to an equal; and what was more extraordinary on his part, he conversed with me exclusively for an hour and a half, to the great surprise of the whole assembly."

Wieland has related part of their conversation, which is, as it could not fail to be, highly interesting. They touched on a variety of subjects; among others, the ancients. Napoleon declared his preference of the Romans to the Greeks. "The eternal squabbles of their petty republics," he said, "were not calculated to give birth to anything grand; whereas the Romans were always occupied with great things, and it was owing to this they

---

4. This versatile writer, the author of *Oberon*, the translator of Lucian and Shakespeare, and the founder of psychological romance in Germany, was then in his seventy-fifth year.
5. The historian (1755-1809), "the Thucydides of Switzerland."

raised up the Colossus which bestrode the world."This preference was characteristic; the following is anomalous: "He preferred Ossian to Homer."

"He was fond only of serious poetry," continues Wieland; "the
pathetic and vigorous writers; and, above all, the tragic poets.
He appeared to have no relish for anything gay; and in spite
of the prepossessing amenity of his manners, an observation
struck me often, he seemed to be of bronze. Nevertheless, he
had put me so much at my ease that I ventured to ask how
it was that the public worship he had restored in France was
not more philosophical and in harmony with the spirit of the
times? 'My dear Wieland,' he replied, 'religion is not meant for
philosophers; they have no faith either in me or my priests. As
to those who do believe, it would be difficult to give them or
to leave them too much of the marvellous. If I had to frame a
religion for philosophers, it would be just the reverse of that of
the credulous part of mankind.'" [6]

Müller, the celebrated Swiss historian, who had a private interview with Napoleon at this period, has left a still fuller account of the
impression he received. "The Emperor [7] began to speak," says Müller,
"of the history of Switzerland, told me that I ought to complete it,
that even the more recent times had their interest. He proceeded from
the Swiss to the old Greek constitutions and history; to the theory of
constitutions; to the complete diversity of those of Asia, and the causes
of this diversity in the climate, polygamy, &c.; the opposite characters
of the Arabian and the Tartar races; the peculiar value of European
culture, and the progress of freedom since the sixteenth century; how
everything was linked together, and in the inscrutable guidance of an
invisible hand; how he himself had become great through his enemies;
the great confederation of nations, the idea of which Henry IV. had;
the foundation of all religion, and its necessity; that man could not
bear clear truth, and required to be kept in order; admitting the possibility, however, of a more happy condition if the numerous feuds
ceased, which were occasioned by too complicated constitutions
(such as the German), and the intolerable burden suffered by states
from excessive armies."

These opinions clearly mark the guiding motives of Napoleon's

---

6. Home's *History of Napoleon* (1841).
7. *Ibid.*

attempts to enforce upon different nations uniformity of institutions and customs.

"I opposed him occasionally," says Müller, "and he entered into discussion. Quite impartially and truly, as before God, I must say that the variety of his knowledge, the acuteness of his observations, the solidity of his understanding (not dazzling wit), his grand and comprehensive views, filled me with astonishment, and his manner of speaking to me, with love for him. By his genius and his disinterested goodness, he has also conquered me." Slowly but surely they are conquering the world. Of his goodness we have the well-weighed verdict of Lord Acton, that it was "the most splendid that has appeared on earth." Of his goodness, we may at least concur in the opinion of the old British tar at Elba, quoted by Sir Walter, and evidently his own view, that "Boney was a d——d good fellow after all."

With regard to the character of *Josephine* opinions still differ about every quality but one. Like the friend of Goldsmith's mad dog—

> *A kind and gentle heart she had*
> *To comfort friends and foes:*

Either her brother Mason Cambacérès, or her brother Catholic and unbrotherly brother-in-law Lucien.

From early days she had learnt "how to flirt and how to fib." Morality was at a low ebb during the French Revolution, when women often saved their necks at the expense of their bodies, and there is unfortunately no doubt that Josephine was no exception. It is certain, however, from his first letters to Josephine, that Napoleon knew nothing of this at the time of his honeymoon (solus) in Italy. Gradually, but very unwillingly, his eyes were opened, and by the time he had reached Egypt he felt himself absolved from the absolute faithfulness he had hitherto preserved towards his wife.

On his return Josephine becomes once more his consort, and even his friend—never again his only love. Josephine's main characteristic henceforward is to make everybody happy and comfortable—in spite of Napoleon's grumblings at her reckless prodigality; never to say No! (except to her husband's accusations) suits her Creole disposition best, especially as it costs her no active exertion, and the Emperor pays for all. And so, having been in turn Our Lady of Victories and Saint Mary the Egyptian, she becomes from her coronation to her death-day "The Mother of the Poor."

The sources of the letters.—These may be divided into three parts (1st) the Early Love-Letters of 1796; (2nd) the Collection published by Didot Frères in 1833; and (3rd) the few scattered Letters gathered from various outside sources.

(1st) With regard to the Early Love-Letters of 1796, these are found most complete in a work published by Longmans in 1824, in two volumes, with the title, *A Tour through Parts of the Netherlands, Holland, Germany, Switzerland, Savoy, and France, in the year 1821-2, by Charles Tennant, Esq.; also containing in an Appendix Facsimile Copies of Eight Letters in the handwriting of Napoleon Bonaparte to his wife Josephine.*

The author introduces them with an interesting preface, which shows that then, as now, the interest in everything connected with Napoleon was unabated:—

> Long after this fleeting book shall have passed away, and with its author shall have been forgotten, these documents will remain; for here, perhaps, is to be found the purest source of information which exists, touching the private character of Napoleon Bonaparte, known, probably, but to the few whose situations have enabled them to observe that extraordinary man in the undisguised relations of domestic life. Although much already has been said and written of him, yet the eagerness with which every little anecdote and incident of his life is sought for shows the interest which still attaches to his name, and these, no doubt, will be bequests which posterity will duly estimate. From these it will be the province of future historians to cull and select simple and authenticated facts, and from these only can be drawn a true picture of the man whose fame has already extended into every distant region of the habitable globe.
>
> I will now proceed to relate the means by which I am enabled to introduce into this journal facsimile copies of eight letters in the handwriting of Napoleon Bonaparte, the originals of which are in my possession. Had these been of a political nature, much as I should prize any relics of such a man, yet they would not have appeared in a book from which I have studiously excluded all controversial topics, and more especially those of a political character. Neither should I have ventured upon their publication if there were a possibility that by so doing I might wound the feelings of any human being. Death has

closed the cares of the individuals connected with these letters. Like the memorials of Alexander the Great or of Charlemagne, they are the property of the possessor, and through him of the public; but not like ancient documents, dependent upon legendary evidence for their identity and truth.

These have passed to me through two hands only, since they came into possession of the Empress Josephine, to whom they are written by their illustrious author. One of the individuals here alluded to, and from whom I received these letters, is a Polish nobleman, who attached himself and his fortunes to Bonaparte, whose confidence he enjoyed in several important diplomatic negotiations.

This book and these letters were known to Sir Walter Scott, who made use of some of them in his *History of Napoleon*. M. Aubenas, in his *Histoire de l'impératrice Josephine*, published in 1857, which has been lavishly made use of in a recent work on the same subject, seems to have known, at any rate, four of these letters, which were communicated to him by M. le Baron Feuillet de Conches. Monsieur Aubenas seems never to have seen the Tennant Collection, of which these undoubtedly form part, but as Baron Feuillet de Conches was an expert in deciphering Bonaparte's extraordinary calligraphy, these letters are very useful for reference in helping us to translate some phrases which had been given up as illegible by Mr. Tennant and Sir Walter Scott.

(2nd) The Collection Didot. This enormously valuable collection forms by far the greater part of the Letters that we possess of Napoleon to his wife. They are undoubtedly authentic, and have been utilised largely by Aubenas, St. Amand, Masson, and the *Correspondance de Napoleon I*. They were edited by Madame Salvage de Faverolles. As is well known, Sir Walter Scott was very anxious to obtain possession of these letters for his *Life of Napoleon*, and his visit to Paris was partly on this account. In *Archibald Constable and his Literary Correspondents*, edited in 1873 by his son, we find the following:—

Letter from Archibald Constable to Sir Walter Scott.
August 30, 1825.

I have had various conversations with Mr. Thomson on the subject of Napoleon's correspondence with Josephine. Mr. Thomson communicated with Count Flahault for me in the view of its being published, and whether the letters could not, in the meantime, be rendered accessible. The publication, it seems, under any circumstances, is by no means determined on, but should they be given, the price expected is five thousand guineas, which I should imagine greatly too much. I have an enumeration of the letters, from whence written, &c. I shall subjoin a copy of it.

When they were finally published in 1833, they seem to have been stimulated into existence by publication of the *Mémorial de Saint-Helene*, better known in England as *Las Cases*. Doubtless Hortense only allowed such letters to be published as would not injure the reputation of her mother or her relations. In the Preface it is stated: "We think that these letters will afford an interest as important as delightful. Everything that comes from Napoleon, and everything that appertains to him, will always excite the lively attention of contemporaries and posterity. If the lofty meditation of philosophy concerns itself only with the general influence of great men upon their own generation and future ones, a curiosity of another nature, and not less greedy, loves to penetrate into the inmost recesses of their soul, in order to elicit their most secret inclinations. It likes to learn what has been left of the *man*, amid the preoccupations of their projects and the elevation of their fortune. It requires to know in what manner their character has modified their genius, or has been subservient to it.

> It is this curiosity that we hope to satisfy by the publication of these letters. They reveal the inmost thought of Napoleon, they will reflect his earliest impulses, they will show how the General, the Consul, and the Emperor felt and spoke, not in his discourses or his proclamations—the official garb of his thought—but in the free outpourings of the most passionate or the most tender affections. . . . This correspondence will prove, we strongly believe, that the conqueror was human, the master of the world a good husband, the great man in fact an excellent man. . . . We shall see in them how, up to the last moment, he lavished on his wife proofs of his tenderness. Without doubt the letters of the Emperor Napoleon are rarer and shorter than those of the First Consul, and the First Consul writes no longer like General Bonaparte, but everywhere the sentiment is fundamentally the same.
>
> We make no reflection on the style of these letters, written in haste and in all the *abandon* of intimacy. We can easily perceive they were not destined to see the light. Nevertheless we publish

them without changing anything in them.

The *Collection Didot* contains 228 letters from Napoleon to Josephine, and 70 from Josephine to Hortense, and two from Josephine to Napoleon, which seem to be the only two in existence of Josephine to Napoleon whose authenticity is unquestioned.

(3rd) The fugitive letters are collected from various sources, and their genuineness does not seem to be quite as well proved as those of the Tennant or Didot Series. We have generally taken the *Correspondence of Napoleon I.* as the touchstone of their merit to be inserted here, although one of them—that republished from *Las Cases* (No. 85, Series G.)—is manifestly mainly the work of that versatile author, who is utterly unreliable except when confirmed by others. As Lord Rosebery has well said, the book is "an arsenal of spurious documents."

We have relegated to an Appendix those published by Madame Ducrest, as transparent forgeries, and have to acknowledge with thanks a letter from M. Masson on this subject which thoroughly confirms these views. There seems some reason to doubt No. I., Series E, but being in the *Correspondence*, I have translated it.

The *Correspondence of Napoleon I.* is a splendid monument to the memory of Napoleon. It is alluded to throughout the Notes as *The Correspondence*, and it deserves special recognition here. Its compilation was decreed by Napoleon III. from Boulogne, on 7th September 1854, and the first volume appeared in 1858, and the last in 1870. With the first volume is inserted the Report of the Commission to the Emperor, part of which we subjoin:

Report of the Commission to the Emperor.

Sire,—Augustus numbered Caesar among the gods, and dedicated to him a temple; the temple has disappeared, the Commentaries remain. Your Majesty, wishing to raise to the chief of your dynasty an imperishable monument, has ordered us to gather together and publish the political, military, and administrative correspondence of Napoleon I. It has realised that the most conspicuous (*éclatant*) homage to render to this incomparable genius was to make him known in his entirety. No one is ignorant of his victories, of the laws with which he has endowed our country, the institutions that he has founded and which dwell immovable after so many revolutions; his prosperity and his reverses are in every mouth; history has recounted what he has done, but it has not always known his designs: it has not had the secret of so many admirable combinations that have been the spoil of fortune (*que la fortune a dejouèes*), and so many grand projects for the execution of which time alone was wanting. The traces of Napoleon's thoughts were scattered; it was necessary to reunite them and to give them to the light.

Such is the task which your Majesty confided to us, and of which we were far from suspecting the extent. The thousands of letters which were received from all parts have allowed us to follow, in spite of a few regrettable *lacunæ*, the thoughts of Napoleon day by day, and to assist, so to say, at the birth of his projects, at the ceaseless workings of his mind, which knew no other rest than change of occupation. But what is perhaps most surprising in the reading of a correspondence so varied, is the power of that universal intelligence from which nothing escaped, which in turn raised itself without an effort to the most sublime conceptions, and which descends with the same facility to the smallest details. . . . Nothing seems to him unworthy of his attention that has to do with the realisation of his designs; and it is not sufficient for him to give the most precise orders, but he superintends himself the execution of them with an indefatigable perseverance.

The letters of Napoleon can add nothing to his glory, but they better enable us to comprehend his prodigious destiny, the prestige that he exercised over his contemporaries '*le culte universel dont sa mémoire est l'objet, enfin, l'entraînement irrésistible par lequel la France a replacé sa dynastie au sommet de l'édifice qu'il avait construit.*'

These letters also contain the most fruitful sources of information . . . for peoples as for governments; for soldiers and for statesmen no less than for historians. Perhaps some persons, greedy of knowing the least details concerning the intimate life of great men, will regret that we have not reproduced those letters which, published elsewhere for the most part, have only dealt with family affairs and domestic relations. Collected together by us as well as the others, they have not found a place in the plan of which your Majesty has fixed for us the limits.

Let us haste to declare that, in conformity with the express intentions of your Majesty, we have scrupulously avoided, in the reproduction of the letters of the Emperor, any alteration, curtailment, or modification of the text. Sometimes, thinking of the legitimate sorrow which blame from so high a quarter may cause, we have regretted not to be able to soften the vigorous judgment of Napoleon on many of his contemporaries, but it was not our province to discuss them, still less to explain them; but if, better informed or calmer, the Emperor has rendered justice to those of his servants that he had for a moment misunderstood, we have been glad to indicate that these severe words have been followed by reparation.

We have found it necessary to have the spelling of names of places and of persons frequently altered, but we have allowed to remain slight incorrectnesses of language which denote the impetuosity of composition, and which often could not be rectified without weakening the originality of an energetic style running right to its object, brief and precise as the words of command. Some concise notes necessary for clearing up obscure passages are the sole conditions which we have allowed ourselves. . . .

The Commission has decided in favour of chronological order throughout. It is, moreover, the only one which can reproduce faithfully the sequence of the Emperor's thoughts. It is also the best for putting in relief his universal aptitude and his marvellous fecundity.

Napoleon wrote little with his own hand; nearly all the items of his correspondence were dictated to his secretaries, to his *aides-de-camp* and his chief of staff, or to his ministers. Thus the Commission has not hesitated to comprise in this collection a great number of items which, although bearing another signature, evidently emanate from Napoleon. . . .

"By declaring that his public life dated from the siege of Toulon, Napoleon has himself determined the point of departure which the Commission should choose. It is from this immortal date that commences the present publication.

(Signed)　　　　The Members of the Commission.
Paris, January 20, 1858.

Contemporary Sources.—It is a commonplace that the history of Napoleon has yet to be written. His contemporaries were stunned or overwhelmed by the whirlwind of his glory; the next generation was blinded by meteoric fragments of his "system," which glowed with impotent heat as they fell through an alien atmosphere into oblivion.

Such were the Bourriennes, the Jominis, the Talleyrands, and other traitors of that ilk. But

> *The tumult and the shouting dies;*
> *The captains and the kings depart;*

and now, when all the lesser tumults and lesser men *have* passed away, each new century will, as Lockhart foretold, *inscribe one mighty era with the majestic name of Napoleon.* And yet the writings of no contemporary can be ignored; neither Alison nor Scott, certainly not Bignon, Montgaillard, Pelet, Mathieu Dumas, and Pasquier. Constant, Bausset, Méneval, Rovigo, and D'Abrantès are full of interest for their personal details, and D'Avrillon, Las Cases, Marmont, Marbot, and Lejeune only a degree less so. Jung's *Memoirs of Lucien* are invaluable, and those of Joseph and Louis Bonaparte useful.

But the *Correspondence* is worth everything else, including Panckouke (1796-99), where, in spite of shocking arrangement, print, and paper, we get the replies as well as the letters. The *Biographic Universelle Michaud* is hostile, except the interesting footnotes of Begin. It must, however, be read. The article in the *Encyclopaedia Britannica* was the work of an avowed enemy of the Napoleonic system, the editor of the *Life and Times of Stein.*

For the Diary, the *Revue Chronologique de l'Histoire de France* or Montgaillard (1823) has been heavily drawn upon, especially for the later years, but wherever practicable the dates have been verified from the *Correspondence* and bulletins of the day. On the whole, the records of respective losses in the battles are slightly favourable to the French, as their figures have been usually taken; always, however, the maximum French loss and the minimum of the allies is recorded, when unverified from other sources.

The late Professor Seeley, in his monograph, asserts that Napoleon, tried by his plan, is a failure that even before death his words and actions merited no monument, We must seek, however, for the mightiest heritage of Napoleon in his brain-children of the second generation, the Genii of the Code.

The Code Napoleon claims today its two hundred million subjects. "The Law should be clean, precise, uniform; to interpret is to corrupt it." So ruled the Emperor; and now, a century later, Archbishop Temple (born in one distant island the year Napoleon died in another) bears testimony to the beneficent sway of Napoleon's Word-Empire. Criticising English legal phraseology, the Archbishop of Canterbury said, "The French Code is always welcome in every country where it has been introduced; and where people have once got hold of it, they are unwilling to have it changed for any other, because it is *a marvel of clearness*." Surely if ever Style is the Man, it is Napoleon, otherwise the inspection of over seven million words, as marshalled forth in his *Correspondence*, would not only confuse but confound. As it is, its "hum of armies, gathering rank on rank," has left behind what Bacon calls a conflation of sound, from which, however, as from Kipling's steel-sinewed symphony,

The clanging chorus goes Law, —
Order, Duty and Restraint, Obedience, Discipline.

Series A

(1796)

Only those who knew Napoleon in the intercourse of private life can render justice to his character. For my own part, I know him, as it were, by heart; and in proportion as time separates us, he appears to me like a beautiful dream. And would you believe that, in my recollections of Napoleon, that which seems to me to approach most nearly to ideal excellence is not the hero, filling the world with his gigantic fame, but the man, viewed in the relations of private life?—Recollections of Caulaincourt, Duke of Vicenza, vol. 1 197.

February 23rd.—Bonaparte made Commander-in-Chief of the Army of Italy.

No.1.

Seven o'clock in the morning. My waking thoughts are all of thee. Your portrait and the remembrance of last night's delirium have robbed my senses of repose. Sweet and incomparable Josephine, what an extraordinary influence you have over my heart. Are you vexed? do I see you sad? are you ill at ease? My soul is broken with grief, and there is no rest for your lover. But is there more for me when, delivering ourselves up to the deep feelings which master me, I breathe out upon your lips, upon your heart, a flame which burns me up—ah, it was this past night I realised that your portrait was not you. You start at noon; I shall see you in three hours. Meanwhile, *mio dolce amor*, accept a thousand kisses,[1] but give me none, for they fire my blood.   N. B.
A Madame Beauharnais.

March 9th.—Bonaparte marries Josephine.

---

1 *Un millier de baise* (sic).

March 11th.—Bonaparte leaves Paris to join his army.

No. 2.

Chanceaux Post House,
March 14, 1796.

I wrote you at Chatillon, and sent you a power of attorney to enable you to receive various sums of money in course of remittance to me. Every moment separates me further from you, my beloved, and every moment I have less energy to exist so far from you. You are the constant object of my thoughts; I exhaust my imagination in thinking of what you are doing. If I see you unhappy, my heart is torn, and my grief grows greater. If you are gay and lively among your friends (male and female), I reproach you with having so soon forgotten the sorrowful separation three days ago; thence you must be fickle, and henceforward stirred by no deep emotions. So you see I am not easy to satisfy; but, My Dear, I have quite different sensations when I fear that your health may be affected, or that you have cause to be annoyed; then I regret the haste with which I was separated from my darling.

I feel, in fact, that your natural kindness of heart exists no longer for me, and it is only when I am quite sure you are not vexed that I am satisfied. If I were asked how I slept, I feel that before replying I should have to get a message to tell me that you had had a good night. The ailments, the passions of men influence me only when I imagine they may reach you, my dear. May my good genius, which has always preserved me in the midst of great dangers, surround you, enfold you, while I will face my fate unguarded. Ah! be not gay, but a trifle melancholy; and especially may your soul be free from worries, as your body from illness: you know what our good Ossian says on this subject. Write me, dear, and at full length, and accept the thousand and one kisses of your most devoted and faithful friend.

[This letter is translated from St. Amand's *La Citoyenne Bonaparte*, p. 3, 1892.]

March 27th.—Arrival at Nice and proclamation to the soldiers.

No. 3.

April 3rd.—He is at Mentone.

Port Maurice, April 3rd.

I have received all your letters, but none has affected me like the last. How can you think, my charmer, of writing me in such terms? Do you believe that my position is not already painful enough without further increasing my regrets and subverting my reason. What eloquence, what feelings you portray; they are of fire, they inflame my poor heart! My unique Josephine, away from you there is no more joy—away from thee the world is a wilderness, in which I stand alone, and without experiencing the bliss of unburdening my soul. You have robbed me of more than my soul; you are the one only thought of my life. When I am weary of the worries of my profession, when I mistrust the issue, when men disgust me, when I am ready to curse my life, I put my hand on my heart where your portrait beats in unison. I look at it, and love is for me complete happiness; and everything laughs for joy, except the time during which I find myself absent from my beloved.

By what art have you learnt how to captivate all my faculties, to concentrate in yourself my spiritual existence—it is witchery, dear love, which will end only with me. To live for Josephine, that is the history of my life. I am struggling to get near you, I am dying to be by your side; fool that I am, I fail to realise how far off I am, that lands and provinces separate us. What an age it will be before you read these lines, the weak expressions of the fevered soul in which you reign.

Ah, my winsome wife, I know not what fate awaits me, but if it keeps me much longer from you it will be unbearable—my strength will not last out. There was a time in which I prided myself on my strength, and, sometimes, when casting my eyes on the ills which men might do me, on the fate that destiny might have in store for me, I have gazed steadfastly on the most incredible misfortunes without a wrinkle on my brow or a vestige of surprise: but today the thought that my Josephine might be ill; and, above all, the cruel, the fatal thought that she might love me less, blights my soul, stops my blood, makes me wretched and dejected, without even leaving me the courage of fury and despair.

I often used to say that men have no power over him who dies without regrets; but, today, to die without your love, to die in uncertainty of that, is the torment of hell, it is a lifelike and terrifying figure of absolute annihilation—I feel passion strangling me. My unique companion! you whom Fate has destined to walk with me the painful path of life! the day on which I no longer possess your heart will be that on which parched Nature will be for me without warmth and without vegetation. I stop, dear love! my soul is sad, my body tired, my spirit dazed, men worry me—I ought indeed to detest them; they keep me from my beloved.

I am at Port Maurice, near Oneille; tomorrow I shall be at Albenga. The two armies are in motion. We are trying to deceive each other—victory to the most skilful! I am pretty well satisfied with Beaulieu; he need be a much stronger man than his predecessor to alarm me much. I expect to give him a good drubbing. Don't be anxious; love me as thine eyes, but that is not enough; as thyself, more than thyself; as thy thoughts, thy mind, thy sight, thy all. Dear love, forgive me, I am exhausted; nature is weak for him who feels acutely, for him whom you inspire.   N. B.

Kind regards to Barras, Sussi, Madame Tallien; compliments to Madame Chateau Renard; to Eugène and Hortense best love. *Adieu, adieu!* I lie down without thee, I shall sleep without thee; I pray thee, let me sleep. Many times I shall clasp thee in my arms, but, but it is not thee.

A la citoyenne Bonaparte chez la
    citoyenne Beauharnais,
        Rue Chanterelne No. 6, Paris.

No. 4.

Albenga, April 5th.

It is an hour after midnight. They have just brought me a letter. It is a sad one, my mind is distressed—it is the death of Chauvet. He was *commissionaire ordinateur en chef* of the army; you have sometimes seen him at the house of Barras. My love, I feel the need of consolation. It is by writing to thee, to thee alone, the thought of whom can so influence my moral being, to whom I must pour out my troubles. What means the future? what means the past? what are we ourselves? what magic fluid surrounds and hides from us the things that it behoves us most to know? We are born, we live, we die in the midst of marvels; is it astounding that priests, astrologers, charlatans have profited by this propensity, by this strange circumstance, to exploit our ideas, and direct them to their own advantage.

Chauvet is dead. He was attached to me. He has rendered essential service to the fatherland. His last words were that he was starting to join me. Yes, I see his ghost; it hovers everywhere, it whistles in the air. His soul is in the clouds, he will be propitious to my destiny. But, fool that I am, I shed tears for our friendship, and who shall tell me that I have not already to bewail the irreparable. Soul of my life, write me by every courier, else I shall not know how to exist. I am very busy here. Beaulieu is moving his army again. We are face to face. I am rather tired; I am every day on horseback.

Adieu, adieu, adieu; I am going to dream of you. Sleep consoles me; it places you by my side, I clasp you in my arms. But on waking, alas! I find myself three hundred leagues from you. Remembrances to Barras, Tallien, and his wife.

N. B.

A la citoyenne Bonaparte chez la
    citoyenne Beauharnais,
        Rue Chantereine No, 6, Paris.

No. 5.

Albenga, April 7th.

I have received the letter that you break off, in order, you say, to go into the country; and in spite of that you give me to understand that you are jealous of me, who am here, overwhelmed with business and fatigue. Ah, My Dear,—it is true I am wrong. In the spring the country is beautiful, and then the lover of nineteen will doubtless find means to spare an extra moment to write to him who, distant three hundred leagues from thee, lives, enjoys, exists only in thoughts of thee, who reads thy letters as one devours, after six hours' hunting, the meat he likes best. I am not satisfied with your last letter; it is cold as friendship. I have not found that fire which kindles your looks, and which I have sometimes fancied I found there.

But how infatuated I am. I found your previous letters weigh too heavily on my mind. The revolution which they produced there invaded my rest, and took my faculties captive. I desired more frigid letters, but they gave me the chill of death. Not to be loved by Josephine, the thought of finding her inconstant but I am forging troubles—there are so many real ones, there is no need to manufacture more! You cannot have inspired a boundless love without sharing it, for a cultured mind and a soul like yours cannot requite complete surrender and devotion with the death-blow.

I have received the letter from Madame Chateau Renard. I have written to the Minister. I will write to the former tomorrow, to whom you will make the usual compliments. Kind regards to Madame Tallien and Barras.

You do not speak of your wretched indigestion—I hate it. *Adieu*, till tomorrow, *mio dolce amor*. A remembrance from my unique wife, and a victory from Destiny—these are my wishes: a unique remembrance entirely worthy of him who thinks of thee every moment.

My brother is here; he has learnt of my marriage with pleasure. He longs to see you. I am trying to prevail on him to go to Paris—his wife has just borne him a girl. He sends you a gift of a box of Genoa *bonbons*. You will receive oranges, perfumes, and orange-flower water, which I am sending.

Junot and Murat present their respects to you.

A la citoyenne Bonaparte,
   Rue Chantereine No. 6, (Address not in B.'s writing.)
      Chaussèe d'Antin, Paris.

April 10th.—Campaign opens (Napoleon's available troops about 35,000).

April 11th.—Colonel Rampon, with 1200 men, treats the attack of D'Argenteau, giving Napoleon time to come up.

April 12th.—Battle of Montenotte, Austrians defeated. Lose 3500 men (2000 prisoners), 5 guns, and 4 stand of colours.

April 14th.—Battle of Millesimo, Austrians and Sardinians defeated. Lose over 6000 prisoners, 2 generals, 4500 killed and wounded, 32 guns, and 15 stand of colours. Lannes made Colonel on the battlefield.

April 15th.—Battle of Dego, the allies defeated and separated.

April 22nd.—Battle of Mondovi, Sardinians defeated. Lose 3000 men, 8 guns, 10 stand of colours.

No. 6.

Carru, April 24th.

To My Sweet Love.—My brother will remit you this letter. I have for him the most lively affection. I trust he will obtain yours; he merits it. Nature has endowed him with a gentle, even, and unalterably good disposition; he is made up of good qualities. I am writing Barras to help him to the Consulate of some Italian port. He wishes to live with his little wife far from the great whirlwind, and from great events. I recommend him to you. I have received your letters of (April) the fifth and tenth. You have been several days without writing me.

What *are* you doing then? Yes, my kind, kind love, I am not jealous, but sometimes uneasy. Come soon. I warn you, if you tarry you will find me ill; fatigue and your absence are too much for me at the same time.

Your letters make up my daily pleasure, and my happy days are not often. Junot bears to Paris twenty-two flags. You ought to return with him, do you understand? Be ready, if that is not disagreeable to you. Should he not come, woe without remedy; should he come back to me alone, grief without consolation, constant anxiety. My Beloved, he will see you, he will breathe on your temples; perhaps you will accord him the unique and priceless favour of kissing your cheek, and I, I shall be alone and very far away; but you are about to come, are you not? You will soon be beside me, on my breast, in my arms, over your mouth. Take wings, come quickly, but travel gently. The route is long, bad, fatiguing. If you should be overturned or be taken ill, if fatigue—go gently, my beloved.

I have received a letter from Hortense. She is entirely lovable. I am going to write to her. I love her much, and I will soon send her the perfumes that she wants.   N. B.

I know not if you want money, for you never speak to me of business. If you do, will you ask my brother for it—he has 200 *louis* of mine! If you want a place for anyone you can send him; I will give him one. Chateau Renard may come too.

A la citoyenne Bonaparte, &c.

April 28th.—Armistice of Cherasco (submission of Sardinia to France): peace signed May 15th.

May 7th.—Bonaparte passed the Po at Placentia, and attacks Beaulieu, who has 40,000 Austrians.

May 8th.—Austrians defeated at Fombio. Lose 2500 prisoners, guns, and 3 standards. Skirmish of Codogno—death of General La Harpe.

May 9th.—Capitulation of Parma by the Grand Duke, who pays ransom of 2 million *francs*, 1600 artillery horses, food, and 2O paintings.

May 10th.—Passage of Bridge of Lodi, Austrians lose 2000 men and 20 cannon.

May 14th.—Bonaparte was requested to divide his command, and thereupon tendered his resignation.

May 15th.—Bonaparte enters Milan. Lombardy pays ransom of 20 million *francs*; and the Duke of Modena 10 millions, and 20 pictures.

May 24th-25th.—Revolt of Lombardy, and punishment of Pavia by the French.

May 30th-31st.—Bonaparte defeats Beaulieu at Borghetto, crosses the Mincio, and makes French cavalry fight (a new feature for the Republican troops).

June 3rd.—Occupies Verona, and secures the line of the Adige.

June 4th.—Battle of Altenkirchen (Franconia) won by Jourdan.

June 5th.—Armistice with Naples. Their troops secede from the Austrian army.

No. 7.
To Josephine.

Tortona, Noon, June 15th.

My life is a perpetual nightmare. A presentiment of ill oppresses me. I see you no longer. I have lost more than life, more than happiness, more than my rest. I am almost without hope. I hasten to send a courier to you. He will stay only four hours in Paris, and then bring me your reply. Write me ten pages. That alone can console me a little. You are ill, you love me, I have made you unhappy, you are in delicate health, and I do not see you!—that thought overwhelms me. I have done you so much wrong that I know not how to atone for it; I accuse you of staying in Paris, and you were ill there. Forgive me, my dear; the love with which you have inspired me has bereft me of reason.

I shall never find it again. It is an ill for which there is no cure. My presentiments are so ominous that I would confine myself to merely seeing you, to pressing you for two hours to my heart—and then dying with you. Who looks after you? I expect you have sent for Hortense. I love that sweet child a thousand times more when I think she can console you a little, though for me there is neither consolation nor repose, nor hope until the courier that I have sent comes back; and until, in a long letter, you explain to me what is the nature of your illness, and to what extent it is serious; if it be dangerous, I warn you, I start at once for Paris. My coming shall coincide with your illness. I have always been fortunate, never has my destiny resisted my will, and today I am hurt in what touches me solely (*uniquement*). Josephine, how can you remain so long without writing to me; your last laconic letter is dated May 22. Moreover, it is a distressing one for me, but I always keep it in my pocket; your portrait and letters are perpetually before my eyes.

I am nothing without you. I scarcely imagine how I existed without knowing you. Ah! Josephine, had you known my heart would you have waited from May 18th to June 4th before starting? Would you have given an ear to perfidious friends who are perhaps desirous of keeping you away from me? I openly avow it to everyone, I hate everybody who is near you. I expected you to set out on May 24th, and arrive on June 3rd.

Josephine, if you love me, if you realise how everything depends on your health, take care of yourself. I dare not tell you not to undertake so long a journey, and that, too, in the hot weather. At least, if you are fit to make it, come by short stages; write me at every sleeping-place, and despatch your letters in advance.

All my thoughts are concentrated in thy *boudoir*, in thy bed, on thy heart. Thy illness!—that is what occupies me night and day. Without appetite, without sleep, without care for my friends, for glory, for fatherland, you, you alone—the rest of the world exists no more for me than if it were annihilated. I prize honour since you prize it, I prize victory since it pleases you; without that I should leave everything in order to fling myself at your feet.

Sometimes I tell myself that I alarm myself unnecessarily; that even now she is better, that she is starting, has started, is perhaps already at Lyons. Vain fancies! you are in bed suffering, more beautiful, more interesting, more lovable. You are pale and your eyes are more languishing, but when will you be cured? If one of us ought to be ill it is I—more robust, more courageous; I should support illness more easily. Destiny is cruel, it strikes at me through you.

What consoles me sometimes is to think that it is in the power of destiny to make you ill; but it is in the power of no one to make me survive you.

In your letter, dear, be sure to tell me that you are convinced that I love you more than it is possible to imagine; that you are persuaded that all my moments are consecrated to you; that to think of any other woman has never entered my head—they are all in my eyes without grace, wit, or beauty; that you, you alone, such as I see you, such as you are, can please me, and absorb all the faculties of my mind; that you have traversed its whole extent; that my heart has no recess into which you have not seen, no thoughts which are not subordinate to yours; that my strength, my prowess, my spirit are all yours; that my soul is in your body; and that the day on which you change or cease to live will be my death-day; that Nature, that Earth, is beautiful only because you dwell therein.

If you do not believe all this, if your soul is not convinced, penetrated by it, you grieve me, you do not love me—there is a magnetic fluid between people who love one another—you know perfectly well that I could not brook a rival, much less offer you one.[2] To tear out his heart and to see him would be for me one and the same thing, and then if I were to carry my hands against your sacred person no, I should never dare to do it; but I would quit a life in which the most virtuous of women had deceived me.

But I am sure and proud of your love; misfortunes are the trials which reveal to each mutually the whole force of our passion. A child as charming as its mamma will soon see the daylight, and will pass many years in your arms. Hapless me! I would be happy with one *day*. A thousand kisses on your eyes, your lips, your tongue, your heart. Most charming of thy sex, what is thy power over me? I am very sick of thy sickness; I have still a burning fever! Do not keep the courier more than six hours,

---

2. So Tennant (*t'en offrir un*): but Baron Feuillet de Conches, an expert in Napoleonic graphology, renders the expression *t'en souffrir un*.

and let him return at once to bring me the longed-for letter of my Beloved.

Do you remember my dream, in which I was your boots, your dress, and in which I made you come bodily into my heart? Why has not Nature arranged matters in this way; she has much to do yet.   N. B.

A la citoyenne Bonaparte, &c.

June 18th.—Bonaparte enters Modena, and takes 50 cannon at Urbino.

June 19th.—Occupies Bologna, and takes 114 cannon.

June 23rd.—Armistice with Rome. The Pope to pay 21 millions, 100 rare pictures, 200 MSS., and to close his ports to the English.

June 24th.—Desaix, with part of Moreau's army, forces the passage of the Rhine.

No. 8.
To Josephine.

Pistoia, Tuscany, June 26th.

For a month I have only received from my dear love two letters of three lines each. Is she so busy, that writing to her dear love is not then needful for her, nor, consequently, thinking about him? To live without thinking of Josephine would be death and annihilation to your husband. Your image gilds my fancies, and enlivens the black and sombre picture of melancholy and grief. A day perhaps may come in which I shall see you, for I doubt not you will be still at Paris, and verily on that day I will show you my pockets stuffed with letters that I have not sent you because they are too foolish (*bête*). Yes, that's the word. Good heavens! tell me, you who know so well how to make others love you without being in love yourself, do you know how to cure me of love??? I will give a good price for that remedy.

You ought to have started on May 24th. Being good-natured, I waited till June 1st, as if a pretty woman would give up her habits, her friends, both Madame Tallien and a dinner with Barras, and the acting of a new play, and Fortuné; yes, Fortuné, whom you love much more than your husband, for whom you have only a little of the esteem, and a share of that benevolence with which your heart abounds. Every day I count up your misdeeds. I lash myself to fury in order to love you no more. Bah, don't I love you the more?

In fact, my peerless little mother, I will tell you my secret. Set me at defiance, stay at Paris, have lovers—let everybody know it—never write me a monosyllable! then I shall love you ten times more for it; and it is not folly, a delirious fever! and I shall not get the better of it. Oh! would to heaven I could get better! but don't tell me you are ill, don't try to justify yourself. Good heavens! you are pardoned. I love you to distraction, and never will my poor heart cease to give all for love. If you did not love me, my fate would be indeed grotesque. You have not written me; you are ill, you do not come. But you have passed Lyons; you will be at Turin on the 28th, at Milan on the 30th, where you will wait for me. You will be in Italy, and I shall be still far from you. *Adieu*, my well-beloved; a kiss on thy mouth, another on thy heart.

We have made peace with Rome—who gives us money. To-morrow we shall be at Leghorn, and as soon as I can in your arms, at your feet, on your bosom.

A la citoyenne Bonaparte, &c.

June 27th.—Leghorn occupied by Murat and Vaubois.

June 29th.—Surrender of citadel of Milan; 1600 prisoners and 150 cannon taken.

Series B
(1796-97)

Des 1796, lorsque, avec 30,000 hommes, il fait la conquête de 1'Italie, il est non-seulement grand général, mais profond politique.—Des Idées Napoléonniennes.

Your Government has sent against me four armies without Generals, and this time a General without an army.—Napoleon to the Austrian Plenipotentiaries, at Leoben.

No. 1

July 5th.—Archduke Charles defeated by Moreau at Radstadt.

July 6th.—Sortie from Mantua: Austrians fairly successful.

To Josephine, at Milan.

Roverbella, July 6, 1796.

I have beaten the enemy. Kilmaine will send you the copy of the despatch. I am tired to death. Pray start at once for Verona. I need you, for I think that I am going to be very ill.
I send you a thousand kisses. I am in bed.

Bonaparte.

July 9th.—Bonaparte asks Kellermann for reinforcements.

July 14th.—Frankfort on the Main captured by Kléber.

July 16th.—Sortie from Mantua: Austrians defeated.

No. 2.

July 17th.—Attempted *coup de main* at Mantua: French unsuccessful.

To Josephine, at Milan.

Marmirolo, July 17, 1796, 9 p.m.

I got your letter, my beloved; it has filled my heart with joy. I am grateful to you for the trouble you have taken to send me news; your health should be better today—I am sure you are cured. I urge you strongly to ride, which cannot fail to do you good.

Ever since I left you, I have been sad. I am only happy when by your side. Ceaselessly I recall your kisses, your tears, your enchanting jealousy; and the charms of the incomparable Josephine keep constantly alight a bright and burning flame in my heart and senses.

When, free from every worry, from all business, shall I spend all my moments by your side, to have nothing to do but to love you, and to prove it to you? I shall send your horse, but I am hoping that you will soon be able to rejoin me. I thought I loved you some days ago; but, since I saw you, I feel that I love you even a thousand times more. Ever since I have known you, I worship you more every day; which proves how false is the maxim of La Bruyère that *"Love comes all at once."*

Everything in nature has a regular course, and different degrees of growth. Ah! pray let me see some of your faults; be less beautiful, less gracious, less tender, and, especially, less kind; above all never be jealous, never weep; your tears madden me, fire my blood. Be sure that it is no longer possible for me to have a thought except for you, or an idea of which you shall not be the judge.

Have a good rest. Haste to get well. Come and join me, so that, at least, before dying, we could say—"We were happy for so many days!!"

Millions of kisses, and even to Fortuné, in spite of his naughtiness.

Bonaparte.

No. 3.

July 18th.—Trenches opened before Mantua.

July 18th.—Stuttgard occupied by Saint-Cyr, who, like Kléber, is under Moreau.

July 18th.—Wurtzburg captured by Klein and Ney (acting under Jourdan).

To Josephine, at Milan.

Marmirolo, July 18, 1796, 2 p.m.

I passed the whole night under arms. I ought to have had Mantua by a plucky and fortunate *coup*: but the waters of the lake have suddenly fallen, so that the column I had shipped could not land. This evening I shall begin a new attempt, but one that will not give such satisfactory results.

I got a letter from Eugène, which I send you. Please write for me to these charming children of yours, and send them some trinkets. Be sure to tell them that I love them as if they were my own. What is yours or mine is so mixed up in my heart, that there is no difference there.

I am very anxious to know how you are, what you are doing? I have been in the village of Virgil, on the banks of the lake, by the silvery light of the moon, and not a moment without dreaming of Josephine.

The enemy made a general sortie on June 16th; it has killed or wounded two hundred of our men, but lost five hundred of its own in a precipitous retreat.

I am well. I am Josephine's entirely, and I have no pleasure or happiness except in her society.

Three Neapolitan regiments have arrived at Brescia; they have sundered themselves from the Austrian army, in consequence of the convention I have concluded with M. Pignatelli.

I've lost my snuff-box; please choose me another, rather flat-shaped, and write something pretty inside, with your own hair. A thousand kisses as burning as you are cold. Boundless love, and fidelity up to every proof. Before Joseph starts, I wish to speak to him. Bonaparte.

No. 4.
To Josephine, at Milan.

Marmirolo, July 19, 1796.

I have been without letters from you for two days. That is at least the thirtieth time today that I have made this observation to myself; you are thinking this particularly wearisome; yet you cannot doubt the tender and unique anxiety with which you inspire me.

We attacked Mantua yesterday. We warmed it up from two batteries with red-hot shot and from mortars. All night long that wretched town has been on fire. The sight was horrible and majestic. We have secured several of the outworks; we open the first parallel tonight. Tomorrow I start for Castiglione with the

Staff, and I reckon on sleeping there. I have received a courier from Paris. There were two letters for you; I have read them. But though this action appears to me quite natural, and though you gave me permission to do so the other day, I fear you may be vexed, and that is a great trouble to me. I should have liked to have sealed them up again: fie! that would have been atrocious. If I am to blame, I beg your forgiveness. I swear that it is not because I am jealous; assuredly not. I have too high an opinion of my beloved for that. I should like you to give me full permission to read your letters, then there would be no longer either remorse or apprehension.

Achille has just ridden post from Milan; no letters from my beloved! *Adieu*, my unique joy. When will you be able to rejoin me? I shall have to fetch you myself from Milan.

A thousand kisses as fiery as my soul, as chaste as yourself.

I have summoned the courier; he tells me that he crossed over to your house, and that you told him you had no commands. Fie! naughty, undutiful, cruel, tyrannous, jolly little monster. You laugh at my threats, at my infatuation; ah, you well know that if I could shut you up in my breast, I would put you in prison there!

Tell me you are cheerful, in good health, and very affectionate.

Bonaparte.

No. 5.
To Josephine, at Milan.

Castiglione , July 21, 1796, 8 a.m.

I am hoping that when I arrive tonight I shall get one of your letters. You know, my dear Josephine, the pleasure they give me; and I am sure you have pleasure in writing them. I shall start tonight for Peschiera, for the mountains of ——, for Verona, and thence I shall go to Mantua, and perhaps to Milan, to receive a kiss, since you assure me they are not made of ice. I hope you will be perfectly well by then, and will be able to accompany me to headquarters, so that we may not part again. Are you not the soul of my life, and the quintessence of my heart's affections?

Your *protégés* are a little excitable; they are like the will-o'-the-wisp. How glad I am to do something for them which will please you. They will go to Milan. A little patience is requisite in everything.

Adieu, belle et bonne, quite unequalled, quite divine. A thousand loving kisses.   Bonaparte.

No. 6.
To Josephine, at Milan.

Castiglione, July 22, 1796.

The needs of the army require my presence hereabouts; it is impossible that I can leave it to come to Milan. Five or six days would be necessary, and during that time movements may occur whereby my presence here would be imperative.

You assure me your health is good; I beg you therefore to come to Brescia. Even now I am sending Murat to prepare apartments for you there in the town, as you desire.

I think you will do well to spend the first night (July 24th) at Cassano, setting out very late from Milan; and to arrive at Brescia on July 25th, where the most affectionate of lovers awaits you. I am disconsolate that you can believe, dear, that my heart can reveal itself to others as to you; it belongs to you by right of conquest, and that conquest will be durable and forever. I do not know why you speak of Madame T., with whom I do not concern myself in the slightest, nor with the women of Brescia. As to the letters which you are vexed at my opening, this shall be the last; your letter had not come.

Adieu, ma tendre amie, send me news often, come forthwith and join me, and be happy and at ease; all goes well, and my heart is yours for life.

Be sure to return to the Adjutant-General Miollis the box of medals that he writes me he has sent you. Men have such false tongues, and are so wicked, that it is necessary to have everything exactly on the square.

Good health, love, and a prompt arrival at Brescia.

I have at Milan a carriage suitable alike for town or country; you can make use of it for the journey. Bring your plate with you, and some of the things you absolutely require.

Travel by easy stages, and during the coolth, so as not to tire yourself. Troops only take three days coming to Brescia. Travelling post it is only a fourteen hours' journey. I request you to sleep on the 24th at Cassano; I shall come to meet you on the 25th at latest.

Adieu, my own Josephine. A thousand loving kisses.

Bonaparte.

July 29th.—Advance of Wurmser, by the Adige valley, on Mantua, and of Quesdonoivich on Brescia, who drives back Massena and Sauret.

July 31st.—Siege of Mantua raised.

August 3rd.—Bonaparte victorious at Lonato.

August 5th.—Augereau victorious at Castiglione, completing the Campaign of Five Days, in which 10,000 prisoners are taken.

August 8th.—Verona occupied by Serrurter.

August 15th.—(Moreau arrives on the Danube) Wurmser retreats upon Trent) the capital of Italian Tyrol.

August 18th.—Alliance, offensive and defensive, between France and Spain.

September 3rd.—Jourdan routed by Archduke Charles at Wurtzburg.

No. 7.
To Josephine, at Milan.

Brescia, August 30, 1796.

Arriving, my beloved, my first thought is to write to you. Your health, your sweet face and form have not been absent a moment from my thoughts the whole day. I shall be comfortable only when I have got letters from you. I await them impatiently. You cannot possibly imagine my uneasiness. I left you vexed, annoyed, and not well. If the deepest and sincerest affection can make you happy, you ought to be. . . . I am worked to death. *Adieu*, my kind Josephine: love me, keep well, and often, often think of me.

Bonaparte.

No. 8.
To Josephine, at Milan

Brescia, August 31, 1796.

I start at once for Verona. I had hoped to get a letter from you; and I am terribly uneasy about you. You were rather ill when I left; I beg you not to leave me in such uneasiness. You promised me to be more regular; and, at the time, your tongue was in harmony with your heart. You, to whom nature has given

44

a kind, genial, and wholly charming disposition, how can you forget the man who loves you with so much fervour? No letters from you for three days; and yet I have written to you several times. To be parted is dreadful, the nights are long, stupid, and wearisome; the day's work is monotonous.

This evening, alone with my thoughts, work and correspondence, with men and their stupid schemes, I have not even one letter from you which I might press to my heart.

The Staff has gone; I set off in an hour. Tonight I get an express from Paris; there was for you only the enclosed letter, which will please you.

Think of me, live for me, be often with your well-beloved, and be sure that there is only one misfortune that he is afraid of that—of being no longer loved by his Josephine. A thousand kisses, very sweet, very affectionate, very exclusive.

Send M. Monclas at once to Verona; I will find him a place. He must get there before September 4th.

Bonaparte.

September 1st.—Bonaparte leaves Verona and directs his troops on Trent. Wurmser, reinforced by 20,000 men, leaves his right wing at Roveredo, and marches *via* the Brent a Gorge on Verona.

No. 9.
To Josephine, at Milan.

Ala, September 3, 1796.

We are in the thick of the fight, my beloved; we have driven in the enemy's outposts; we have taken eight or ten of their horses with a like number of riders. My troops are good-humoured and in excellent spirits. I hope that we shall do great things, and get into Trent by the fifth.

No letters from you, which really makes me uneasy; yet they tell me you are well, and have even had an excursion to Lake Como. Every day I wait impatiently for the post which will bring me news of you—you are well aware how I prize it. Far from you I cannot live, the happiness of my life is near my gentle Josephine.

Think of me! Write me often, very often: in absence it is the only remedy: it is cruel, but, I hope, will be only temporary.

Bonaparte.

September 4th.—Austrian right wing defeated at Roveredo.

September 5th.—Bonaparte enters Trent, cutting off Wurmser from his base. Defeats Davidowich on the Lavis and leaves Vaubois to contain this general while he follows Wurmser.

September 6th.—Wurmser continues his advance, his outposts occupy Vicenza and Montebello.

September 7th.—Combat of Primolano: Austrians defeated. Austrian vanguard attack Verona, but are repulsed by General Kilmaine.

September 8th.—Battle of Bassano: Wurmser completely routed, and retires on Legnago.

No. 10.
To Josephine, at Milan.

Montebello, Noon, September 10, 1796.

My Dear,—The enemy has lost 1 8,000 men prisoners; the rest killed or wounded. Wurmser, with a column of 1 500 cavalry, and 500 infantry, has no resource but to throw himself into Mantua.

Never have we had successes so unvarying and so great. Italy, Friuli, the Tyrol, are assured to the Republic. The Emperor will have to create a second army: artillery, pontoons, baggage, everything is taken.

In a few days we shall meet; it is the sweetest reward for my labours and anxieties.

A thousand fervent and very affectionate kisses.

Bonaparte.

September 11th.—Skirmish at Cerea: Austrians successful. Bonaparte arrives alone, and is nearly captured.

No. 11.
To Josephine, at Milan.

Ronco, September 12, 1796, 10 a.m.

My dear Josephine,—I have been here two days, badly lodged, badly fed, and very cross at being so far from you.

Wurmser is hemmed in, he has with him 3000 cavalry and 5000 infantry. He is at Porto-Legnago; he is trying to get back into Mantua, but for him that has now become impossible. The moment this matter shall be finished I will be in your arms.

I embrace you a million times.   Bonaparte.

September 13th.—Wurmser, brushing aside the few French who oppose him, gains the suburbs of Mantua.

September 14th.—Massena attempts a surprise, but is repulsed.

September 15th.—Wurmser makes a sortie from St. Georges, but is driven back.

September 16th.—And at La Favorite, with like result.

No. 12.
To Josephine, at Milan.

Verona, September 17, 1796.

My Dear,—I write very often and you seldom. You are naughty, and undutiful; very undutiful, as well as thoughtless. It is disloyal to deceive a poor husband, an affectionate lover. Ought he to lose his rights because he is far away, up to the neck in business, worries and anxiety. Without his Josephine, without the assurance of her love, what in the wide world remains for him. What will he do?

Yesterday we had a very sanguinary conflict; the enemy has lost heavily, and been completely beaten. We have taken from him the suburbs of Mantua.

Adieu, charming Josephine; one of these nights the door will be burst open with a bang, as if by a jealous husband, and in a moment I shall be in your arms.

A thousand affectionate kisses   Bonaparte.

October 2nd.—(Moreau defeats Latour at Biberach, but then continues his retreat.)

October 8th.—Spain declares war against England.

October 10th.—Peace with Naples signed.

No. 13.
To Josephine, at Milan.

Modena, October 17, 1796, 9 p.m.

The day before yesterday I was out the whole day. Yesterday I kept my bed. Fever and a racking headache both prevented me writing to my beloved; but I got your letters. I have pressed them to my heart and lips, and the grief of a hundred miles of separation has disappeared. At the present moment I can see you by my side, not capricious and out of humour, but gentle, affectionate, with that mellifluent kindness of which my Josephine is the sole proprietor. It was a dream, judge if it has cured my fever.

Your letters are as cold as if you were fifty; we might have been married fifteen years. One finds in them the friendship and feelings of that winter of life. Fie! Josephine. It is very naughty, very unkind, very undutiful of you. What more can you do to make me indeed an object for compassion? Love me no longer? Eh, that is already accomplished! Hate me? Well, I prefer that! Everything grows stale except ill-will; but indifference, with its marble pulse, its rigid stare, its monotonous demeanour! . . .
A thousand thousand very heartfelt kisses.

I am rather better. I start tomorrow. The English evacuate the Mediterranean. Corsica is ours. Good news for France, and for the army. Bonaparte.

October 25th.—(Moreau recrosses the Rhine.)

November 1st.—Advance of Marshal Alvinzi. Vaubois defeated by Davidovich on November 5th, after two days' fight.

November 6th.—Napoleon successful, but Vaubois' defeat compels the French army to return to Verona.

No. 14.
To Josephine, at Milan.

Verona, November 9, 1796.
My Dear,—I have been at Verona since the day before yesterday. Although tired, I am very well, very busy; and I love you passionately at all times. I am just off on horseback.

I embrace you a thousand times. Bonaparte.

November 12th.—Combat of Caldiero: Napoleon fails to turn the Austrian position, owing to heavy rains. His position desperate.

November 15th.—First battle of Arcola. French gain partial victory.

November 16th and 17th.—Second battle of Arcola. French completely victorious. "Lodi was nothing to Arcola" (Bourrienne).

November 17th.—Death of Czarina Catherine II. of Russia.

November 18th.—Napoleon victoriously re-enters Verona by the Venice gate, having left it, apparently in full retreat, on the night of the 14th by the Milan gate.

No. 15.
From Bourrienne's Life of Napoleon, vol. 1. chap. 4.

Verona , November 19th, Noon.

My Adored Josephine,—Once more I breathe freely. Death is no longer before me, and glory and honour are once more re-established. The enemy is beaten at Arcola. Tomorrow we will repair Vaubois' blunder of abandoning Rivoli. In a week Mantua will be ours, and then your husband will clasp you in his arms, and give you a thousand proofs of his ardent affection. I shall proceed to Milan as soon as I can; I am rather tired. I have received letters from Eugène and Hortense—charming young people. I will send them to you as soon as I find my belongings, which are at present somewhat dispersed.

We have made five thousand prisoners, and killed at least six thousand of the enemy. Goodbye, my adored Josephine. Think of me often. If you cease to love your Achilles, if for him your heart grows cold, you will be very cruel, very unjust. But I am sure you will always remain my faithful mistress, as I shall ever remain your fond lover. Death alone can break the chain which sympathy, love, and sentiment have forged. Let me have news of your health. A thousand and a thousand kisses.

No. 16.
To Josephine, at Milan.

Verona, November 23, 1796.

I don't love you an atom; on the contrary, I detest you. You are a good for nothing, very ungraceful, very tactless, very tatterdemalion. You never write to me; you don't care for your husband; you know the pleasure your letters give him, and you write him barely half-a-dozen lines, thrown off anyhow.

How, then, do you spend the livelong day, madam? What business of such importance robs you of the time to write to your very kind lover? What inclination stifles and alienates love, the affectionate and unvarying love which you promised me? Who may this paragon be, this new lover who engrosses all your time, is master of your days, and prevents you from concerning yourself about your husband? Josephine, be vigilant; one fine night the doors will be broken in, and I shall be before you.

Truly, My Dear,—I am uneasy at getting no news from you. Write me four pages immediately, and some of those charming

remarks which fill my heart with the pleasures of imagination.
I hope that before long I shall clasp you in my arms, and cover
you with a million kisses as burning as if under the equator.

Bonaparte.

No. 17.

Verona, November 24, 1796.
I hope soon, darling, to be in your arms. I love you to distraction. I am writing to Paris by this courier. All goes well. Wurmser was beaten yesterday under Mantua. Your husband only
needs Josephine's love to be happy.

Bonaparte.

No. 18.
To Josephine, at Genoa.

Milan, November 27, 1796, 3 p.m.
I get to Milan; I fling myself into your room; I have left all in
order to see you, to clasp you in my arms. . . . You were not
there. You gad about the towns amid junketings; you run farther from me when I am at hand; you care no longer for your
dear Napoleon. A passing fancy made you love him; fickleness
renders him indifferent to you.
Used to perils, I know the remedy for weariness and the ills of
life. The ill-luck that I now suffer is past all calculations; I did
right not to anticipate it.
I shall be here till the evening of the 20th. Don't alter your
plans; have your fling of pleasure; happiness was invented for
you. The whole world is only too happy if it can please you, and
only your husband is very, very unhappy.

Bonaparte.

No. 19.
To Josephine, at Genoa.

Milan, November 28, 1796, 8 p.m.
I have received the courier whom Berthier had hurried on
to Genoa. You have not had time to write me, I feel it intuitively. Surrounded with pleasures and pastimes, you would be
wrong to make the least sacrifice for me. Berthier has been
good enough to show me the letter which you wrote him. My
intention is that you should not make the least change in your

plans, nor with respect to the pleasure parties in your honour; I am of no consequence, either the happiness or the misery of a man whom you don't love is a matter of no moment.

For my part, to love you only, to make you happy, to do nothing which may vex you, that is the object and goal of my life.

Be happy, do not reproach me, do not concern yourself in the happiness of a man who lives only in your life, rejoices only in your pleasure and happiness. When I exacted from you a love like my own I was wrong; why expect lace to weigh as heavy as gold? When I sacrifice to you all my desires, all my thoughts, every moment of my life, I obey the sway which your charms, your disposition, and your whole personality have so effectively exerted over my unfortunate heart. I was wrong, since nature has not given me attractions with which to captivate you; but what I do deserve from Josephine is her regard and esteem, for I love her frantically and uniquely.

Farewell, beloved wife; farewell, my Josephine. May fate concentrate in my breast all the griefs and troubles, but may it give Josephine happy and prosperous days. Who deserves them more? When it shall be quite settled that she can love me no more, I will hide my profound grief, and will content myself with the power of being useful and serviceable to her.

I reopen my letter to give you a kiss . . . Ah! Josephine! . . . Josephine! Bonaparte.

December 24th.—French under Hoche sail for Ireland; return "foiled by the elements."

January 7th, 1797.—Alvinzi begins his new attack on Rivoli, 'while Provera tries to get to Mantua with 11,000 men *via* Padua and Legnago. Alvinzi's total forces 48,000, but only 28,000 at Rivoli against Bonaparte's 23,000.

January 9th.—Kehl (after 48 days' siege) surrenders to Archduke Charles.

January 10th.—Napoleon at Bologna advised of the advance, and hastens to make Verona, as before, the pivot of his movements.

No. 20.

January 12th.—Combat of St. Michel: Massena defeats Austrians.

To Josephine, at Milan.

Verona, January 12, 1797.

Scarcely set out from Roverbella, I learnt that the enemy had appeared at Verona. Massena made some dispositions, which have been very successful. We have made six hundred prisoners, and have taken three pieces of cannon. General Brune got seven bullets in his clothes, without being touched by one of them—this is what it is to be lucky.

I give you a thousand kisses. I am very well. We have had only ten men killed, and a hundred wounded.

Bonaparte.

January 13th.—Joubert attacked; retires from Corona on Rivoli in the morning, joined by Bonaparte at night.

January 14th.—Battle of Rivoli: Austrian centre defeated. Bonaparte at close of day hurries off with Massena's troops to overtake Provera, marching sixteen leagues during the night. Massena named next day *enfant chéri de la victoire* by Bonaparte, and later Duc de Rivoli.

January 15th.—Joubert continues battle of Rivoli: complete defeat of Austrians. Provera, however, has reached St. Georges, outside Mantua.

January 16th.—Sortie of Wurmser at La Favorite repulsed. Provera, hurled back by Victor (named the Terrible on this day), is surrounded by skilful manoeuvres of Bonaparte, and surrenders with 6000 men. In three days Bonaparte had taken 18,000 prisoners and all Alvinzi's artillery. Colonel Graham gives Austrian losses at 14,000 to 15,000, exclusive of Provera's 6000.

January 26th.—Combat of Carpenedolo: Massena defeats the Austrians.

February 2nd.—Joubert occupies Lawis. Capitulation of Mantua, by Wurmser, with 13,000 men (and 6000 in hospital), but he, his staff, and 200 cavalry allowed to return. Enormous capture of artillery, including siege-train abandoned by Bonaparte before the battle of Castiglione. Advance of Victor on Rome.

No. 21.
To Josephine, at Bologna.

Forli, February 3, 1797.

I wrote you this morning. I start tonight. Our forces are at Rimini. This country is beginning to be tranquillised. My cold makes me always rather tired.

I idolise you, and send you a thousand kisses.

A thousand kind messages to my sister.

Bonaparte.

February 9th.—Capture of Ancona.

No. 22.
To Josephine, at Bologna.

Ancona, February 10, 1797.

We have been at Ancona these two days. We took the citadel, after a slight fusillade, and by a *coup de main*. We made 1200 prisoners. I sent back the fifty officers to their homes.

I am still at Ancona. I do not press you to come, because everything is not yet settled, but in a few days I am hoping that it will be. Besides, this country is still discontented, and everybody is nervous.

I start tomorrow for the mountains. You don't write to me at all, yet you ought to let me have news of you every day.

Please go out every day; it will do you good.

I send you a million kisses. I never was so sick of anything as of this vile war.

Goodbye, my darling. Think of me!   Bonaparte.

No. 23.
To Josephine, at Bologna.

Ancona, February 13, 1797.

I get no news from you, and I feel sure that you no longer love me. I have sent you the papers, and various letters. I start immediately to cross the mountains. The moment that I know something definite, I will arrange for you to accompany me; it is the dearest wish of my heart.

A thousand and a thousand kisses.   Bonaparte.

No. 24.
To Josephine, at Bologna.

February 16, 1797.

You are melancholy, you are ill; you no longer write to me, you want to go back to Paris. Is it possible that you no longer love your comrade? The very thought makes me wretched. My darling, life is unbearable to me now that I am aware of your melancholy.

I make haste to send you Moscati, so that he may look after you. My health is rather bad; my cold gets no better. Please take care of yourself, love me as much as I love you, and write me every day. I am more uneasy than ever.

I have told Moscati to escort you to Ancona, if you care to come there. I will write to you there, to let you know where I am.

Perhaps I shall make peace with the Pope, then I shall soon be by your side; it is my soul's most ardent wish.

I send you a hundred kisses. Be sure that nothing equals my love, unless it be my uneasiness. Write to me every day yourself. Goodbye, dearest. Bonaparte.

No. 25.

February 19th.—Peace of Tolentino with the Pope, who has to pay for his equivocal attitude and broken treaty.

To Josephine, at Bologna.

Tolentino, February 19, 1797.

Peace with Rome has just been signed. Bologna, Ferrara, Romagna, are ceded to the Republic. The Pope is to pay us thirty millions shortly, and various works of art.

I start tomorrow morning for Ancona, and thence for Rimini, Ravenna, and Bologna. If your health permit, come to Rimini or Ravenna, but, I beseech you, take care of yourself.

Not a word from you—what on earth have I done? To think only of you, to love only Josephine, to live only for my wife, to enjoy happiness only with my dear one—does this deserve such harsh treatment from her? My Dear, I beg you, think often of me, and write me every day.

You are ill, or else you do not love me! Do you think, then, that I have a heart of stone? and do my sufferings concern you so little? You must know me very ill! I cannot believe it! You to whom nature has given intelligence, tenderness, and beauty, you who alone can rule my heart, you who doubtless know only too well the unlimited power you hold over me! Write to me, think of me, and love me.—Yours ever, for life.

Bonaparte.

March 16th.—Bonaparte defeats Archduke Charles on the Tagliamento.

March 25th.—Bonaparte writes the Directory from Goritz that "up till now Prince Charles has manoeuvred worse than Beaulieu and Wurmser"

March 29th.—Klagenfurt taken by Massena.

April 1st.—Laybach by Bernadotte.

April 17th.—Preliminaries of peace at Leoben signed by Bonaparte.

April 18th.—Hoche crosses the Rhine at Neuwied.

April 21st.—Moreau at Kehl.

April 23rd.—Armistice of two Rhine armies follows preliminaries of Leoben.

May 16th.—Augereau enters Venice.

June 28th.—French capture Corfu, and 600 guns.

July 8th.—Death of Edmund Burke, aged sixty-eight.

July 18th.—Talleyrand becomes French Minister of Foreign Affairs.

September 4th.—Day of 18th *Fructidor* at Paris. *Coup d'Etat* of Rewbell, Larévellière-Lépeaux, and Barras, secretly aided by Bonaparte, who has sent them Augereau to command Paris.

September 18th.—Death of Lazare Hoche, aged twenty-nine, probably poisoned by the Directory, which has recalled Moreau, retired Bernadotte, and will soon launch Bonaparte on the seas, so that he may find failure and Bantry Bay at Aboukir (Montgaillard).

September 30th.—National bankruptcy admitted in France, the sixth time in two centuries.

October 17th.—Treaty of Campo-Formio; Bonaparte called thereupon by Talleyrand "General Pacificator."

November 16th.—Death of Frederick William II., King of Prussia, aged fifty-three; succeeded by his son, Frederick William III., aged twenty-seven.

December 1st.—Bonaparte Minister Plenipotentiary at Congress of Rastadt, and

December 5th.—Arrives at Paris.

December 10th.—Bonaparte presented to the Directory by Talleyrand.

December 27th.—Riots at Rome: Joseph Bonaparte (ambassador} insulted; General Duphot (engaged to Joseph's sister-in-law, Desirée) killed.

Series C

THE MARENGO CAMPAIGN, 1800

3rd Outlaw. "By the bare scalp of Robin Hood's fat friar, This fellow were a king for our wild faction!

1st Outlaw. "We'll have him; sirs, a word.

Speed. "Master, be one of them,
It is an honourable kind of thievery."
> *The Two Gentlemen of Verona*,
>> Act 4., Scene 1.

EVENTS OF 1798.

Napoleonic History.—*May 20th.*—Napoleon sails from Toulon for Egypt.

June 11th.—Takes Malta; sails for Egypt (June 20th).

July 4th.—Captures Alexandria.

July 21st.—Defeats Mamelukes at Battle of the Pyramids, and enters Cairo the following day.

August 1st.—French fleet destroyed by Nelson at the Battle of the Nile.

October 7th.—Desaix defeats Mourad Bey at Sedyman (Upper Egypt).

General History.—*January 4th.*—Confiscation of all English merchandise in France. Commencement of Continental system.

January 5th.—Directory fail to float a loan of 80 millions (*francs*), and:

January 28th.—Forthwith invade Switzerland, ostensibly to defend the Vaudois, under a sixteenth-century treaty, really to revolutionise the country, and seize upon the treasure of Berne.

February 15th.—Republic proclaimed at Rome. French occupy the Vatican, and

February 20th.—Drive Pope Pius VI. into exile to the convent of Sienna.

March 5th.—Capture of Berne by General Brune.

April 13th.—Bernadotte, ambassador, attacked at the French Embassy in Vienna.

May 19th.—Fitzgerald, a leader in the Irish rebellion, arrested.

August 22nd.—General Humbert and 1100 French troops land at Killala, County Mayo.

September 8th.—Humbert and 800 men taken by Lord Cornwallis at Ballinamack.

September 12th.—Turkey declares war with France, and forms alliance with England and Russia.

November 19th.—Wolfe-Tone commits suicide.

December 5th.—Macdonald defeats Mack and 40,000 Neapolitans at Civita Castellana.

December 9th.—Joubert occupies Turin.

December 15th.—French occupy Rome.

December 29th.—Coalition of Russia, Austria, and England against France.

EVENTS OF 1799.

Napoleonic History.—*January 23rd.*—Desaix defeats Mourad Bey at Samhoud (Upper Egypt). February 3rd.—Desaix defeats Mourad Bey at the Isle of Philae (near Assouan)—furthest limit of the Roman Empire. Napoleon crosses Syrian desert and takes El Arish (February 20th) and Gaza (February 25th), captures Jaffa (March 7th) and Sour , formerly Tyre (April 3rd). Junot defeats Turks and Arabs at Nazareth (April 8th), and Kléber defeats them at Mount Tabor (April 16th). Napoleon invests Acre but retires (May 2 1st), re-enters Cairo (June 14th), annihilates Turkish army at Aboukir (July 25th); secretly sails for France (August 23rd), lands at Frejus (October 9th), arrives at Paris (October 13th); dissolves the Directory (November 9th) and Council of Five Hundred (November 10th), and is proclaimed First Consul (December 24th).

General History.—January 10th.—Championnet occupies Capua.

January 20th.—Pacification of La Vendée by General Hédouville.

January 23rd.—Championnet occupies Naples.

March 3rd.—Corfu taken from the French by a Russo-Turkish force.

March 7th.—Massena defeats the Austrians, and conquers the country of the Grisons.

March 25th.—Archduke Charles defeats Jourdan at Stockach.

March 30th.—Kray defeats French (under Schérer) near Verona,

April 5th.—And again at Magnano.

April 14th.—Suwarrow takes command of Austrian army at Verona;

April 22nd.—Defeats French at Cassano, with heavy loss.

April 28th.—French plenipotentiaries, returning from Radstadt, murdered by men in Austrian uniforms Montgaillard☐thinks by creatures of the Directory.

May 4th.—Capture of Seringapatam by General Baird.

May 12th.—Austro-Russian army checked at Bassignana.

May 16th.—Sièyes becomes one of the Directory.

May 20th.—Suwarrow takes Brescia,

May 24th.—And Milan (citadel).

June 5th.—Massena defeated at Zurich by Archduke Charles; and Macdonald (*June 19th*) by Suwarrow at the Trebbia.

June 18th.—Gohier, Roger-Ducos, and Moulin replace Treilhard, Laréveillère-Lepeaux, and Merlin on the Directory.

June 20th.—Turin surrenders to Austro- Russians.

June 22nd.—Turkey, Portugal, and Naples join the coalition against France.

July 14th.—French carry their prisoner, Pope Pius VI., to Valence, where he dies (*August 29th*)

July 22nd.—Alessandria surrenders to Austro- Russians.

July 30th.—Mantua, after 72 days' siege, surrenders to Kray.

August 15th.—French defeated at Novi by Suwarrow. French lose Joubert and 20,000 men.

August 17th.—French, under Lecombe, force the St. Gothard.

August 27th.—English army disembark at the Helder.

August 30th.—Dutch fleet surrendered to the British Admiral.

September 19th.—Brune defeats Duke of York at Bergen.

September 25th.—Massena defeats allies at Zurich, who lose 16,000 men and 100 guns. "Massena saves France at Zurich, as Villars saved it at Denain."—*Montgaillard.*

October 6th.—Brune defeats Duke of York at Kastrikum.

October 7th.—French take Constance.

October 16th.—Saint-Cyr, without cavalry or cannon, defeats Austrians at Bosco.

October 18th.—Capitulation at Alkmaar by Duke of York to General Brune. "The son of George III. capitulates at Alkmaar as little honourably as the son of George II. had capitulated at Kloster-Seven in 1757."—*Montgaillard.*

November 4th.—Melas defeats French at Fossano.

November 13th.—Ancona surrendered to the Austrians by Monnier, after a six months' siege.

November 24th.—Moreau made commander of the armies of the Rhine (being in disgrace, has served as a volunteer in Italy most of this year); Massena sent to the army of Italy.

December 5th.—Coni, the key of Piedmont, surrenders to the Austrians.

December 14th.—Death of George Washington.

December 15th.—Battle of Montefaccio, near Genoa. Saint-Cyr defeats Austrians.

EVENTS OF 1800.

February 11th.—Bank of France constituted.

February 20th.—Kléber defeats Turks at Heliopolis.

May 3rd.—Battle of Engen. Moreau defeats Kray, who loses 10,000 men, and—

May 5th.—Again defeats Austrians at Moeskirch.

May 6th.—Napoleon leaves Paris.

May 8th.—Arrives at Auxnnne, and on the 9th at Geneva, from thence moves to Lausanne (*May 12th*), where he is delighted with reception accorded to the French t roofs, and hears of Moreau's victory at Bibernach (*May 11th*). On the 14th he hears of Desaix's safe arrival at Toulon from Egypt, together 'with Davoust, and orders the praises of their past achievements to be sung in the *Moniteur*. The same day writes Massena that in Genoa a man like himself (Massena) is worth 20,000. On the 16th is still at Lausanne.

No. 1.
To Josephine, at Paris.

Lausanne, May 15th, 1800.

I have been at Lausanne since yesterday. I start tomorrow. My health is fairly good. The country round here is very beautiful. I see no reason why, in ten or twelve days, you should not join me here; you must travel *incognito*, and not say where you are going, because I want no one to know what I am about to do. You can say you are going to Plombières.

I will send you Moustache, [1] who has just arrived.

My very kindest regards to Hortense. Eugène will not be here for eight days; he is *en route*.

Bonaparte.

No. 2.
To Josephine, at Paris.

Torre di Garofolo, May 16, 1800.

I start immediately to spend the night at Saint-Maurice. I have not received a single letter from you; that is not well. I have written you by every courier.

Eugène may arrive the day after tomorrow. I have rather a cold, but it will have no ill effects.

My very kindest regards to you, my good little Josephine, and to all who belong to you.

Bonaparte.

May 17th-19th.—At Martigny, "struggling against ice, snow-storms, and avalanches," and astonishing the great St. Bernard "with the passage of our 'pieces of 8,' and especially of our limbers a new experience for it" On May 20th he climbed the St. Bernard on a mule, and descended it on a sledge. On May 21st he is at Aosta, hoping to be back in Paris within a fortnight. His army had passed the mountain in

---

1 Bonaparte's courier.

four days. On May 27th he is at Ivrea, taken by Lannes on the 24th.

No. 3.[1]
(From *Tennant's Tour*, &c., vol. 2.)

11 p.m.

I hardly know which way to turn. In an hour I start for Vercelli.
Murat ought to be at Novaro tonight. The enemy is thoroughly
demoralised; he cannot even yet understand us. I hope within
ten days to be in the arms of my Josephine, who is always very
good when she is not crying and not flirting. Your son arrived
this evening. I have had him examined; he is in excellent health.
Accept a thousand tender thoughts. I have received M.'s letter. I
will send her by the next courier a box of excellent cherries.
We are here—within two months for Paris.—Yours entirely,

N. B.

To Madame Bonaparte. (*Address not in Bonaparte's writing.*)

June 1st.—First experiments with vaccination at Paris, with fluid
sent from London.

On June 2nd Napoleon enters Milan, where he spends a week.

No. 4.
To Josephine, at Paris.

Milan.

I am at Milan, with a very bad cold. I can't stand rain, and I have
been wet to the skin for several hours, but all goes well. I don't
persuade you to come here. I shall be home in a month. I trust
to find you flourishing. I am just starting for Pavia and Stradella.
We are masters of Brescia, Cremona, and Placentia. Kindest regards. Murat has borne himself splendidly.

June 5th.—Massena gives up Genoa, but leaves with all the honours of war.

June 7th.—Lannes takes Pavia, 350 cannon, and 10,000 muskets.

June 9th.—Battle of Montebello. Bonaparte defeats Austrians, who
lose 8000 men.

June 14th.—Bonaparte wins Marengo, but loses Desaix—"the man
I loved and esteemed the most." In his bulletin he admits the battle at
one time was lost, until he cried to his troops "Children, remember it

---

1 The date of this letter is May 29, 1800. See Notes.

is my custom to sleep upon the battlefield." He mentions the charges of Desaix and Kellermann, and especially eulogises the latter—a fact interesting on account of the false statements made of his ignoring it. In the bulletin of June 21st he blames the "punic faith" of Lord Keith at Genoa, a criticism the Admiral repaid with usury fifteen years later.

June 14th.—Assassination of Kléber, in Egypt.

June 16th.—Convention of Alessandria between Bonaparte and Melas; end of the "Campaign of Thirty Days."

June 19th.—Moreau defeats Kray at Hochstedt, and occupies Ulm.

June 23rd.—Genoa re-entered by the French.

June 26th.—Bonaparte leaves Massena in command of the Army of Reserve, now united with the Army of Italy.

July 3rd.—The First Consul is back in Paris unexpectedly—not wishing triumphal arches or such-like "*colifichets*" In spite of which the plaudits he receives are very dear to him, "sweet as the voice of Josephine."

September 5th.—Vaubois surrenders Malta to the English, after two years' blockade.

September 15th.—Armistice between France and Austria in Germany.

September 30th.—Treaty of Friendship and Commerce between France and U.S. agreed that the flag covers the goods.

October 3rd.—To facilitate peace King George renounces his title of King of France.

November 12th.—Rupture of Armistice between France and Austria.

December 3rd.—Moreau wins the battle of Hohenlinden (Austrian loss, 16,000 men, 80 guns; French 3000).

December 20th.—Moreau occupies Lintz (100 miles from Vienna).

December 24th.—Royalist conspirators fail to kill Bonaparte with an infernal machine.

December 25th.—Armistice at Steyer between Moreau and Archduke Charles (tent for by the Austrians a fortnight before as their last hope).

Series D

The peace of Amiens had always been regarded from the side of England as an armed truce: on the side of Napoleon it had a very different character. . . . A careful reader must admit that we were guilty of a breach of faith in not surrendering Malta. The promise of its surrender was the principal article of the treaty.

England and Napoleon in 1803.

(Edited for the R. Hist. S. by Oscar Browning, 1887.)

JOSEPHINE'S TWO VISITS TO PLOMBIÈRES, 1801 AND 1802.

EVENTS OF 1801.

January 1st.—Legislative Union of Great Britain and Ireland.

January 3rd.—French under Brune occupy Verona, and

January 8th.—Vicenza.

January 11th.—Cross the Brenta.

January 16th.—Armistice at Treviso between Brune and the Austrian General Bellegarde.

February 9th.—Treaty of Luneville, by which the Thalweg of the Rhine became the boundary of Germany and France.

March 8th.—English land at Aboukir.

March 21st.—Battle of Alexandria (Canopus). Menou defeated by Abercromby, with loss of 2000.

March 24th.—The Czar Paul is assassinated.

March 28th.—Treaty of Peace between France and Naples, who cedes Elba and Piombino.

April 2nd.—Nelson bombards Copenhagen.

May 23rd.—General Baird lands at Kosseir on the Red Sea with 1000 English and 10,000 *Sepoys*.

June 7th.—French evacuate Cairo.

July 1st.—Toussaint-Louverture elected Life-Governor of St. Domingo. Slavery abolished there. The new ruler declares, "I am the Bonaparte of St. Domingo, and the Colony cannot exist without me;" and heads his letters to the First Consul, "From the First of the Blacks to the First of the Whites."

July 15th.—*Concordat* between Bonaparte and the Pope, signed at Paris by Bonaparte, ratified by the Pope (August 15th).

August 4th.—Nelson attacks Boulogne flotilla and is repulsed.

August 15th.—Attacks again, and suffers severely.

August 31st.—Menou capitulates to Hutchinson at Alexandria.

September 29th.—Treaty of Peace between France and Portugal; boundaries of French Guiana extended to the Amazon.

October 1st.—Treaty between France and Spain, who restores Louisiana. Preliminaries of Peace between France and England signed in London.

October 8th.—Treaty of Peace between France and Russia.

October 9th.—And between France and Turkey.

December 14th.—Expedition sent out to St. Domingo by the French under General Leclerc.

No. 1
To Josephine, at Plombières.

Paris the "27" . . ., 1801.

The weather is so bad here that I have remained in Paris. Malmaison, without you, is too dreary. The fête has been a great success; it has rather tired me. The blister they have put on my arm gives me constant pain.

Some plants have come for you from London, which I have sent to your gardener. If the weather is as bad at Plombières as it is here, you will suffer severely from floods.

Best love to "*Maman*" and Hortense.

Bonaparte.

EVENTS OF 1802.

January 4th.—Louis Bonaparte marries Hortense Beauharnais, both unwilling.

January 9th.—The First Consul, with Josephine, leaves for Lyons, where,

January 25th.—He remodels the Cisalpine Republic as the Italian Re- public, under his Presidency.

March 25th.—Treaty of Amiens signed in London. French lose only Ceylon and Trinidad. Malta to be restored to the Order of Knights, reconstituted.

May 7th.—Toussaint surrenders to Leclerc.

May 19th.—Institution of the Legion of Honour.

No. 2.
To Josephine, at Plombières.

Malmaison, June 19, 1802.

I have as yet received no news from you, but I think you must already have begun to take the waters. It is rather dull for us here, although your charming daughter does the honours of the house to perfection. For the last two days I have suffered slightly from my complaint. The fat Eugène arrived yesterday evening; he is very hale and hearty.

I love you as I did the first hour, because you are kind and sweet beyond compare.

Hortense told me that she was often writing you.

Best wishes, and a love-kiss.—Yours ever,

Bonaparte.

No. 3.
To Josephine, at Plombières.

Malmaison, June 23, 1802.

My Good Little Josephine,—Your letter has come. I am sorry to see you have been poorly on the journey, but a few days' rest will put you right. I am very fairly well. Yesterday I was at the Marly hunt, and one of my fingers was very slightly injured whilst shooting a boar.

Hortense is usually in good health. Your fat son has been rather unwell, but is getting better. I think the ladies are playing *The Barber of Seville* tonight. The weather is perfect.

Rest assured that my truest wishes are ever for my little Josephine.—Yours ever,

Bonaparte.

No. 4.
To Josephine, at Plombières.

Malmaison, June 27, 1802.

Your letter, dear little wife, has apprised me that you are out of sorts. Corvisart tells me that it is a good sign that the baths are having the desired effect, and that your health will soon be re-established. But I am most truly grieved to know that you are in pain.

Yesterday I went to see the Sevres manufactory at St. Cloud.

Best wishes to all.—Yours for life, Bonaparte.

June 29th.—Pope withdraws excommunication from Talleyrand.

No. 5.
To Josephine, at Plombières.

Malmaison, July 1, 1802.

Your letter of June 20th has arrived. You say nothing of your health nor of the effect of the baths. I see that you expect to be home in a week; that is good news for your lover, who is tired of being alone!

You ought to have seen General Ney, who started for Plombières; he will be married on his return.

Yesterday Hortense played Rosina in *The Barber of Seville* with her usual skill.

Rest assured of my love, and that I await your return impatiently. Without you everything here is dreary.

Bonaparte.

August 2nd.—Napoleon Bonaparte made First Consul for life. "The conduct and the language of Bonaparte represents at once Augustus, Mahomet, Louis XI., Masaniello" (Montgaillard, an avowed enemy).

September 22nd.—Opening of the Ourcq Waterworks for the supply of Paris.

September 25th.—Mass celebrated at St. Cloud for the first time. In this month Napoleon annexes Piedmont, and the next sends Ney to occupy Switzerland.

October 11th.—Birth of Napoleon Charles, son of Louis Bonaparte and Hortense.

October 29th.—Napoleon and Josephine visit Normandy, and, contrary to expectation, receive ovations everywhere. They return to Paris, November 14th.

EVENTS OF 1803.

February 19th.—New constitution imposed by France on Switzerland.

April 14th.—Bank of France reorganised by Bonaparte; it alone allowed to issue notes.

April 27th.—Death of Toussaint-Louverture at Besancon.

April 30th.—France sells Louisiana to U.S. for £4,000,000 (15 million dollars).

May 22nd.—France declares war against England, chiefly respecting Malta. England having seized all French ships in British harbours previous to war being declared, Napoleon seizes all British tourists in France.

May 31st.—His soldiers occupy Electorate of Hanover.

June 14th.—He visits North of France and Belgium, accompanied by Josephine, and returns to Paris August 12th.

September 27th.—Press censorship established in France.

November 30th.—French evacuate St. Domingo.

Series E
1804

Everywhere the king of the earth found once more, to put a bridle on his pride, the inevitable lords of the sea.—Bignon, 5. 130.

LETTERS OF THE EMPEROR NAPOLEON TO THE EMPRESS
JOSEPHINE DURING HIS JOURNEY ALONG THE COAST, 1804.
EVENTS OF 1804.

February 15th.—The conspiracy of Pichegru. Moreau arrested, Pichegru (*February 28th*), and Georges Cadoudal (*March 9th*).

March 21st.—Duc D'Enghien shot at Vincennes.

April 6th.—Suicide of Pichegru.

April 30th.—Proposal to make Bonaparte Emperor.

May 4th.—Tribune adopts the proposal.

May 18th.—The First Consul becomes the Emperor Napoleon.

May 19th.—Napoleon confers the dignity of Marshal of the Empire on Berthier, Murat, Moncey, Jourdan, Massena, Augereau, Bernadotte, Soult, Brune, Lannes, Mortier, Ney, Davoust, Bessières, Kellermann, Lefebvre, Perignon, Serrurier.

July 14th.—Inauguration of the Legion of Honour.

No. 1.
To the Empress Josephine.

Pont-de-Bricques, July 21, 1804.

Madame and dear Wife,—During the four days that I have been away from you I have always been either on horseback or in a conveyance, without any ill effect on my health.

M. Maret tells me that you intend starting on Monday; travelling by easy stages, you can take your time and reach the Spa without tiring yourself.

The wind having considerably freshened last night, one of our gunboats, which was in the harbour, broke loose and ran on the rocks about a league from Boulogne.—I believed all lost men and merchandise; but we managed to save both. The spectacle was grand: the shore sheeted in fire from the alarm guns, the sea raging and bellowing, the whole night spent in anxiety to save these unfortunates or to see them perish! My soul hovered between eternity, the ocean, and the night. At 5 a.m. all was calm, everything saved; and I went to bed with the feeling of having had a romantic and epic dream—a circumstance which might have reminded me that I was all alone, had weariness and soaked garments left me any other need but that of sleep.

Napoleon.

[*Correspondence of Napoleon I.*, No. 7861, communicated by M. Chambry.]

No. 2.
To The Empress, at Aix-La-Chapelle.

Boulogne, August 3, 1804.

My Dear,—I trust soon to learn that the waters have done you much good. I am sorry to hear of all the vexations you have undergone. Please write me often. My health is very good, although I am rather tired. I shall be at Dunkirk in a very few days, and shall write you from there.

Eugène has started for Blois.

Je te couvre de baisers. Napoleon.

No. 3.
To the Empress, at Aix-La-Chapelle.

Calais, August 6, 1804.

My Dear,—I arrived at Calais at midnight; I expect to start tonight for Dunkirk. I am in very fair health, and satisfied with what I see. I trust that the waters are doing you as much good as exercise, camp, and seascape are doing me.

Eugène has set off for Blois. Hortense is well. Louis is at Plombières.

I am longing to see you. You are always necessary to my happiness. My very best love. Napoleon.

No. 4.
To the Empress, at Aix-La-Chapelle.

Ostend, August 14, 1804.

My Dear,—I have had no letter from you for several days; yet I should be more comfortable if I knew that the waters were efficacious, and how you spend your time. During the past week I have been at Ostend. The day after tomorrow I shall be at Boulogne for a somewhat special fete. Advise me by the courier what you intend to do, and how soon you expect to end your baths.

I am very well satisfied with the army and the flotillas. Eugène is still at Blois. I hear no more of Hortense than if she were on the Congo. I am writing to scold her.

My best love to all. Napoleon.

No. 5.
To the Empress, at Aix-La-Chapelle.

Arras, Wednesday, August 29, 1804.

Madame and dear Wife,—I have just reached Arras. I shall stay there tomorrow. I shall be at Mons on Friday, and on Sunday at Aix-la-Chapelle. I am as well satisfied with my journey as with the army. I think I shall pass through Brussels without stopping there; thence I shall go to Maestricht. I am rather impatient to see you. I am glad to hear you have tried the waters; they cannot fail to do you good. My health is excellent. Eugène is well, and is with me.

Very kindest regards to everyone. Bonaparte.

[Translated from a Letter in the *Collection of Baron Heath, Philobiblon Society*, vol. 14]

October 2nd.—Sir Sydney Smith attacks flotilla at Boulogne unsuccessfully.

No. 6.
To Josephine, at St. Cloud.

Trèves, October 6, 1804.

My Dear,—I arrive at Trèves the same moment that you arrive at St. Cloud. I am in good health. Do not grant an audience to T——, and refuse to see him. Receive B—— only in general company, and do not give him a private interview. Make prom-

ises to sign marriage contracts only after I have signed them.—
Yours ever,   Napoleon.

December 1st.—Plebiscite confirms election of Napoleon as Emperor, by 3,500,000 votes to 2000.

December 2nd.—Napoleon crowns himself Emperor, and Josephine Empress, in the presence and with the benediction of the Pope.

General Events.—*October 8th*—The negro Dessalines crowned Emperor of St. Domingo, under title of James I.

December 12th.—Spain declares war against England.

Series F

CAMPAIGN OF AUSTERLITZ, 1805.

To convey an idea of the brilliant campaign of 1805 . . . I should, like the almanac-makers, be obliged to note down a victory for every day.—Bourrienne, vol. 2. 323.

Si jamais correspondance de mari à femme à été intime et fréquente, si jamais continuité et permanence de tendresse à été marquée, c'est bien dans ces lettres écrites, chaque jour presque, par Napoléon à sa femme durant la campagne de l'an XIV.—F. Masson, *Joséphine, Impératrice et Reine*, 1899, p. 427.

LETTERS OF THE EMPEROR NAPOLEON TO THE EMPRESS JOSEPHINE, DURING THE AUSTERLITZ CAMPAIGN, 1805.

EVENTS OF 1805.

March 13th.—Napoleon proclaimed King of Italy.

May 26th.—Crowned at Milan.

June 8th.—Prince Eugène named Viceroy of Italy.

June 23rd.—Lucca made a principality, and given to Elisa Bonaparte.

July 22nd.—Naval battle between Villeneuve and Sir Robert Calder, which saves England from invasion.

August 16th.—Napoleon breaks up camp of Boulogne.

September 8th.—Third Continental Coalition (Russia, Austria, and England against France). Austrians cross the Inn, and invade Bavaria.

September 21st.—Treaty of Paris between France and Naples, which engages to take no part in the war.

September 23rd.—*Moniteur* announces invasion of Bavaria by Austria.

September 24th.—Napoleon leaves Paris.

September 27th.—Joins at Strasburg his Grand Army (160,000 strong}.

October 1st.—Arrives at Ettlingen.

October 2nd.—Arrives at Louisbourg. Hostilities commence.

No. 1
To Josephine, at Strasburg

Imperial Headquarters, Ettlingen,
October 2, 1805, 10 a.m.

I am well, and still here. I am starting for Stuttgard, where I shall be tonight. Great operations are now in progress. The armies of Wurtemberg and Baden have joined mine. I am well placed for the campaign, and I love you. Napoleon.

No. 2.
To Josephine, at Strasburg

Louisbourg, October 4, 1805, Noon.

I am at Louisbourg. I start tonight. There is as yet nothing new. My whole army is on the march. The weather is splendid. My junction with the Bavarians is effected. I am well. I trust in a few days to have something interesting to communicate.

Keep well, and believe in my entire affection. There is a brilliant Court here, a new bride who is very beautiful, and upon the whole some very pleasant people, even our Electress, who appears extremely kind, although the daughter of the King of England. Napoleon.

No. 3.
To Josephine, at Strasburg

Louisbourg, October 5, 1805.

I continue my march immediately. You will, My Dear, be five or six days without hearing from me; don't be uneasy, it is connected with operations now taking place. All goes well, and just as I could wish.

I have assisted at a marriage between the son of the Elector and a niece of the King of Prussia. I wish to give the young princess a wedding present to cost 36,000 to 40,000 *francs*. Please attend to this, and send it to the bride by one of my chamberlains, when they shall come to rejoin me. This matter must be attended to immediately.

Adieu, dear, I love you and embrace you.   Napoleon.

October 6th-7th.—French cross the Danube and turn Mack's army.

October 8th.—Battle of Wertingen. (Murat defeats the Austrians.)

October 9th.—Battle of Gunzburg. (Ney defeats Mack.)

No. 4.

October 10th.—French enter Augsbourg.

To Josephine, at Strasburg

Augsbourg, Thursday, October 10, 1805,
11 a.m.

I slept last night [1] with the former Elector of Trèves, who is very well lodged. For the past week I have been hurrying forward. The campaign has been successful enough so far. I am very well, although it rains almost every day. Events crowd on us rapidly. I have sent to France 4000 prisoners, 8 flags, and have 14 of the enemy's cannon.

Adieu, dear, I embrace you.   Napoleon.

October 11th.—Battle of Hasslach. Dupont holds his own against much superior forces.

No. 5.

October 12th.—French enter Munich.

To Josephine, at Strasburg

October 12, 1805, 11 p.m.

My army has entered Munich. On one side the enemy is beyond the Inn; I hold the other army, 60,000 strong, blocked on the Iller, between Ulm and Memmingen. The enemy is beaten, has lost its head, and everything points to a most glorious campaign, the shortest and most brilliant which has been made. In an hour I start for Burgau-sur-l'Iller.

I am well, but the weather is frightful. It rains so much that I change my clothes twice a day.

I love and embrace you.   Napoleon.

October 14th.—Capture of Memmingen and 4000 Austrians by

---

1. *J'ai couché aujourd'hui*—*i.e.* a few hours' morning sleep.

Soult.

October 15th.—Battle of Elchingen. Ney defeats Laudon.

October 17th.—Capitulation of Ulm.

No. 6.

October 19th.—Werneck and 8000 men surrender to Murat.

To Josephine, at Strasburg

Abbaye d'Elchingen, October 19, 1805.

My dear Josephine,—I have tired myself more than I ought. Soaked garments and cold feet every day for a week have made me rather ill, but I have spent the whole of today indoors, which has rested me.

My design has been accomplished; I have destroyed the Austrian army by marches alone; I have made 60,000 prisoners, taken 120 pieces of cannon, more than 90 flags, and more than 30 generals. I am about to fling myself on the Russians; they are lost men. I am satisfied with my army. I have only lost 1500 men, of whom two-thirds are but slightly wounded.

Prince Charles is on his way to cover Vienna. I think Massena should be already at Vicenza.

The moment I can give my thoughts to Italy, I will make Eugène win a battle.

Very best wishes to Hortense.

Adieu, my Josephine; kindest regards to everyone.

Napoleon.

October 20th.—Mack and his army defile before Napoleon.

No. 7.

October 21st.—Battle of Trafalgar; Franco-Spanish fleet destroyed after a five hours' fight. "The result of the battle of Trafalgar compensates, for England, the results of the operations of Ulm. It has been justly observed that this power alone, of all those who fought France from 1793 to 1812, never experienced a check in her political or military combinations without seeing herself compensated forthwith by a signal success in some other part of the world "(*Montgaillard*).

To the Empress, at Strasburg

Elchingen, October 21, 1805, Noon.

I am fairly well, my dear. I start at once for Augsbourg. I have made 33,000 men lay down their arms, I have from 60,000 to 70,000 prisoners, more than 90 flags, and 200 pieces of cannon. Never has there been such a catastrophe in military annals! Take care of yourself. I am rather jaded. The weather has been fine for the last three days. The first column of prisoners files off for France today. Each column consists of 6000 men.

Napoleon.

No. 8.

October 25th.—The Emperor of Russia and King of Prussia swear, at the tomb of the Great Frederick, to make implacable war on France (Convention signed November 3rd).

To the Empress, at Strasburg

Augsburg, October 25, 1805.

The two past nights have thoroughly rested me, and I am going to start tomorrow for Munich. I am sending word to M. de Talleyrand and M. Maret to be near at hand. I shall see something of them, and I am going to advance upon the Inn in order to attack Austria in the heart of her hereditary states. I should much have liked to see you; but do not reckon upon my sending for you, unless there should be an armistice or winter quarters. *Adieu*, dear; a thousand kisses. Give my compliments to the ladies.

Napoleon.

No. 9.

To the Empress, at Strasburg

Munich, Sunday, October 27, 1805.

I received your letter *per* Lemarois. I was grieved to see how needlessly you have made yourself unhappy. I have heard particulars which have proved how much you love me, but you should have more fortitude and confidence. Besides, I had advised you that I should be six days without writing you.

Tomorrow I expect the Elector. At noon I start to support my advance on the Inn. My health is fair. You need not think of crossing the Rhine for two or three weeks. You must be cheerful, amuse yourself, and hope that before the end of the month[2] we shall meet.

I am advancing against the Russian army. In a few days I shall

---

2. The month *Brumaire*—*i.e,* before November 21st.

have crossed the Inn.

Adieu, my dear; kindest regards to Hortense, Eugène, and the two Napoleons.

Keep back the wedding present a little longer.

Yesterday I gave a concert to the ladies of this court. The precentor is a superior man.

I took part in the Electors pheasant-shoot; you see by that that I am not so tired. M. de Talleyrand has come.

Napoleon.

October 28th.—Grand Army cross the Inn. Lannes occupies Braunau.

October 28th to October 29-30th.—Battle of Catchero.—Massena with 55,000 men attacks Archduke Charles entrenched with 70,000; after two days' fight French repulsed at this place, previously disastrous to their arms.

No. 10.
To the Empress, at Strasburg

Haag, November 3, 1805, 10 p.m.

I am in full march; the weather is very cold, the earth covered with a foot of snow. This is rather trying. Luckily there is no want of wood; here we are always in forests. I am fairly well. My campaign proceeds satisfactorily; my enemies must have more anxieties than I.

I wish to hear from you and to learn that you are not worrying yourself.

Adieu, dear; I am going to lie down. Napoleon.

November 4th.—Combat of Amstetten. Lannes and Murat drive back the Russians. Davoust occupies Steyer. Army of Italy takes Vicenza.

No. 2.
To the Empress, at Strasburg

Tuesday, November 5, 1805.

I am at Lintz. The weather is fine. We are within seventy miles of Vienna. The Russians do not stand; they are in full retreat. The house of Austria is at its wit's end, and in Vienna they are removing all the court belongings. It is probable that something new will occur within five or six days. I much desire to see you again. My health is good.

I embrace you.   Napoleon.

November 7th.—Ney occupies Innsbruck.

November 9th.—Davoust defeats Meerfeldt at Marienzell.

November 10th.—Marmont arrives at Leoben.

November 11th.—Battle of Diernstein; Mortier overwhelmed by Russians, but saved by Dupont.

November 13th.—Vienna entered and bridge over the Danube seized. Massena crosses the Tagliamento.

November 14th.—Ney enters Trent.

No. 12.
To the Empress, at Strasburg

November 15, 1805, 9 p.m.

I have been at Vienna two days, My Dear, rather fagged. I have not yet seen the city by day; I have traversed it by night. To-morrow I receive the notables and public bodies. Nearly all my troops are beyond the Danube, in pursuit of the Russians.
Adieu, Josephine; as soon as it is possible I will send for you. My very best love.   Napoleon.

No. 13.

November 16th.—Jellachich surrenders to Augereau at Feldkirch with 7000 men.

To the Empress, at Strasburg

Vienna, November 16, 1805.

I am writing to M. d'Harville, so that you can set out and make your way to Baden, thence to Stuttgard, and from there to Munich. At Stuttgard you will give the wedding present to the Princess Paul. If it costs fifteen to twenty thousand *francs*, that will suffice; the rest will do for giving presents at Munich to the daughters of the Electress of Bavaria. All that Madame de Serent[3] has advised you is definitely arranged. Take with you the wherewithal to make presents to the ladies and officers who will wait upon you. Be civil, but receive full homage; they owe everything to you, and you owe nothing save civility. The Elec-

---

3. Countess de Serent, the Empress's lady-in-waiting.

79

tress of Wurtemberg is daughter of the King of England. She is an excellent woman; you should be very kind to her, but yet without affectation.

I shall be very glad to see you, the moment circumstances permit me. I start to join my vanguard. The weather is frightful; it snows heavily. Otherwise my affairs go excellently.

Adieu, my dear. Napoleon.

November 19th.—French occupy Brunn, and Napoleon establishes his headquarters at Wischau.

November 24th.—Massena occupies Trieste.

November 28th.—Army of Italy joins troops of the Grand Army at Klagenfurt.

December 2nd.—Battle of the Three Emperors (Austerlitz). French forces 80,000; allies 95,000.

No. 14.
To the Empress, at Strasburg

Austerlitz, December 3, 1805.

I have despatched to you Lebrun from the field of battle. I have beaten the Russian and Austrian army commanded by the two Emperors. I am rather fagged. I have bivouacked eight days in the open air, through nights sufficiently keen. Tonight I rest in the chateau of Prince Kaunitz, where I shall sleep for the next two or three hours. The Russian army is not only beaten, but destroyed.

I embrace you. Napoleon.

December 4th.—Haugwitz, the Prussian Minister, congratulates Napoleon on his victory. "*Voilà!*" replied the Emperor; "*un compliment dont la fortune a changé l'addresse.*"

No. 15.
To the Empress, at Munich

Austerlitz, December 5, 1805.

I have concluded a truce. The Russians have gone. The battle of Austerlitz is the grandest of all I have fought. Forty-five flags, more than 150 pieces of cannon, the standards of the Russian Guard, 20 generals, 30,000 prisoners, more than 20,000 slain—a horrible sight.

The Emperor Alexander is in despair, and on his way to Russia. Yesterday, at my bivouac, I saw the Emperor of Germany. We conversed for two hours; we have agreed to make peace quickly.

The weather is not now very bad. At last behold peace restored to the Continent; it is to be hoped that it is going to be to the world. The English will not know how to face us.

I look forward with much pleasure to the moment when I can once more be near you. My eyes have been rather bad the last two days; I have never suffered from them before.

Adieu, my dear. I am fairly well, and very anxious to embrace you.   Napoleon.

No. 16.
To the Empress, at Munich

> Austerlitz, December 7, 1805.

I have concluded an armistice; within a week peace will be made. I am anxious to hear that you reached Munich in good health. The Russians are returning; they have lost enormously—more than 20,000 dead and 30,000 taken. Their army is reduced by three-quarters. Buxhowden, their general-in-chief, was killed. I have 3000 wounded and 700 to 800 dead.

My eyes are rather bad; it is a prevailing complaint, and scarcely worth mentioning.

Adieu, dear. I am very anxious to see you again.

I am going to sleep tonight at Vienna.   Napoleon.

No. 17.
To the Empress, at Munich

> Brunn, December 10, 1805.

It is a long time since I had news of you. Have the grand fêtes at Baden, Stuttgard, and Munich made you forget the poor soldiers, who live covered with mud, rain, and blood?

I shall start in a few days for Vienna.

We are endeavouring to conclude peace. The Russians have gone, and are in flight far from here; they are on their way back to Russia, well drubbed and very much humiliated.

I am very anxious to be with you again.

Adieu, dear.

My bad eyes are cured.   Napoleon.

December 15th.—Treaty with Prussia.

No. 18.
To the Empress, at Munich

December 19, 1805.

Great Empress,—Not a single letter from you since your departure from Strasburg. You have gone to Baden, Stuttgard, Munich, without writing us a word. This is neither very kind nor very affectionate.

I am still at Brunn. The Russians are gone. I have a truce. In a few days I shall see what I may expect. Deign from the height of your grandeur to concern yourself a little with your slaves.

Napoleon.

No. 19.
To the Empress, at Munich

Schönbrunn, December 20, 1805.

I got your letter of the 16th. I am sorry to learn you are in pain. You are not strong enough to travel two hundred and fifty miles at this time of the year. I know not what I shall do; I await events. I have no will in the matter; everything depends on their issue. Stay at Munich; amuse yourself. That is not difficult when you have so many kind friends and so beautiful a country. I, for my part, am sufficiently busy. In a few days my decision will be made.

Adieu, dear. Kindest and most affectionate regards.

Napoleon.

December 27th.[4]—Peace of Presburg.

December 31st.—Napoleon arrives outside Munich, and joins Josephine the next morning.

---

4. 6 *Nivose*, which for the year 1805 was December 27 (see Harris Nicolas' *Chronology of History*). Haydn, Woodward, Bouillet, all have December 26th; Alison and *Biographie Universelle* have December 27th; but, as usual, the *Correspondence of Napoleon I.* is taken here as the final court of appeal.

Series G

Battles then lasted a few hours, campaigns a few days.
—Bignon, *On Friedland* (vol. 6. 292).

1806.

January 1st.—The Elector of Bavaria and the Duke of Wurtemberg created Kings by France.

January 23rd.—Death of William Pitt, aged 47.

February 15th.—Joseph Bonaparte enters Naples, and on

March 10th is declared King of the Two Sicilies.

April 1st.—Prussia seizes Hanover.

June 5th.—Louis Bonaparte made King of Holland.

July 6th.—Battle of Maida (Calabria. English defeat General Reynier. French loss 4000; English 500).

July 12th.—Napoleon forms Confederation of the Rhine, 'with himself at Chief and Protector.

July 18th.—Gaeta surrenders to Massena.

August 6th.—Francis II., Emperor of Germany, becomes Emperor of Austria as Francis 7.

August 15th.—Russia refuses to ratify peace preliminaries signed by her ambassador at Paris on July 25th.

September 13th.—Death of Charles James Fox, aged 57.

No. 1

October 5th.—Proclamation by the Prince of the Peace against France (germ of Spanish War).

To the Empress, at Mayence

October 5, 1806.

It will be quite in order for the Princess of Baden to come to Mayence. I cannot think why you weep; you do wrong to make yourself ill. Hortense is inclined to pedantry; she loves to air her views. She has written me; I am sending her a reply. She ought to be happy and cheerful. Pluck and a merry heart—that's the recipe.

Adieu, dear. The Grand Duke has spoken to me about you; he saw you at Florence at the time of the retreat.

Napoleon.

No. 2.

To the Empress, at Mayence

Bamberg, October 7, 1806.

I start this evening, My Dear, for Cronach. The whole of my army is advancing. All goes well. My health is perfect. I have only received as yet one letter from you. I have some from Eugène and from Hortense. Stephanie should now be with you. Her husband wishes to make the campaign; he is with me.

Adieu. A thousand kisses and the best of health.

Napoleon.

October 8th.—Prussia, assisted by Saxony, Russia, and England, declares war against France.

October 9th.—Campaign opens. Prussians defeated at Schleitz.

October 10th.—Lannes defeats them at Saalfeld. Prince Louis of Prussia killed; 1000 men and 30 guns taken.

October 11th.—French peace negotiations with England broken off.

No. 3.

To the Empress, at Mayence

Gera, October 13, 1806, 2 a.m.

My Dear,—I am at Gera today. My affairs go excellently well, and everything as I could wish. With the aid of God, they will,

I believe, in a few days have taken a terrible course for the poor King of Prussia, whom I am sorry for personally, because he is a good man. The Queen is at Erfurt with the King. If she wants to see a battle, she shall have that cruel pleasure. I am in splendid health.

I have already put on flesh since my departure; yet I am doing, in person, twenty and twenty-five leagues a day, on horseback, in my carriage, in all sorts of ways. I lie down at eight, and get up at midnight. I fancy at times that you have not yet gone to bed.—Yours ever, Napoleon.

October 14th.—Battles of Jena and Auerstadt.

No. 4.

October 15th.—Napoleon at Weimar. He releases 6000 Saxon prisoners , which soon causes peace with Saxony.

To the Empress, at Mayence

Jena, October 15, 1806, 3 a.m.

My Dear,—I have made excellent manoeuvres against the Prussians. Yesterday I won a great victory. They had 150,000 men. I have made 20,000 prisoners, taken 100 pieces of cannon, and flags. I was in presence of the King of Prussia, and near to him; I nearly captured him and the Queen. For the past two days I have bivouacked. I am in excellent health.

Adieu, dear. Keep well, and love me.

If Hortense is at Mayence, give her a kiss; also to Napoleon and to the little one.

Napoleon.

No. 5.

October 16th.—Soult routs Kalkreuth at Greussen; Erfurt and 16,000 men capitulate to Murat.

To the Empress, at Mayence

Weimar, October 16, 1806, 5 p.m.

M. Talleyrand will have shown you the bulletin, my dear; you will see my successes therein. All has happened as I calculated, and never was an army more thoroughly beaten and more entirely destroyed. I need only add that I am very well, and that fatigue, bivouacs, and night-watches have made me fat.

Adieu, dear. Kindest regards to Hortense and to the great M. Napoleon.—Yours ever,   Napoleon.

October 17th.—Bernadotte defeats Prussian reserve at Halle.

October 18th.—Davoust takes Leipsic, and an enormous stock of English merchandise,

October 19th.—Napoleon at Halle.

October 20th.—Lannes takes Dessau, and Davoust Wittenberg.

October 21st.—Napoleon at Dessau.

No. 6.

October 23rd.—Napoleon males Wittenberg central depot for his army.

To the Empress, at Mayence

Wittenberg, October 23, 1 806, Noon.
I have received several of your letters. I write you only a line. My affairs prosper. Tomorrow I shall be at Potsdam, and at Berlin on the 25th. I am wonderfully well, and thrive on hard work. I am very glad to hear you are with Hortense and Stephanie, *en grande compagnie*. So far, the weather has been fine.
Kind regards to Stephanie, and to everybody, not forgetting M. Napoleon.
Adieu, dear.—Yours ever,   Napoleon.

No. 7.

October 24th.—Lannes occupies Potsdam.

To the Empress, at Mayence

Potsdam, October 24, 1806.
My Dear,—I have been at Potsdam since yesterday, and shall remain there today. I continue satisfied with my undertakings. My health is good; the weather very fine. I find Sans-Souci very pleasant.
Adieu, dear. Best wishes to Hortense and to M. Napoleon.

Napoleon.

October 25th.—Marshal Davoust enters Berlin; Bernadotte occupies Brandenburg.

October 28th.—Prince Hohenlohe surrenders at Prenzlau to Murat with 16,000 men, including the Prussian Guard.

October 30th.—Stettin surrenders with 5000 men and 150 cannon.

No. 8.

November 1st.—Anklam surrenders, with 4000 men, to General Becker.

To the Empress, at Mayence

November 1, 1806, 2 a.m.

Talleyrand has just arrived and tells me, my dear, that you do nothing but cry. What on earth do you want? You have your daughter, your grandchildren, and good news; surely these are sufficient reasons for being happy and contented.

The weather here is superb; there has not yet fallen during the whole campaign a single drop of water. I am very well, and all goes excellently.

Adieu, dear; I have received a letter from M. Napoleon; I do not believe it is from him, but from Hortense. Kindest regards to everybody. Napoleon.

November 2nd.—Kustrin surrenders, with 4000 men and 90 guns, to Davoust.

No. 9.
To the Empress, at Mayence

Berlin, November 2, 1806.

Your letter of October 26th to hand. We have splendid weather here. You will see by the bulletin that we have taken Stettin—it is a very strong place. All my affairs go as well as possible, and I am thoroughly satisfied. One pleasure is alone wanting—that of seeing you, but I hope that will not long be deferred.

Kindest regards to Hortense, Stephanie, and to the little Napoleon.

Adieu, dear.—Yours ever, Napoleon.

No. 9A.
From the *Memoirs of Mademoiselle d'Avrillon* (vol. 1. 128).

To the Empress, at Mayence

Berlin, Monday, Noon.

My Dear,—I have received your letter. I am glad to know that you are in a place which pleases me, and especially to know that you are very well there. Who should be happier than you? You should live without a worry, and pass your time as pleasantly as possible; that, indeed, is my intention.

I forbid you to see Madame Tallien, under any pretext whatever. I will admit of no excuse. If you desire a continuance of my esteem, if you wish to please me, never transgress the present order. She may possibly come to your apartments, to enter them by night; forbid your porter to admit her.

I shall soon be at Malmaison. I warn you to have no lovers there that night; I should be sorry to disturb them. *Adieu*, dear; I long to see you and assure you of my love and affection.

Napoleon.

No. 10.
To the Empress, at Mayence

November 6, 1806, 9 p.m.

Yours to hand, in which you seem annoyed at the bad things I say about women; it is true that I hate intriguing women more than anything. I am used to kind, gentle, persuasive women; these are the kind I like. If I have been spoilt, it is not my fault, but yours. Moreover, you shall learn how kind I have been to one who showed herself sensible and good, Madame d'Hatzfeld. When I showed her husband's letter to her she admitted to me, amid her sobs, with profound emotion, and frankly, "Ah! it is indeed his writing!" While she was reading, her voice went to my heart; it pained me.

I said, "Well, *madame*, throw that letter on the fire, I shall then have no longer the power to punish your husband." She burnt the letter, and seemed very happy. Her husband now feels at ease; two hours later he would have been a dead man. You see then how I like kind, frank, gentle women; but it is because such alone resemble you.

Adieu, dear; my health is good. Napoleon.

November 6th and 7th.—Blucher and his army (17,000 men) surrender at Lubeck to Soult, Murat, and Bernadotte.

November 8th.—Magdeburg surrenders to Ney, with 20,000 men, immense stores, and nearly 800 cannon.

No. 2.

November 9th.—Napoleon levies a contribution of 150 million *francs* on Prussia and her allies.

To the Empress, at Mayence

Berlin, November 9, 1806.

My Dear,—I am sending good news. Magdeburg has capitulated, and on November 7th I took 20,000 men at Lubeck who escaped me last week. The whole Prussian army, therefore, is captured; even beyond the Vistula there does not remain to Prussia 20,000 men. Several of my army corps are in Poland. I am still at Berlin. I am very fairly well.

Adieu, dear; heartiest good wishes to Hortense, Stephanie, and the two little Napoleons.—Yours ever,   Napoleon.

November 10th.—Davoust occupies Posen. Hanover occupied by Marshal Mortier.

No. 12.
To the Empress, at Mayence

Berlin, November 16, 1806.

I received your letter of November 11th. I note with satisfaction that my convictions give you pleasure. You are wrong to think flattery was intended; I was telling you of yourself as I see you. I am grieved to think that you are tired of Mayence. Were the journey less long, you might come here, for there is no longer an enemy, or, if there is, he is beyond the Vistula; that is to say, more than three hundred miles away. I will wait to hear what you think about it. I should also be delighted to see M. Napoleon.

Adieu, my dear.—Yours ever,   Napoleon.

I have still too much business here for me to return to Paris.

November 17th.—Suspension of arms signed at Charlottenburg.

November 19th.—French occupy Hamburg.

November 20th.—French occupy Hameln.

November 21st.—French occupy Bremen. Berlin decree. Napoleon interdicts trade with England.

No. 13.
To the Empress, at Mayence

November 22, 1806, 10 p.m.

Your letter received. I am sorry to find you in the dumps; yet you have every reason to be cheerful. You are wrong to show so much kindness to people who show themselves unworthy of it. Madame L—— is a fool; such an idiot that you ought to know her by this time, and pay no heed to her. Be contented, happy in my friendship, and in the great influence you possess. In a few days I shall decide whether to summon you hither or send you to Paris.

Adieu, dear; you can go at once, if you like, to Darmstadt, or to Frankfort; that will make you forget your troubles.

Kindest regards to Hortense. Napoleon.

November 25th.—Napoleon leaves Berlin.

No. 14.
To the Empress, at Mayence

Kustrin, November 26, 1806.

I am at Kustrin, making a tour and spying out the land a little; I shall see in a day or two whether you should come. You can keep ready. I shall be very pleased if the Queen of Holland be of the party. The Grand Duchess of Baden must write to her husband about it.

It is 2 a.m. I am just getting up; it is the usage of war. Kindest regards to you and to everyone.

Napoleon.

No. 15.

November 27th.—Napoleon arrives at Posen.

To the Empress, at Mayence

Meseritz, November 27, 1806, 2 a.m.

I am about to make a tour in Poland. This is the first town there. Tonight I shall be at Posen, after which I shall send for you to come to Berlin, so that you can arrive there the same day as I. My health is good, the weather rather bad; it has rained for the past three days. My affairs prosper. The Russians are in flight.

Adieu, dear; kindest regards to Hortense, Stephanie, and the little Napoleons.   Napoleon.

November 28th.—Murat enters Warsaw. French occupy Duchies of Mecklenburg.

No. 16.
To The Empress, at Mayence

Posen, November 29, 1806, Noon.

I am at Posen, capital of Great Poland. The cold weather has set in; I am in good health. I am about to take a circuit round Poland. My troops are at the gates of Warsaw.

Adieu, dear; very kindest regards, and a hearty embrace.

No. 17.

December 2nd.—Glogau surrenders to Vandamme.

To the Empress, at Mayence

Posen, December 2, 1806.

Today is the anniversary of Austerlitz. I have been to a city ball. It is raining; I am in good health. I love you and long for you. My troops are at Warsaw. So far the cold has not been severe. All these fair Poles are Frenchwomen at heart; but there is only one woman for me. Would you know her? I could draw her portrait very well; but I should have to flatter it too much for you to recognise yourself; yet, to tell the truth, my heart would only have nice things to say to you. These nights are long, all alone.—Yours ever,

Napoleon,

No. 18.
To the Empress, at Mayence

December 3, 1806, Noon.

Yours of November 26th received. I notice two things in it. You say I do not read your letters: it is an unkind thought. I take your bad opinion anything but kindly. You tell me that perhaps it is a mere phantasy of the night, and you add that you are not jealous. I found out long ago that angry persons always assert that they are not angry; that those who are afraid keep on re-peating that they have no fear; you therefore are convinced of jealousy. I am delighted to hear it! Nevertheless, you are wrong; I think of nothing less, and in the desert plains of Poland one thinks little about beauties. . . .

I had yesterday a ball of the provincial nobility—the women good-looking enough, rich enough, dowdy enough, although in Paris fashions.

Adieu, dear; I am in good health.—Yours ever,

Napoleon.

No. 19.
To the Empress, at Mayence

Posen, December 3, 1806, 6 p.m.

Yours of November 27th received, from which I see that your little head is quite turned. I am reminded of the verse

Désir de femme est un feu qui dévore.

Still you must calm yourself. I wrote you that I was in Poland; that, when we were established in winter quarters, you could come; you will have to wait a few days. The greater one becomes, the less one can consult one's wishes—being dependent on events and circumstances. You can come to Frankfort or Darmstadt. I am hoping to send for you in a few days; that is, if circumstances will permit. The warmth of your letter makes me realise that you, like other pretty women, know no bounds. What you will, must be; but, as for me, I declare that of all men I am the greatest slave; my master has no pity, and this master is the nature of things.

Adieu, dear; keep well. The person that I wished to speak to you about is Madame L——, of whom everyone is speaking ill; they assure me that she is more Prussian than French woman. I don't believe it, but I think her an idiot who talks nothing but trash. Napoleon.

December 6th.—Thorn (on the Vistula) occupied by Ney.

No. 20.
To the Empress, at Mayence

Posen, December 9, 1806.

Yours of December 1st received. I see with pleasure that you are more cheerful; that the Queen of Holland wishes to come with you. I long to give the order; but you must still wait a few days. My affairs prosper.

Adieu, dear; I love you and wish to see you happy.

Napoleon.

<h1 style="text-align:center">No. 21.</h1>

To the Empress, at Mayence

Posen, December 10, 1806, 5 p.m.

An officer has just brought me a rug, a gift from you; it is some-what short and narrow, but I thank you for it none the less. I am in fair health. The weather is very changeable. My affairs prosper pretty well. I love you and long for you much.

Adieu, dear; I shall write for you to come with at least as much pleasure as you will have in coming.—Yours ever,

Napoleon.

A kiss to Hortense, Stephanie, and Napoleon.

December 11th.—Davoust forces the passage of the Bug.

<h1 style="text-align:center">No. 22.</h1>

December 12th.—Treaty of peace and alliance between France and Saxony signed at Posen.

To the Empress, at Mayence

Posen, December 12th, 1806, 7 p.m.

My Dear,—I have not received any letters from you, but know, nevertheless, that you are well. My health is good, the weather very mild; the bad season has not begun yet, but the roads are bad in a country where there are no highways. Hortense will come then with Napoleon; I am delighted to hear it. I long to see things shape themselves into a position to enable you to come.

I have made peace with Saxony. The Elector is King and one of the confederation.

Adieu, my well-beloved Josephine.—Yours ever,

Napoleon.

A kiss to Hortense, Napoleon, and Stephanie.

Päer, the famous musician, his wife, a *virtuoso* whom you saw at Milan twelve years ago, and Brizzi are here; they give me a little music every evening.

<h1 style="text-align:center">No. 23.</h1>

To the Empress, at Mayence

December 15, 1806, 3 p.m.

My Dear,—I start for Warsaw. In a fortnight I shall be back; I hope then to be able to send for you. But if that seems a long time, I should be very glad if you would return to Paris, where you are wanted. You well know that I am dependent on events. All my affairs go excellently. My health is very good; I am as well as possible.

Adieu, dear. I have made peace with Saxony.—Yours ever,

Napoleon.

December 17th.—Turkey declares war on Russia. (So Montgaillard; but Napoleon refers to it in the thirty-ninth bulletin, dated December 7th, while Haydn dates it January 7th.)

No. 24.
To the Empress, at Mayence

Warsaw, December 20, 1806, 3 p.m.

I have no news from you, dear. I am very well. The last two days I have been at Warsaw. My affairs prosper. The weather is very mild, and even somewhat humid. It has as yet barely begun to freeze; it is October weather.

Adieu, dear; I should much have liked to see you, but trust that in five or six days I shall be able to send for you.

Kindest regards to the Queen of Holland and to her little Napoleons.—Yours ever,   Napoleon.

December 22nd.—Napoleon crosses the Narew, and the next day defeats Russians at Czarnowo; also

December 24th.—At Nasielsk.

December 26th.—Ney defeats Lestocq at Soldau; Lannes defeats Beningsen at Pultusk;

December 28th.—And Augereau defeats Buxhowden at Golymin.

No. 25.
To the Empress, at Mayence

Golymin, December 29, 1806, 5 a.m.

I write you only a line, my dear. I am in a wretched barn. I have beaten the Russians, taken thirty pieces of cannon, their baggage, and 6000 prisoners; but the weather is frightful. It is raining; we have mud up to our knees.

In two days I shall be at Warsaw, whence I shall write you.—
Yours ever,   Napoleon.

No. 26.
To the Empress, at Mayence

Pultusk, December 31, 1806.

I have had a good laugh over your last letters. You idealise the fair ones of Great Poland in a way they do not deserve. I have had for two or three days the pleasure of hearing Päer and two lady singers, who have given me some very good music. I received your letter in a wretched barn, having mud, wind, and straw for my only bed. Tomorrow I shall be at Warsaw. I think all is over for this year. The army is entering winter quarters. I shrug my shoulders at the stupidity of Madame de L——; still you should show her your displeasure, and counsel her not to be so idiotic. Such things become common property, and make many people indignant.

For my part, I scorn ingratitude as the worst fault in a human heart. I know that instead of comforting you, these people have given you pain.

Adieu, dear; I am in good health. I do not think you ought to go to Cassel; that place is not suitable. You may go to Darmstadt.

Napoleon.

No. 27.
To the Empress, at Mayence

Warsaw, January 3, 1807.

My Dear,—I have received your letter. Your grief pains me; but one must bow to events. There is too much country to travel between Mayence and Warsaw; you must, therefore, wait till circumstances allow me to come to Berlin, in order that I may write you to come thither. It is true that the enemy, defeated, is far away; but I have many things here to put to rights. I should be inclined to think that you might return to Paris, where you are needed. Send away those ladies who have their affairs to look after; you will be better without people who have given you so much worry.

My health is good; the weather bad. I love you from my heart.

Napoleon.

January 5th.—Capture of Breslau, with 7000 men, by Vandamme and Hédouville.

No. 28.

January 7th.—English Orders in Council against Berlin Decree.

To the Empress, at Mayence

Warsaw, January 7, 1807.

My Dear,—I am pained by all that you tell me; but the season being cold, the roads very bad and not at all safe, I cannot consent to expose you to so many fatigues and dangers. Return to Paris in order to spend the winter there. Go to the Tuileries; receive, and lead the same life as you are accustomed to do when I am there; that is my wish. Perhaps I shall not be long in rejoining you there; but it is absolutely necessary for you to give up the idea of making a journey of 750 miles at this time of the year, through the enemy's country, and in the rear of the army. Believe that it costs me more than you to put off for some weeks the pleasure of seeing you, but so events and the success of my enterprise order it.

Adieu, my dear; be cheerful, and show character.

Napoleon,

No. 29.
To the Empress, at Mayence

Warsaw, January 8, 1807.

My Dear,—I received your letter of the 27th with those of M. Napoleon and Hortense, which were enclosed with it. I had begged you to return to Paris. The season is too inclement, the roads unsafe and detestable; the distances too great for me to permit you to come hither, where my affairs detain me. It would take you at least a month to come. You would arrive ill; by that time it might perhaps be necessary to start back again; it would therefore be folly. Your residence at Mayence is too dull; Paris reclaims you; go there, it is my wish. I am more vexed about it than you. I should have liked to spend the long nights of this season with you, but we must obey circumstances.

Adieu, dear.—Yours ever,

Napoleon.

No. 30.
To the Empress, at Mayence

Warsaw, January 11, 1807.

Your letter of the 27th received, from which I note that you are somewhat uneasy about military events. Everything is settled, as I have told you, to my satisfaction; my affairs prosper. The distance is too great for me to allow you to come so far at this time of year. I am in splendid health, sometimes rather wearied by the length of the nights.

Up to the present I have seen few people here. *Adieu*, dear. I wish you to be cheerful, and to give a little life to the capital. I would much like to be there.—Yours ever,

Napoleon.

I hope that the Queen has gone to the Hague with M. Napoleon.

No. 31.

January 16th.—Capture of Brieg by the French.

To the Empress, at Mayence

January 16, 1807.

My Dear,—I have received your letter of the 5th of January; all that you tell me of your unhappiness pains me. Why these tears, these repinings? Have you then no longer any fortitude? I shall see you soon. Never doubt my feelings; and if you wish to be still dearer to me, show character and strength of mind. I am humiliated to think that my wife can distrust my destinies.

Adieu, dear. I love you, I long to see you, and wish to learn that you are content and happy.   Napoleon.

No. 32.

To the Empress, at Mayence

Warsaw, January 18, 1807.

I fear that you are greatly grieved at our separation and at your return to Paris, which must last for some weeks longer. I insist on your having more fortitude. I hear you are always weeping. Fie! how unbecoming it is! Your letter of January 7th makes me unhappy. Be worthy of me; assume more character. Cut a suitable figure at Paris; and, above all, be contented.

I am very well, and I love you much; but, if you are always crying, I shall think you without courage and without character. I do not love cowards. An empress ought to have fortitude.

Napoleon.

No. 33.
To the Empress, at Mayence

Warsaw, January 19, 1807.

My Dear,—Your letter to hand. I have laughed at your fear of fire. I am in despair at the tone of your letters and at what I hear. I forbid you to weep, to be petulant and uneasy; I want you to be cheerful, lovable, and happy. Napoleon.

No. 34.
To the Empress, at Mayence

Warsaw, January 23, 1807.

Your letter of January 15th to hand. It is impossible to allow women to make such a journey as this—bad roads, miry and unsafe. Return to Paris; be cheerful and content there. Perhaps even I shall soon be there. I have laughed at what you say about your having taken a husband to be with him. I thought, in my ignorance, that the wife was made for the husband, the husband for his country, his family, and glory. Pardon my ignorance; one is always learning from our fair ladies.

Adieu, my dear. Think how much it costs me not to send for you. Say to yourself, "It is a proof how precious I am to him."

Napoleon.

No. 35.

January 25th.—Russians defeated at Mobrungen by Bernadotte.

To the Empress, at Mayence

January 25, 1807.

I am very unhappy to see you are in pain. I hope that you are at Paris; you will get better there. I share your griefs, and do not groan. For I could not risk losing you by exposing you to fatigues and dangers which befit neither your rank nor your sex. I wish you never to receive T—— at Paris; he is a black sheep. You would grieve me by doing otherwise. *Adieu*, my dear. Love me, and be courageous. Napoleon.

No. 36.
To the Empress, at Paris

Warsaw, January 26, 1807, Noon.

My Dear,—I have received your letter. It pains me to see how you are fretting yourself. The bridge of Mayence neither increases nor decreases the distance which separates us. Remain, therefore, at Paris. I should be vexed and uneasy to know that you were so miserable and so isolated at Mayence. You must know that I ought, that I can, consider only the success of my enterprise. If I could consult my heart I should be with you, or you with me; for you would be most unjust if you doubted my love and entire affection. Napoleon.

No. 37.
To the Empress, at Paris

Willemberg, February 1, 1807, Noon.
Your letter of the 11th, from Mayence, has made me laugh. Today, I am a hundred miles from Warsaw; the weather is cold, but fine.
Adieu, dear; be happy, show character.

Napoleon.

No. 38.
To the Empress, at Paris

My Dear,—Your letter of January 20th has given me pain; it is too sad. That's the fault of not being a little more devout! You tell me that your glory consists in your happiness. That is narrow-minded; one should say, my glory consists in the happiness of others. It is not conjugal; one should say, my glory consists in the happiness of my husband. It is not maternal; one should say, my glory consists in the happiness of my children. Now, since nations—your husband, your children—can only be happy with a certain amount of glory, you must not make little of it. Fie, Josephine! your heart is excellent and your arguments weak. You feel acutely, but you don't argue as well.
That's sufficient quarrelling. I want you to be cheerful, happy in your lot, and that you should obey, not with grumbling and tears, but with gaiety of heart and a little more good temper.
Adieu, dear; I start tonight to examine my outposts.

Napoleon.

February 5th.—Combats of Bergfriede, Wallersdorf, and Deppen; Russians forced back.

February 6th.—Combat of Hof. Murat victorious.

February 8th.—Battle of Eylau; retreat of Russians.

No. 39.
To the Empress, at Paris

Eylau, February 9, 1807, 3 a.m.

My Dear,—Yesterday there was a great battle; the victory has remained with me, but I have lost many men. The loss of the enemy, which is still more considerable, does not console me. To conclude, I write you these two lines myself, although I am very tired, to tell you that I am well and that I love you.—Yours ever, Napoleon.

No. 40.
To the Empress, at Paris

Eylau, February 9, 1807, 6 p.m.

My Dear,—I write you a line in order that you may not be uneasy. The enemy has lost the battle, 40 pieces of cannon, 10 flags, 12,000 prisoners; he has suffered frightfully. I have lost many: 1600 killed, 3000 or 4000 wounded.

Your cousin Tascher conducts himself well; I have summoned him near me with the title of orderly officer.

Corbineau has been killed by a shell; I was singularly attached to that officer, who had much merit; I am very unhappy about him. My mounted guard has covered itself with glory. Dahlman is dangerously wounded.

Adieu, dear.—Yours ever, Napoleon.

No. 41.
To the Empress, at Paris

Eylau, February 11 1807, 3 a.m.

My Dear,—I write you a line; you must have been very anxious. I have beaten the enemy in a fight to be remembered, but it has cost many brave lives. The bad weather that has set in forces me to take cantonments.

Do not afflict yourself, please; all this will soon be over, and the happiness of seeing you will make me promptly forget my fatigues. Besides, I have never been in better health.

Young Tascher, of the 4th Regiment, has behaved well; he has had a rough time of it. I have summoned him near me; I have made him an orderly officer—there's an end to his troubles.

This young man interests me.

Adieu, dear; a thousand kisses. Napoleon.

No. 42.
To the Empress, at Paris

Preussich-Eylau, February 12, 1807.
I send you a letter from General Darmagnac. He is a very good soldier, who commanded the 32nd. He is much attached to me. If this Madame de Richmond be well off, and it is a good match, I shall see this marriage with pleasure. Make this known to both of them. Napoleon.

No. 43.
To the Empress, at Paris

Eylau, February 14, 1807.
My Dear,—I am still at Eylau. This country is covered with dead and wounded. It is not the bright side of warfare; one suffers, and the mind is oppressed at the sight of so many victims. My health is good. I have done as I wished, and driven back the enemy, while making his projects fail.

You are sure to be uneasy, and that thought troubles me. Nevertheless, calm yourself, My dear, and be cheerful.—Yours ever,
Napoleon.

Tell Caroline and Pauline that the Grand Duke and the Prince[1] are in excellent health.

February 16th.—Savary defeats Russians at Ostrolenka.

No. 44.
To the Empress, at Paris

Eylau, February 17, 1807, 3 a.m.
Your letter to hand, informing me of your arrival at Paris. I am very glad to know you are there. My health is good.

The battle of Eylau was very sanguinary, and very hardly contested. Corbineau was slain. He was a very brave man. I had grown very fond of him.

Adieu, dear; it is as warm here as in the month of April; everything is thawing. My health is good.
Napoleon.

---

1. Murat and Borghèse.

No. 45.
To the Empress, at Paris

Landsberg, February 18, 1807, 3 a.m.

I write you two lines. My health is good. I am moving to set my army in winter quarters.

It rains and thaws as in the month of April. We have not yet had one cold day.

Adieu, dear.—Yours ever, Napoleon.

No. 46.
To the Empress, at Paris

Liebstadt, February 20, 1807, 2 a.m.

I write you two lines, dear, in order that you may not be uneasy. My health is very good, and my affairs prosper.

I have again put my army into cantonments.

The weather is extraordinary; it freezes and thaws; it is wet and unsettled.

Adieu, dear.—Yours ever, Napoleon.

No. 47.
To the Empress, at Paris

Liebstadt, February 21, 1807, 2 a.m.

Your letter of the 4th February to hand; I see with pleasure that your health is good. Paris will thoroughly re-establish it by giving you cheerfulness and rest, and a return to your accustomed habits.

I am wonderfully well. The weather and the country are vile. My affairs are fairly satisfactory. It thaws and freezes within twenty-four hours; there can never have been known such an extraordinary winter.

Adieu, dear; I love you, I think of you, and wish to know that you are contented, cheerful, and happy.—Yours ever,

Napoleon.

No. 48.
To the Empress, at Paris

Liebstadt, February 21, 1807, Noon.

My Dear,—Your letter of the 8th received; I see with pleasure that you have been to the opera, and that you propose holding receptions weekly. Go occasionally to the theatre, and always into the Royal box. I notice also with pleasure the banquets you are giving.

I am very well. The weather is still unsettled; it freezes and thaws.

I have once more put my army into cantonments in order to rest them.

Never be doleful, love me, and believe in my entire affection.

Napoleon.

No. 49.
To the Empress, at Paris

Osterode, February 23, 1807, 2 p.m.

My Dear,—Your letter of the 10th received. I am sorry to see you are a little out of sorts.

I have been in the country for the past month, experiencing frightful weather, because it has been unsettled, and varying from cold to warm within a week. Still, I am very well.

Try and pass your time pleasantly; have no anxieties, and never doubt the love I bear you. Napoleon.

February 26th.—Dupont defeats Russians at Braunsberg.

No. 50.
To the Empress, at Paris

Osterode, March 2, 1807.

My Dear,—It is two or three days since I wrote to you; I reproach myself for it; I know your uneasiness. I am very well; my affairs prosper. I am in a wretched village, where I shall pass a considerable time; it is not as good as the great city! I again assure you, I was never in such good health; you will find me very much stouter.

It is spring weather here; the snow has gone, the streams are thawing—which is what I want.

I have ordered what you wish for Malmaison; be cheerful and happy; it is my will.

Adieu, dear; I embrace you heartily.—Yours ever,

Napoleon.

March 9th.—The Grand Sanhedrim, which assembled at Paris on February 9, terminates its sittings.

No. 51.
To the Empress, at Paris

Osterode, March 10, 1807, 4 p.m.

My Dear,—I have received your letter of the 25th. I see with pleasure that you are well, and that you sometimes make a pilgrimage to Malmaison.

My health is good, and my affairs prosper.

The weather has become rather cold again. I see that the winter has been very variable everywhere.

Adieu, dear; keep well, be cheerful, and never doubt my affection,—Yours ever, Napoleon.

No. 52.
To the Empress, at Paris

Osterode, March 11, 1807.

My Dear,—I received your letter of the 27th. I am sorry to see from it that you are ill; take courage. My health is good; my affairs prosper. I am waiting for fine weather, which should soon be here. I love you and want to know that you are content and cheerful.

A great deal of nonsense will be talked of the battle of Eylau; the bulletin tells everything; our losses are rather exaggerated in it than minimised.—Yours ever, Napoleon.

No. 53.
To the Empress, at Paris

Osterode, March 13, 1807, 2 p.m.

My Dear,—I learn that the vexatious tittle-tattle that occurred in your salon at Mayence has begun again; make people hold their tongues. I shall be seriously annoyed with you if you do not find a remedy. You allow yourself to be worried by the chatter of people who ought to console you. I desire you to have a little character, and to know how to put everybody into his (or her) proper place.

I am in excellent health. My affairs here are good. We are resting a little, and organising our food supply.

Adieu, dear; keep well. Napoleon.

No. 54.
To the Empress, at Paris

Osterode, March 15, 1807.

I received your letter of the 1st of March, from which I see that you were much upset by the catastrophe of Minerva at the opera. I am very glad to see that you go out and seek distractions.

My health is very good. My affairs go excellently. Take no heed of all the unfavourable rumours that may be circulated. Never doubt my affection, and be without the least uneasiness.— Yours ever,   Napoleon.

No. 55.
To the Empress, at Paris

Osterode, March 17, 1807.

My Dear,—It is not necessary for you to go to the small plays and into a private box; it ill befits your rank; you should only go to the four great theatres, and always into the Royal box. Live as you would do if I were at Paris.

My health is very good. The cold weather has recommenced. The thermometer has been down to 8°.—Yours ever,

Napoleon.

No. 56.
To the Empress, at Paris

Osterode, March 17, 1807, 10 p.m.

I have received yours of March 5th, from which I see with pleasure that you are well. My health is perfect. Yet the weather of the past two days has been cold again; the thermometer to-night has been at 10°, but the sun has given us a very fine day. *Adieu*, dear. Very kindest regards to everybody.

Tell me something about the death of that poor Dupuis; have his brother told that I wish to help him.

My affairs here go excellently.—Yours ever,

Napoleon.

No. 57.

March 25th.—Abolition of slave trade in Great Britain by Parliament.

April, and to go to St. Cloud on May 1st. You may go and spend the Sundays, and a day or two, at Malmaison. At St. Cloud you may have your usual visitors.

My health is good. It is still quite cold enough here. All is quiet.

I have named the little princess Josephine.[2] Eugène should be well pleased.—Yours ever,

Napoleon.

No. 60.
To the Empress, at Paris

Finckenstein, April 2, 1807.

My Dear,—I write you a line. I have just moved my headquarters into a very fine *château*, after the style of Bessières', where I have several fireplaces, which is a great comfort to me; getting up often in the night, I like to see the fire.

My health is perfect. The weather is fine, but still cold. The thermometer is at four to five degrees.

Adieu, dear.—Yours ever,

Napoleon.

No. 61.
To the Empress, at Paris

Finckenstein, April 6, 1807, 3 p.m.

My Dear,—I have received your letter, from which I see you have spent Holy Week at Malmaison, and that your health is better. I long to hear that you are thoroughly well.

I am in a fine *château*, where there are fireplaces, which I find a great comfort. It is still very cold here; everything is frozen.

You will have seen that I have good news from Constantinople.

My health is good. There is nothing fresh here.—Yours ever,

Napoleon.

No. 62.
To the Empress, at Paris

Finckenstein, April 10, 1807, 6 pm.

My Dear,—My health is excellent. Here spring is beginning;

---

2. Eugène's eldest daughter, the Princess Josephine Maximilienne Auguste, born March 14, 1807; married Bernadotte's son, Prince Oscar, June 18, 1827.

but as yet there is no vegetation. I wish you to be cheerful and contented, and never to doubt my attachment. Here all goes well.   Napoleon.

No. 63
To the Empress, at Paris

Finckenstein, April 14, 1807, 7 p.m.
I have received your letter of April 3rd. I see from it that you are well, and that it has been very cold in Paris. The weather here is very unsettled; still I think the spring has come at length; already the ice has almost gone. I am in splendid health.
Adieu, dear. I ordered some time ago for Malmaison all that you ask for,—Yours ever,

Napoleon,

No. 64.
To the Empress, at Paris

Finckenstein, April 18, 1807.
I have received your letter of April 5th. I am sorry to see from it that you are grieved at what I have told you. As usual, your little Creole head becomes flurried and excited in a moment. Let us not, therefore, speak of it again. I am very well, but yet the weather is rainy. Savary is very ill of a bilious fever, before Dantzic; I hope it will be nothing serious. *Adieu*, dear; my very best wishes to you.

Napoleon.

No. 65.
To the Empress, at Paris

Finckenstein, April 24, 1807, 7 p.m.
I have received your letter of the 12th. I see from it that your health is good, and that you are very happy at the thought of going to Malmaison.
The weather has changed to fine; I hope it may continue so. There is nothing fresh here. I am very well.
Adieu, dear.—Yours ever,   Napoleon.

No. 66.
To the Empress, at Paris

Finckenstein, May 2, 1807, 4 p.m.

My Dear,—I have just received your letter of the 23rd; I see with pleasure that you are well, and that you are as fond as ever of Malmaison. I hear the Arch-Chancellor is in love. Is this a joke, or a fact? It has amused me; you might have given me a hint about it!

I am very well, and the fine season commences. Spring shows itself at length, and the leaves begin to shoot. *Adieu*, dear; very best wishes.—Yours ever,

Napoleon.

No. 67.
To the Empress, at Paris

Finckenstein, May 10, 1807.

I have just received your letter. I know not what you tell me about ladies in correspondence with me. I love only my little Josephine, sweet, pouting, and capricious, who can quarrel with grace, as she does everything else, for she is always lovable, except when she is jealous; then she becomes a regular shrew.[3] But let us come back to these ladies. If I had leisure for any among them, I assure you that I should like them to be pretty rosebuds.

Are those of whom you speak of this kind?

I wish you to have only those persons to dinner who have dined with me; that your list be the same for your assemblies; that you never make intimates at Malmaison of ambassadors and foreigners. If you should do the contrary, you would displease me. Finally, do not allow yourself to be duped too much by persons whom I do not know, and who would not come to the house, if I were there.

Adieu, dear.—Yours ever,   Napoleon.

No. 68.
To the Empress, at Paris

Finckenstein, May 12, 1807.

I have just received your letter of May 2nd, in which I see that

---

3. *Toute diablesse.*

you are getting ready to go to St. Cloud. I was sorry to see the bad conduct of Madame ——. Might you not speak to her about mending her ways, which at present might easily cause unpleasantness on the part of her husband?

From what I hear, Napoleon is cured; I can well imagine how unhappy his mother has been; but measles is an ailment to which everyone is liable. I hope that he has been vaccinated, and that he will at least be safe from the smallpox.

Adieu, dear. The weather is very warm, and vegetation has be-gun; but it will be some days before there is any grass.

Napoleon.

No. 69.
To the Empress, at St. Cloud

Finckenstein, May 14, 1807.

I realise the grief which the death of this poor Napoleon[4] must cause you; you can imagine what I am enduring. I should like to be by your side, in order that your sorrow might be kept within reasonable bounds. You have had the good fortune nev-er to lose children; but it is one of the pains and conditions attached to our miseries here below. I trust I may hear you have been rational in your sorrow, and that your health remains good! Would you willingly augment my grief?

Adieu, dear.   Napoleon.

No. 70.
To the Empress, at St. Cloud

Finckenstein, May 16, 1807.

I have just received your letter of May 6th. I see from it how ill you are already; and I fear that you are not rational, and that you are making yourself too wretched about the misfortune which has come upon us.

Adieu, dear.—Yours ever,   Napoleon.

No. 71.
To the Empress, at Lacken

Finckenstein, May 20, 1807.

I have just received your letter of May 10th. I see that you have gone to Lacken. I think you might stay there a fortnight; it

---

4. Charles Napoleon, Prince Royal of Holland, died at the Hague, May 5, 1807.

would please the Belgians and serve to distract you.

I am sorry to see that you have not been rational. Grief has bounds which should not be passed. Take care of yourself for the sake of your friend, and believe in my entire affection.

Napoleon.

No. 72.

May 24th.—Dantzic surrenders to Lefebvre after two months' siege, with 800 guns and immense stores.

To the Empress, at Lacken

Finckenstein, May 24, 1807.

Your letter from Lacken just received. I am sorry to see your grief undiminished, and that Hortense has not yet come; she is unreasonable, and does not deserve our love, since she only loves her children.

Try to calm her, and do not make me wretched. For every ill without a remedy consolations must be found.

Adieu, dear.—Yours ever,   Napoleon.

No. 73.
To the Empress, at Lacken

Finckenstein, May 26, 1807.

I have just received your letter of the 16th. I have seen with pleasure that Hortense has arrived at Lacken. I am annoyed at what you tell me of the state of stupor in which she still is. She must have more courage, and force herself to have it. I cannot imagine why they want her to go to take the waters; she will forget her trouble much better at Paris, and find more sources of consolation.

Show force of character, be cheerful, and keep well. My health is excellent.

Adieu, dear. I suffer much from all your griefs; it is a great trouble to me not to be by your side.   Napoleon.

May 28th.—Lefebvre made Duke of Dantzic by Napoleon.

May 20th.—Selim III. deposed in Turkey by Mustapha IV., his nephew.

June 1st.—22,000 Spanish troops, sent by Charles IV., join the French army in Germany.

No. 74.
To the Empress, at Malmaison

Dantzig, June 2, 1807.

My Dear,—I note your arrival at Malmaison. I have no letters from you; I am vexed with Hortense, she has never written me a line. All that you tell me about her grieves me. Why have you not found her some distractions? Weeping won't do it! I trust you will take care of yourself in order that I may not find you utterly woebegone.

I have been the two past days at Dantzic; the weather is very fine, my health excellent. I think more of you than you are thinking of a husband far away.

Adieu, dear; very kindest regards. Pass on this letter to Hortense. Napoleon.

No. 75.
To the Empress, at St. Cloud

Marienburg, June 3, 1807.

This morning I slept at Marienburg. Yesterday I left Dantzic; my health is very good. Every letter that comes from St. Cloud tells me you are always weeping. That is not well; it is necessary for you to keep well and be cheerful.

Hortense is still unwell; what you tell me of her makes me very sorry for her.

Adieu, dear; think of all the affection I bear for you.

Napoleon.

June 5th.—Russians defeated at Spanden; Bernadotte wounded.

No. 76.

June 6th.—Russians defeated at Deppen by Soult.

To the Empress, at St. Cloud

Finckenstein, June 6, 1807.

My Dear,—I am in flourishing health. Your yesterday's letter pained me; it seems to me that you are always grieving, and that you are not reasonable. The weather is very fine.

Adieu, dear; I love you and wish to see you cheerful and contented. Napoleon.

June 9th.—Russians defeated at Guttstadt by Napoleon, and . . . . .

June 10th.—At Heilsberg.

June 14th.—Battle of Friedland, completing the "Campaign of Ten Days."

No. 77.
To the Empress, at St. Cloud

Friedland, June 15, 1807.

My Dear,—I write you only a line, for I am very tired, by reason of several days' bivouacking. My children have worthily celebrated the anniversary of the battle of Marengo.

The battle of Friedland will be as celebrated for my people, and equally glorious. The entire Russian army routed, 80 pieces of cannon captured, 30,000 men taken or slain, 25 Russian generals killed, wounded, or taken, the Russian Guard wiped out. The battle is worthy of her sisters—Marengo, Austerlitz, Jena. The bulletin will tell you the rest. My loss is not considerable. I out-manoeuvred the enemy successfully.

Be content and without uneasiness.

Adieu, dear; my horse is waiting.

Napoleon.

You may give this news as official, if it arrives before the bulletin. They may also fire salvoes. Cambacérès will make the proclamation.

No. 78.

June 16th.—Königsberg captured by Soult—"what was left to the King of Prussia is conquered."

To the Empress, at St. Cloud

Friedland, June 16, 1807, 4 p.m.

My Dear,—Yesterday I despatched Moustache with the news of the battle of Friedland. Since then I have continued to pursue the enemy. Königsberg, which is a town of 80,000 souls, is in my power. I have found there many cannon, large stores, and, lastly, more than 160,000 muskets, which have come from England.

Adieu, dear. My health is perfect, although I have a slight catarrh caused by bivouacking in the rain and cold. Be happy and cheerful.—Yours ever, Napoleon.

June 17th.—Neisse, in Silesia, with 6000 men, surrenders to the

French; also

June 18th.—Glatz.

No. 79.
To the Empress, at St. Cloud

Tilsit, June 19, 1807.

This morning I despatched Tascher to you, to calm all your fears. Here all goes splendidly. The battle of Friedland has decided everything. The enemy is confounded, overwhelmed, and greatly weakened.

My health is good, and my army is superb.

Adieu, dear. Be cheerful and contented.   Napoleon.

June 21st.—Armistice concluded at Tilsit.

No. 80.
To the Empress, at St. Cloud

Tilsit, June 22, 1807.

My Dear,—I have your letter of June 10th. I am sorry to see you are so depressed. You will see by the bulletin that I have concluded a suspension of arms, and that we are negotiating peace. Be contented and cheerful.

I despatched Borghese to you, and, twelve hours later, Moustache; therefore you should have received in good time my letters and the news of the grand battle of Friedland.

I am wonderfully well, and wish to hear that you are happy.— Yours ever,   Napoleon.

No. 81.
To the Empress, at St. Cloud

Tilsit, June 25, 1807.

My Dear,—I have just seen the Emperor Alexander. I was much pleased with him. He is a very handsome, young, and kind-hearted Emperor; he has more intelligence than people usually give him credit for. Tomorrow he will lodge in the town of Tilsit.

Adieu, dear. I am very anxious to hear that you are well and happy. My health is very good.   Napoleon.

No. 82.
To the Empress, at St. Cloud

Tilsit, July 3, 1807.

My Dear,—M. de Turenne will give you full details of all that has occurred here. Everything goes excellently. I think I told you that the Emperor of Russia drinks your health with much cordiality. He, as well as the King of Prussia, dines with me every day. I sincerely trust that you are happy. *Adieu*, dear. A thousand loving remembrances. Napoleon.

No. 83.
To the Empress, at St. Cloud

Tilsit, July 6, 1807

I have your letter of June 25th. I was grieved to see that you were selfish, and that the success of my arms should have no charm for you.

The beautiful Queen of Prussia is to come tomorrow to dine with me.

I am well, and am longing to see you again, when destiny shall so order it. Still, it may be sooner than we expect.

Adieu, dear; a thousand loving remembrances.

Napoleon.

No. 84.

July 7th.—Peace signed between France and Russia.

To the Empress, at St. Cloud

Tilsit, July 7, 1807.

My Dear,—Yesterday the Queen of Prussia dined with me. I had to be on the defence against some further concessions she wished me to make to her husband; but I was very polite, and yet held firmly to my policy. She is very charming. I shall soon give you the details, which I could not possibly give you now unless at great length. When you read this letter, peace with Prussia and Russia will be concluded, and Jerome acknowledged King of Westphalia, with a population of three millions. This news is for yourself alone.

Adieu, dear; I love you, and wish to know that you are cheerful and contented. Napoleon.

No. 85.
To the Empress, at St. Cloud

Tilsit, July 8,[5] 1807.

The Queen of Prussia is really charming; she is full of *coquetterie* for me; but don't be jealous; I am an oil-cloth over which all that can only glide. It would cost me too much to play the lover.   Napoleon.

No. 12,875 of the Correspondence (taken from Las Cases).

July 9th.—Peace signed between France and Prussia, the latter resigning all its possessions between the Rhine and the Elbe.

No. 86.
To the Empress, at St. Cloud

Dresden, July 18, 1807, Noon.

My Dear,—Yesterday I arrived at Dresden at 5 p.m., in excellent health, although I remained a hundred hours in the carriage without getting out. I am staying here with the King of Saxony, with whom I am highly pleased. I have now therefore traversed more than half the distance that separates us.

It is very likely that one of these fine nights I may descend upon St. Cloud like a jealous husband, so beware.

Adieu, dear; I shall have great pleasure in seeing you.—Yours ever,   Napoleon.

July 25th.—Plot of Prince Ferdinand of Asturias against his parents, the King and Queen of Spain.

July 27th.—Napoleon arrives at St. Cloud, 5 a.m.

August 19th.—Napoleon suppresses the French Tribunate.

August 20th.—Marshal Brune captures Stralsund from the Swedes.

September 1st.—The Ionian Isles become part of the French Empire.

September 5th to 7th.—Bombardment of Copenhagen by the English.

September 7th.—Occupation of Rugen by Marshal Brune.

October 6th.—War between Russia and Sweden.

October 16th.—Treaty of alliance between France and Denmark.

---

5. Presumed date.

October 17th.—Junot with 27,000 men starts for Portugal, with whom France has been nominally at war since 1801.

October 27th.—Treaty of Fontainebleau signed between France and Spain. (Plot of Prince Ferdinand against his father discovered at Madrid the same day.)

November 8th.—Russia declares war against England.

November 15th.—Napoleon constitutes the kingdom of Westphalia, with his brother Jerome as king.

November 26th.—Junot enters Abrantes, and on

November 30th,—enters Lisbon.

December 9th.—Trade suspended between England and the United States (*re* rights of neutrals).

December 23rd.—France levies a contribution of 100 million *francs* on Portugal.

Series H

Napoleon was received with unbounded adulation by all the towns of Italy. . . . He was the Redeemer of France, but the Creator of Italy.—Alison, *Hist, of Europe* (vol. 11. 280).

LETTERS OF THE EMPEROR NAPOLEON TO THE EMPRESS JOSEPHINE DURING THE JOURNEY HE MADE IN ITALY, 1807.

November 16th.—Napoleon leaves Fontainebleau.

November 22nd-25th.—At Milan.

No. 1.
To the Empress, at Paris.

Milan, November 25, 1807.

My Dear,—I have been here two days. I am very glad that I did not bring you here; you would have suffered dreadfully in crossing Mont Cenis, where a storm detained me twenty-four hours.

I found Eugène in good health; I am very pleased with him. The Princess is ill; I went to see her at Monza. She has had a miscarriage; she is getting better.

Adieu, dear.   Napoleon.

November 29th to December 7th.—At Venice (writes Talleyrand, "This land is a phenomenon of the power of commerce").

No. 2.
To the Empress, at Paris

Venice, November 30, 1807.

I have your letter of November 22nd. The last two days I have been at Venice. The weather is very bad, which has not prevented me from sailing over the lagoons in order to see the

EUGÈNE BEAUHARNAIS
AFTERWARDS VICEROY OF ITALY

different forts.

I am glad to see you are enjoying yourself at Paris.

The King of Bavaria, with his family, as well as the Princess Eliza, are here.

I am spending December 2nd[1] here, and that past I shall be on my way home, and very glad to see you.

Adieu, dear.   Napoleon.

No. 3.
To the Empress, at Paris

Udine, December 11, 1807.

My Dear,—I have your letter of December 3rd, from which I note that you were much pleased with the Jardin des Plantes. Here I am at the extreme limit of my journey; it is possible I may soon be in Paris, where I shall be very glad to see you again. The weather has not as yet been cold here, but very rainy. I have profited by this good season up to the last moment, for I suppose that at Christmas the winter will at length make itself felt.

Adieu, dear.—Yours ever,   Napoleon.

December 12th.—At Udine.

December 14th.—At Mantua.

December 16th.—At Milan (till December 26th).

December 17th.—His Milan decree against English commerce.

December 27th-28th.—At Turin.

1808.

January 1st.—At Paris.

---

1 His Coronation Day.

Series I

The imbecility of Charles IV., the vileness of Ferdinand, and the corruption of Godoy were undoubtedly the proximate causes of the calamities which overwhelmed Spain.—Napier's *Peninsular War* (vol. 1. preface).

LETTERS OF THE EMPEROR NAPOLEON TO THE EMPRESS
JOSEPHINE DURING THE STAY THAT HE MADE AT BAYONNE,
1808.

This year offers a strange picture. The Emperor Napoleon was at Venice in the month of January, surrounded by the homage of all the courts and princes of Italy; in the month of April he was at Bayonne, surrounded by that of Spain, and the great personages of that country; and, finally, in the month of October he is at Erfurth, with his parterre of kings.—Mémoires du Duc de Rovigo.

January 27th.—Queen and Prince Regent of Portugal reach Rio de Janeiro.

February 2nd.—French troops enter Rome.

February 17th.—French occupy Pampeluna, and

February 29th.—Barcelona.

March 19th.—Charles IV. abdicates, and his son proclaimed Ferdinand VII.

March 20th.—Godoy imprisoned by Ferdinand.

March 23rd.—Murat enters Madrid.

March 27th.—Napoleon excommunicated.

April 15th.—Napoleon arrives at Bayonne.

No. 1.
To the Empress, at Bordeaux

Bayonne, April 16, 1808.

I have arrived here in good health, rather tired by a dull journey and a very bad road.

I am very glad you stayed behind, for the houses here are wretched and very small.

I go today into a small house in the country, about a mile from the town.

Adieu, dear. Take care of yourself.

No. 2.
To the Empress, at Bordeaux

Bayonne, April 17, 1808.

I have just received yours of April 15th. What you tell me of the owner of the country-house pleases me. Go and spend the day there sometimes.

I am sending an order for you to have 20,000 *francs* per month additional while I am away, counting from the 1st of April.

I am lodged atrociously. I am leaving this place in an hour, to occupy a country-house (*bastide*) about a mile away. The Infant Don Carlos and five or six Spanish *grandees* are here, the Prince of the Asturias fifty miles away. King Charles and the Queen are due. I know not how I shall lodge all these people. Everything here is still most primitive (*a l'auberge*). The health of my troops in Spain is good.

It took me some time to understand your little jokes; I have laughed at your recollections. O you women, what memories you have!

My health is fairly good, and I love you most affectionately. I wish you to give my kind regards to everybody at Bordeaux; I have been too busy to send them to anybody.

Napoleon.

April 20th.—Ferdinand arrives at Bayonne.

No. 3.
To the Empress, at Bordeaux

April 21, 1808.

I have just received your letter of April 19th. Yesterday I had the Prince of the Asturias and his suite to dinner, which occasioned me considerable embarrassment. I am waiting for Charles IV. and the Queen.

My health is good. I am now sufficiently recovered for the campaign.

Adieu, dear. Your letters always give me much pleasure.

Napoleon.

No. 4.
To the Empress, at Bordeaux

Bayonne, April 23, 1808.

My Dear,—A son has been born to Hortense;[1] I am highly delighted. I am not surprised that you tell me nothing of it, since your letter is dated the 21st, and the child was only born on the 20th,[2] during the night.

You can start on the 26th, sleep at Mont de Marsan, and arrive here on the 27th. Have your best dinner-service sent on here on the 25th, in the evening. I have made arrangements for you to have a little house in the country, next to the one I have. My health is good.

I am waiting for Charles IV. and his wife.

Adieu, dear. Napoleon.

April 30th.—Charles IV. and the Queen arrive at Bayonne.

May 1st.—Ferdinand gives back the crown to his father.

May 2nd.—Murat subdues insurrection at Madrid.

May 5th.—Treaty of Bayonne; Charles IV. and Ferdinand (*May 6*) surrender to Napoleon their rights to the Spanish crown.

May 13th.—Spanish Junta ask for Joseph Bonaparte to be their king.

June 6th.—King Joseph proclaimed King of Spain and the Indies by Napoleon, in an imperial decree, dated Bayonne.

June 7th.—French, under Dupont, sacked Cordova.

June 9th.—Emperor of Austria calls out his militia.

June 15th.—French fleet at Cadiz surrender to the Spanish.

July 4th.—English cease hostilities with Spain, and recognise Ferdinand VII.

---

1. Charles Louis Napoleon, afterwards Napoleon III.
2. At 17 Rue Lafitte.

To the Empress, at Paris

March 25, 1807.

I have received your letter of March 13th. If you really wish to please me, you must live exactly as you live when I am at Paris. Then you were not in the habit of visiting the second-rate theatres or other places. You ought always to go into the Royal box. As for your home life: hold receptions there, and have your fixed circles of friends; that, my dear, is the only way to deserve my approbation. Greatness has its inconveniences; an Empress cannot go where a private individual may.

Very best love. My health is good. My affairs prosper.

Napoleon.

No. 58.
To the Empress, at Paris

Osterode, March 27, 1807, 7 p.m.

My Dear,—Your letter pains me. There is no question of your dying. You are in good health, and you can have no just ground for grief.

I think you should go during May to St. Cloud; but you must spend the whole month of April at Paris.

My health is good. My affairs prosper.

You must not think of travelling this summer; nothing of that sort is feasible. You ought not to frequent inns and camps. I long as much as you for our meeting and for a quiet life.

I can do other things besides fight; but duty stands first and foremost. All my life long I have sacrificed everything to my destiny—peace of mind, personal advantage, happiness.

Adieu, dear. See as little as possible of that Madame de P——. She is a woman who belongs to the lowest grade of society; she is thoroughly common and vulgar.   Napoleon.

I have had occasion to find fault with M. de T——. I have sent him to his country house in Burgundy. I wish no longer to hear his name mentioned.

No. 59.
To the Empress, at Paris

Osterode, April 1, 1807.

My Dear,—I have just got your letter of the 20th. I am sorry to see you are ill. I wrote you to stay at Paris the whole month of

July 7th.—Spanish new constitution sworn to by Joseph and by the Junta.

July 9th.—Commences the siege of Saragassa.

July 14th.—Bessières defeats 40,000 Spaniards at Medina de Rio Seco.

July 15th.—Murat declared King of Naples.

July 20th.—Joseph enters Madrid. Mahmoud deposed by his younger brother at Constantinople.

July 22nd.—Dupont capitulates at Baylen "the only stain on French arms for twenty years (17921812)." Montgaillard.

July 30th.—French protest against Austrian armaments.

August 1st.—Wellington landed in Portugal.

August 21st.—Battle of Vimiera, creditable to Junot.

August 25th.—Spanish troops reoccupy Madrid.

August 30th.—Convention of Cintra. French only hold Barcelona, Biscay, Navarre, and Alava, In the 'whole of Spain.

September 8th.—Convention of Paris (Prussia and France); Prussian army not to exceed 40,000 men.

Series J

When he shows as seeking quarter, with paws like hands in prayer,
That is the time of peril—the time of the truce of the Bear!

—Kipling.

No. 1.
To the Empress, at St. Cloud

Erfurt, September 29, 1808.

I have rather a cold. I have received your letter, dated Malmaison. I am well pleased with the Emperor and everyone here.
It is an hour after midnight, and I am tired. *Adieu*, dear; take care of yourself.

Napoleon.

No. 2.
To the Empress, at St. Cloud

October 9, 1808.

My Dear,—I have received your letter. I note with pleasure that you are well. I have just been shooting over the battle field of Jena. We had breakfast (*déejeuné*) at the spot where I bivouacked on the night of the battle.
I assisted at the Weimar ball. The Emperor Alexander dances; but not I. Forty years are forty years.
My health is really sound, in spite of a few trifling ailments.
Adieu, dear; I hope to see you soon.—Yours ever,

Napoleon.

No. 3.
To the Empress, at St. Cloud

My Dear,—I write you seldom; I am very busy. Conversations which last whole days, and which do not improve my cold. Still all goes well. I am pleased with Alexander; he ought to be with me. If he were a woman, I think I should make him my sweetheart.

I shall be back to you shortly; keep well and let me find you plump and rosy.

Adieu, dear.   Napoleon.

Series K

The winter campaign commenced on the 1st of November 1808, and terminated on the 1st of March 1809, to the advantage of the French, who, for that reason, denominate it the Imperial Campaign. The Spaniards were long before they could recover from the terror caused by the defeat of their armies, the capture of Madrid, the surrender of Saragossa, and the departure of the English from Corunna.—Sarrazin's History of the War in Spain and Portugal, 1815.

LETTERS OF THE EMPEROR NAPOLEON TO THE EMPRESS JOSEPHINE DURING THE SPANISH CAMPAIGN, 1808 AND 1809.

October 29th.—English enter Spain.

October 31st.—Blake defeated by Lefebvre at Tornosa.

No. 1.
To the Empress, at Paris

November 3, 1808.

I arrived tonight[1] with considerable trouble. I had ridden several stages at full speed. Still, I am well. Tomorrow I start for Spain. My troops are arriving in force. *Adieu*, dear.—Yours ever,

Napoleon.

November 4th.—Napoleon enters Spain.

No. 2..
To the Empress, at Paris

Tolosa, November 5, 1808.

I am at Tolosa. I am starting for Vittoria, where I shall be in a few hours. I am fairly well, and I hope everything will soon be completed.   Napoleon.

1. At Bayonne.

No. 3.
To the Empress, at Paris

Vittoria, November 7.

My Dear,—I have been the last two days at Vittoria. I am in good health. My troops are arriving daily; the Guard arrived today.

The King is in very good health. I am very busy. I know that you are in Paris. Never doubt my affection.

Napoleon.

November 10th.—Battle of Burgos. Soult and Bessières defeat Spaniards, who lose 3000 killed and 3000 prisoners, and 20 cannon.

November 12th.—Battle of Espinosa. Marshal Victor defeats La Romano and Blake, who lose 20,000 men and 50 cannon.

No. 4..

November 14th.—Third revolution at Constantinople. Mahmoud IV. assassinated (November 15th).

To the Empress, at Paris

Burgos, November 14, 1808.

Matters here are progressing at a great rate. The weather is very fine. We are successful. My health is very good.

Napoleon.

November 23rd.—Battle of Tudela. Castaños and Palafox defeated, with loss of 7000 men and 30 cannon, by Marshal Lannes. "The battle of Tudela makes the pendant of that of Espinosa." *Napoleon.*

No. 5.
To the Empress, at Paris

November 26, 1808.

I have received your letter. I trust that your health be as good as mine is, although I am very busy. All goes well here.

I think you should return to the Tuileries on December 21st, and from that date give a concert daily for eight days.—Yours ever, Napoleon.

Kind regards to Hortense and to M. Napoleon.

December 3rd.—French voluntarily evacuate Berlin.

December 4th.—Surrender of Madrid. Napoleon abolishes the Inquisition and feudal rights. ("He regards the taking of a capital as decisive for the submission of a whole kingdom; thus in 1814 will act his adversaries, pale but judicious imitators of his strategy."—Montgaillard.)

No. 6.
To the Empress, at Paris

December 7, 1808.

Your letter of the 28th to hand. I am glad to see that you are well. You will have seen that young Tascher has distinguished himself, which has pleased me. My health is good.

Here we are enjoying Parisian weather of the last fortnight in May. We are hot, and have no fires; but the nights are rather cool.

Madrid is quiet. All my affairs prosper.

Adieu, dear.—Yours ever, Napoleon.

Kind regards to Hortense and to M. Napoleon.

No. 7.
To the Empress, at Paris

Chamartin, December 10, 1808.

My Dear,—Yours to hand, in which you tell me what bad weather you are having in Paris; here it is the best weather imaginable. Please tell me what mean these alterations Hortense is making; I hear she is sending away her servants. Is it because they have refused to do what was required? Give me some particulars. Reforms are not desirable.

Adieu, dear. The weather here is delightful. All goes excellently, and I pray you to keep well. Napoleon.

No. 8.
To the Empress, at Paris

December 21, 1808.

You ought to have been at the Tuileries on the 12th. I trust you may have been pleased with your rooms.

I have authorised the presentation of Kourakin to you and the family; be kind to him, and let him take part in your plays.

Adieu, dear. I am well. The weather is rainy; it is rather cold.

Napoleon.

No. 9.

December 22nd.—Napoleon quits Madrid.

To the Empress, at Paris

Madrid, December 22, 1808.

I start at once to outmanoeuvre the English, who appear to have received reinforcements and wish to look big.

The weather is fine, my health perfect; don't be uneasy.

Napoleon.

No. 10.
To the Empress, at Paris

Benavento, December 31, 1808.

My Dear,—The last few days I have been in pursuit of the English, but they flee panic-stricken. They have pusillanimously abandoned the remnant of La Romana's army in order not to delay its retreat a single half day. More than a hundred wagons of their baggage have already been taken. The weather is very bad.

Lefebvre [2] has been captured. He took part in a skirmish with 300 of his *chasseurs*; these idiots crossed a river by swimming and threw themselves in the midst of the English cavalry; they killed several, but on their return Lefebvre had his horse wounded; it was swimming, the current took him to the bank where the English were; he was taken. Console his wife.

Adieu, dear. Bessières, with 10,000 cavalry, is at Astorga.

Napoleon.

A happy New Year to everybody.

No. 11.
To the Empress, at Paris

January 3, 1809.

My Dear,—I have received your letters of the 18th and 21st. I am close behind the English.

The weather is cold and rigorous, but all goes well.

Adieu, dear.—Yours ever,   Napoleon.

A happy New Year, and a very happy one, to my Josephine.

---

2. General Lefebvre—Desnouettes.

No. 12.
To the Empress, at Paris

Benavento, January 5, 1809.

My Dear,—I write you a line. The English are in utter rout; I have instructed the Duke of Dalmatia to pursue them closely (*l'épee dans les reins*). I am well; the weather bad.

Adieu, dear.   Napoleon.

No. 13.
To the Empress, at Paris

January 8, 1809.

I have received yours of the 23rd and 26th. I am sorry to see you have toothache. I have been here two days. The weather is what we must expect at this season. The English are embarking. I am in good health.

Adieu, dear.

I am writing Hortense. Eugène has a daughter.

Yours ever,   Napoleon.

No. 14.
To the Empress, at Paris

January 9, 1809.

Moustache brings me your letter of 31st December. I see from it, dear, that you are sad and have very gloomy disquietudes. Austria will not make war on me; if she does, I have 150,000 men in Germany and as many on the Rhine, and 400,000 Germans to reply to her. Russia will not separate herself from me. They are foolish in Paris; all goes well.

I shall be at Paris the moment I think it worthwhile. I advise you to beware of ghosts; one fine day, at two o'clock in the morning.

But *adieu*, dear; I am well, and am yours ever,

Napoleon.

131

Series L

Berthier, incapable of acting a principal part, was surprised, and making a succession of false movements that would have been fatal to the French army, if the Emperor, journeying night and day, had not arrived at the very hour when his lieutenant was on the point of consummating the ruin of the army. But then was seen the supernatural force of Napoleon's genius. In a few hours he changed the aspect of affairs, and in a few days, maugre their immense number, his enemies, baffled and flying in all directions, proclaimed his mastery in an art which, up to that moment, was imperfect; for never, since troops first trod a field of battle, was such a display of military genius made by man.—Napier.

LETTERS OF THE EMPEROR NAPOLEON TO THE EMPRESS JOSEPHINE DURING THE AUSTRIAN CAMPAIGN, 1809.

EVENTS OF 1809.

January 7th.—Ring and Queen of Prussia visit Alexander at St. Petersburg.

January 12th.—Cayenne and French Guiana captured by Spanish and Portuguese South Americans.

January 13th.—Combat of Alcazar. Victor defeats Spaniards.

January 14th.—Treaty of Alliance between England and Spain.

January 16th.—Battle of Corunna. Moore killed; Baird wounded.

January 17th.—English army sails for England.

January 22nd.—King Joseph returns to Madrid.

January 27th.—Soult takes Ferrol (retaken by English, June 22nd).

February 21st.—Lannes takes Saragossa.

February 23rd.—English capture Martinique.

March 4th.—Madison made President of United States.

March 29th.—Soult fights battle of Oporto. Spaniards lose 20,000 men and 200 guns. Gustavus Adolphus abdicates throne of Sweden.

April 9th.—Austrians under Archduke Charles cross the Inn, enter Bavaria, and take Munich. Napoleon receives this news April 12th, and reaches Strasburg April 15th.

April 15th.—Eugène defeated on the Tagliamento.

April 16th.—And at Sacile.

April 19th.—Combat of Pfafferhofen. Oudinot repulses Austrians, while Davoust wins the Battle of Thann. Napoleon joins the army.

April 20th.—Battle of Abensberg. Archduke Louis defeated. Austrians take Ratisbon, and 1800 prisoners. Poles defeated by Archduke Ferdinand at Baszy.

April 21st.—Combat of Landshut; heavy Austrian losses. Austrians under Archduke Ferdinand take Warsaw.

April 22nd.—Battle of Eckmühl. Napoleon defeats Archduke Charles.

April 23rd.—French take Ratisbon.

April 25th.—King of Bavaria re-enters Munich.

April 26th.—French army crosses the Inn.

April 28th-30th.—French force the Salza, and cut in two the main Austrian army "One of the most beautiful manoeuvres of modern tactics" (Montgaillard).

April 29th.—Combat of Caldiero. Eugène defeats Archduke John.

May 3rd.—Russia declares war on Austria, and enters Galicia.

May 4th.—Combat of Ebersberg. Massena defeats Austrians, but loses a large number of men.

No. 1
To the Empress, at Strasburg

Donauwoerth, April 17, 1809.

I arrived here yesterday at 4 a.m.; I am just leaving it. Everything is under way. Military operations are in full activity. Up to the present, there is nothing new.

My health is good.—Yours ever,   Napoleon.

No. 2
To the Empress, at Strasburg

Enns, May 6, 1809, Noon.

My Dear,—I have received your letter. The ball that touched me has not wounded me; it barely grazed the tendon Achilles. My health is very good. You are wrong to be uneasy. My affairs here go excellently.—Yours ever, Napoleon.

Kind regards to Hortense and the Duke de Berg.[1]

May 8th.—Eugène crosses the Piave, and defeats Archduke John.

No. 3.
To the Empress, at Strasburg

Saint-Polten, May 9, 1809.

My Dear,—I write you from Saint-Polten. Tomorrow I shall be before Vienna; it will be exactly a month to the day after the Austrians crossed the Inn, and violated peace.

My health is good, the weather splendid, and the soldiery very cheerful; there is wine here.

Keep well.—Yours ever, Napoleon.

May 13th.—French occupy Vienna, after a bombardment of thirty-six hours.

May 17th.—Roman States united to the French Empire.

May 18th.—French occupy Trieste.

May 19th.—Lefebvre occupies Innsbruck.

May 20th.—Eugène reaches Klagenfurt.

May 21st-22nd.—Battle of Essling. A drawn battle, unfavourable to the French, who lose Marshal Lannes, three generals killed, and 500 officers and 18,000 men wounded. The Archduke admits a loss of 4200 killed and 16,000 wounded.

May 22nd.—Meerveldt with 4000 men surrenders at Laybach to Macdonald.

May 25th.—Eugène reaches Leoben in Styria, and captures most of the corps of Jellachich.

May 26th.—Eugène joins the army of Germany, at Bruck in Styria.

---

1. Napoleon Louis, Prince Royal of Holland, and Grand Duke of Berg from March 3, 1809.

No. 4

May 12th.—Soult evacuates Portugal. Wellington crosses the Douro, and enters Spain.

To the Empress, at Strasburg

Schoenbrunn, May 12, 1809.

I am despatching the brother of the Duchess of Montebello to let you know that I am master of Vienna, and that everything here goes perfectly.

My health is very good. Napoleon.

No. 5.

To the Empress, at Strasburg

Ebersdorf, May 27, 1809.

I am despatching a page to tell you that Eugène has rejoined me with all his army; that he has completely performed the task that I entrusted him with; and has almost entirely destroyed the enemy's army opposed to him.

I send you my proclamation to the army of Italy, which will make you understand all this.

I am very well.—Yours ever, Napoleon.

P.S.—You can have this proclamation printed at Strasburg, and have it translated into French and German, in order that it may be scattered broadcast over Germany. Give a copy of the proclamation to the page who goes on to Paris.

May 28th.—Hofer defeats Bavarians at Innsbruck.

No. 6.

To the Empress, at Strasburg

Ebersdorf, May 29, 1809, 7 p.m.

My Dear,—I have been here since yesterday; I am stopped by the river. The bridge has been burnt; I shall cross at midnight. Everything here goes as I wish it, *viz.*, very well.

The Austrians have been overwhelmed (*frappés de la foudre*).

Adieu, dear.—Yours ever, Napoleon.

No. 7

To the Empress, at Strasburg

Ebersdorf, May 31, 1809.

Your letter of the 26th to hand. I have written you that you can go to Plombières. I do not care for you to go to Baden; it is not necessary to leave France. I have ordered the two princes to re-enter France. [2]

The loss of the Duke of Montebello, who died this morning, has grieved me exceedingly. Thus everything ends!!

Adieu, dear; if you can help to console the poor *Maréchale*, do so.—Yours ever,   Napoleon.

June 1st.—Archduke Ferdinand evacuates Warsaw.

June 6th.—Regent of Sweden proclaimed King as Charles XIII.

No. 8
To the Empress, at Strasburg

Schoenbrunn, June 9, 1809.

I have received your letter; I see with pleasure that you are going to the waters at Plombières, they will do you good.

Eugène is in Hungary with his army. I am well, the weather very fine. I note with pleasure that Hortense and the Duke of Berg are in France.

Adieu, dear.—Yours ever,   Napoleon.

June 10th.—Union of the Papal States to France promulgated in Rome.

June 11th.—Napoleon and all his abettors excommunicated.

June 14th.—Eugène, aided by Macdonald and Lauriston, defeats Archduke Ferdinand at Raab.

No. 9.
To the Empress, at Plombières

Schoenbrunn, June 16, 1809.

I despatch a page to tell you that, on the 14th, the anniversary of Marengo, Eugène won a battle against the Archduke John and the Archduke Palatine, at Raab, in Hungary; that he has taken 3000 men, many pieces of cannon, 4 flags, and pursued them a long way on the road to Buda-Pesth.

Napoleon.

June 18th.—Combat of Belchite. Blake defeated by Suchet near Saragossa.

---

2. Her two grandsons, who, with Hortense, their mother, were at Baden.

No. 10.
To the Empress, at Plombières

Schoenbrunn, June 19, 1809, Noon.

I have your letter, which tells me of your departure for Plombières. I am glad you are making this journey, because I trust it may do you good.

Eugène is in Hungary, and is well. My health is very good, and the army in fighting trim.

I am very glad to know that the Grand Duke of Berg is with you.

Adieu, dear. You know my affection for my Josephine; it never varies.—Yours ever,   Napoleon.

July 4th-5th.—French cross Danube, and win battle of Enzersdorff.

July 5th-6th.—Pope Pius VII. carried off from Rome by order of Murat; eventually kept at Savona.

July 6th.—Battle of Wagram. The most formidable artillery battle ever fought up to this date (900 guns in action). The Austrians had 120,000 men, with more guns and of larger calibre than those of the French.

No. 11.

July 7th.—St. Domingo surrenders to the English.

To the Empress, at Plombières

Ebersdorf, July 7, 1809, 5 a.m.

I am despatching a page to bring you the good tidings of the victory of Enzersdorf, which I won on the 5th, and that of Wagram, which I won on the 6th.

The enemy's army flies in disorder, and all goes according to my prayers (*voeux*).

Eugène is well. Prince Aldobrandini is wounded, but slightly.

Bessières has been shot through the fleshy part of his thigh; the wound is very slight. Lasalle was killed. My losses are full heavy, but the victory is decisive and complete. We have taken more than 100 pieces of cannon, 12 flags, many prisoners.

I am sunburnt.

Adieu, dear. I send you a kiss. Kind regards to Hortense.

Napoleon.

No. 12.
To the Empress, at Plombières

Wolkersdorf, July 9, 1809, 2 a.m.

My Dear,—All goes here as I wish. My enemies are defeated, beaten, utterly routed. They were in great numbers; I have wiped them out. Today my health is good; yesterday I was rather ill with a surfeit of bile, occasioned by so many hardships, but it has done me much good.

Adieu, dear. I am in excellent health.   Napoleon.

July 12th.—Armistice of Znaim. Archduke Charles resigns his command.

No. 13.
To the Empress, at Plombières

In the Camp, before Znaim, July 13, 1809.

I send you the suspension of arms concluded yesterday with the Austrian General. Eugène is on the Hungary side, and is well. Send a copy of the suspension of arms to Cambacérès, in case he has not yet received one.

I send you a kiss, and am very well.   Napoleon.

You may cause this suspension of arms to be printed at Nancy.

July 14th.—English seize Senegal. Oudinot, Marmont, Macdonald made Marshals.

No. 14.
To the Empress, at Plombières

Schoenbrunn, July 17, 1809.

My Dear,—I have sent you one of my pages. You will have learnt the result of the battle of Wagram, and, later, of the suspension of arms of Znaim.

My health is good. Eugène is well, and I long to know that you, as well as Hortense, are the same.

Give a kiss for me to *Monsieur*, the Grand Duke of Berg.

Napoleon.

No. 15.
To the Empress, at Plombières

Schoenbrunn, July 24, 1809.

I have just received yours of July 18th. I note with pleasure that

the waters are doing you good. I see no objection to you going back to Malmaison after you have finished your treatment. It is hot enough here in all conscience. My health is excellent.
Adieu, dear. Eugène is at Vienna, in the best of health.—Yours ever,   Napoleon.

July 28th.—Battle of Talavera. Wellington repulses Victor, who attacks by King Joseph's order, without waiting for the arrival of Souk with the main army. Wellington retires on Portugal.

July 29th-31st.—Walcheren Expedition; 17,000 English land in Belgium.

No. 16.
To the Empress, at Plombières

Schoenbrunn, August 7, 1809.

I see from your letter that you are at Plombières, and intend to stay there. You do well; the waters and the fine climate can only do you good.

I remain here. My health and my affairs follow my wishes.

Please give my kind regards to Hortense and the Napoleons.—Yours ever,   Napoleon.

August 8th—Combat of Arzobispo. Soult defeats the Spaniards.

August 15th.—Flushing surrenders to the English.

No. 17.
To the Empress, at Paris

Schoenbrunn, August 21, 1809.

I have received your letter of August 14th, from Plombières; I see from it that by the 18th you will be either at Paris or Malmaison. The heat, which is very great here, will have upset you. Malmaison must be very dry and parched at this time of year. My health is good. The heat, however, has brought on a slight catarrh.

Adieu, dear.   Napoleon.

No. 18.
To the Empress, at Malmaison

Schoenbrunn, August 26, 1809.

I have your letter from Malmaison. They bring me word that you are plump, florid, and in the best of health. I assure you Vienna is not an amusing city. I would very much rather be back again in Paris.

Adieu, dear. Twice a week I listen to the comedians (*bouffons*); they are but very middling; it, however, passes the evenings. There are fifty or sixty women of Vienna, but outsiders (*au parterre*), as not having been presented.

Napoleon.

No. 19.
To the Empress, at Malmaison

Schoenbrunn, August 31, 1809.

I have had no letter from you for several days; the pleasures of Malmaison, the beautiful greenhouses, the beautiful gardens, cause the absent to be forgotten. It is, they say, the rule of your sex. Every one speaks only of your good health; all this is very suspicious.

Tomorrow I am off with Eugène for two days in Hungary.

My health is fairly good.

Adieu, dear.—Yours ever,   Napoleon.

No. 20.
To the Empress, at Malmaison

Krems, September 9, 1809.

My Dear,—I arrived here yesterday at 2 a.m.; I have come here to see my troops. My health has never been better. I know that you are very well.

I shall be in Paris at a moment when nobody will expect me. Everything here goes excellently and to my satisfaction.

Adieu, dear.   Napoleon.

No. 21.
To the Empress, at Malmaison

Schoenbrunn, September 23, 1809.

I have received your letter of the 16th, and note that you are well. The old maid's house is only worth 120,000[3] *francs*; they will never get more for it. Still, I leave you mistress to do what you like, since it amuses you; only, once purchased, don't pull it down to put a rockery there.

Adieu, dear.   Napoleon.

---

3. Boispréau, belonging to Mademoiselle Julien

No. 22.
To the Empress, at Malmaison

Schoenbrunn, September 25, 1809.

I have received your letter. Be careful, and I advise you to be vigilant, for one of these nights you will hear a loud knocking. My health is good. I know nothing about the rumours; I have never been better for many a long year. Corvisart was no use to me.

Adieu, dear; everything here prospers.—Yours ever,

Napoleon.

September 26th.—Battle of Silistria; Turks defeat Russians.

No. 23.

October 14th.—Treaty of Vienna, between France and Austria.

To the Empress, at Malmaison

Schoenbrunn, October 14, 1809.

My Dear,—I write to advise you that Peace was signed two hours ago between Champagny and Prince Metternich.

Adieu, dear. Napoleon.

October 19th.—Mortier routs Spaniards at Oçana.

No. 24.
To the Empress, at Malmaison

Nymphenburg, near Munich, October 21, 1809.

I arrived here yesterday in the best of health, but shall not start till tomorrow. I shall spend a day at Stuttgard. You will be advised twenty-four hours in advance of my arrival at Fontainebleau. I look forward with pleasure to seeing you again, and I await that moment impatiently.

I send you a kiss.—Yours ever, Napoleon.

No. 25.
To the Empress, at Malmaison

Munich, October 22, 1809.

My Dear,—I start in an hour. I shall be at Fontainebleau from the 26th to 27th; you may meet me there with some of your

November 25th.—Disappearance of Benjamin Bathurst, erroneously thought to have been murdered by the French, really by robbers.

December 1st.—Capture of Gerona and 200 cannon by Augereau.

December 16th.—French Senate pronounce the divorce of Napoleon and Josephine.

December 24th.—English re-embark from Flushing.

Series M

Josephine, my excellent Josephine, thou knowest if I have loved thee! To thee, to thee alone do I owe the only moments of happiness which I have enjoyed in this world. Josephine, my destiny overmasters my will. My dearest affections must be silent before the interests of France.—

Bourrienne's Napoleon.[1]

LETTERS OF THE EMPEROR NAPOLEON TO THE EMPRESS JOSEPHINE AFTER THE DIVORCE AND BEFORE HIS MARRIAGE WITH MARIE LOUISE.
DECEMBER, 1809, TO APRIL 2, 1810.

No. 1.
To the Empress, at Malmaison

December 1809, 8 p.m.

My Dear,—I found you today weaker than you ought to be. You have shown courage; it is necessary that you should maintain it and not give way to a doleful melancholy. You must be contented and take special care of your health, which is so precious to me.

If you are attached to me and if you love me, you should show strength of mind and force yourself to be happy. You cannot question my constant and tender friendship, and you would know very imperfectly all the affection I have for you if you imagined that I can be happy if you are unhappy, and contented if you are ill at ease.

Adieu, dear. Sleep well; dream that I wish it.

Napoleon.

---

1 Also Meme's *Memoirs of Josephine*, p. 333.

No. 2.
To the Empress, at Malmaison

Tuesday, 6 o'clock.

The Queen of Naples, whom I saw at the hunt in the Bois de Boulogne, where I rode down a stag, told me that she left you yesterday at 1 p.m. in the best of health.

Please tell me what you are doing today. As for me, I am very well. Yesterday, when I saw you, I was ill. I expect you will have been for a drive.

Adieu, dear.   Napoleon.

No. 3.
To the Empress, at Malmaison

Trianon, 7 p.m.

My Dear,—I have just received your letter. Savary tells me that you are always crying; that is not well. I trust that you have been a drive today. I sent you my quarry. I shall come to see you when you tell me you are reasonable, and that your courage has the upper hand.

Tomorrow, the whole day, I am receiving Ministers.

Adieu, dear. I also am sad today; I need to know that you are satisfied and to learn that your equilibrium (*aplomb*) is restored. Sleep well.   Napoleon.

No. 4.
To the Empress, at Malmaison

Thursday, Noon, 1809.

My Dear,—I wished to come and see you today, but I was very busy and rather unwell. Still, I am just off to the Council. Please tell me how you are. This weather is very damp, and not at all healthy.   Napoleon.

No. 5.
To the Empress, at Malmaison

Trianon.

I should have come to see you today if I had not been obliged to come to see the King of Bavaria, who has just arrived in Paris.

I shall come to see you tonight at eight o'clock, and return at ten. I hope to see you tomorrow, and to see you cheerful and placid.

Adieu, dear. Napoleon.

No. 6.
To the Empress, at Malmaison

Trianon, Tuesday.

My Dear,—I lay down after you left me yesterday;[2] I am going to Paris. I wish to hear that you are cheerful. I shall come to see you during the week.

I have received your letters, which I am going to read in the carriage. Napoleon.

No. 7.
To the Empress, at Malmaison

Paris, Wednesday, Noon, 27th December 1809.

Eugène told me that you were very miserable all yesterday. That is not well, my dear; it is contrary to what you promised me.

I have been thoroughly tired in revisiting the Tuileries; that great palace seemed empty to me, and I felt lost in it.

Adieu, dear. Keep well. Napoleon.

No. 8.
To the Empress, at Malmaison

Paris, Sunday, December 31, 10 a.m., 1809.

My Dear,—The Empress, with Hortense, had been to dine at Trianon. Today I have a grand parade; I shall see all my Old Guard and more than sixty artillery trains.

The King of Westphalia is returning home, which will leave a house vacant in Paris. I am sad not to see you. If the parade finishes before 3 o'clock, I will come; otherwise, tomorrow.

Adieu, dear. Napoleon.

No. 9.
To the Empress, at Malmaison

Thursday Evening, 1810.

My Dear,—The Empress, with Hortense, had been to dine at Trianon. Hortense, whom I saw this afternoon, has given me news of you. I trust that you will have been able to see your

---

2. The Empress, with Hortense, had been to dine at Trianon.

plants today, the weather having been fine. I have only been out for a few minutes at three o'clock to shoot some hares.

Adieu, dear; sleep well. Napoleon.

No. 10.
To the Empress, at Malmaison

Friday, 8 p.m., 1810.

I wished to come and see you today, but I cannot; it will be, I hope, in the morning. It is a long time since I heard from you. I learnt with pleasure that you take walks in your garden these cold days.

Adieu, dear; keep well, and never doubt my affection.

Napoleon.

No. 11.
To the Empress, at Malmaison

Sunday , 8 p.m., 1810.

I was very glad to see you yesterday; I feel what charms your society has for me.

Today I walked with Estève.[3] I have allowed £4000 for 1810, for the extraordinary expenses at Malmaison. You can therefore do as much planting as you like; you will distribute that sum as you may require. I have instructed Esteve to send £8000 the moment the contract for the Maison Julien shall be made. I have ordered them to pay for your *parure* of rubies, which will be valued by the Department, for I do not wish to be robbed by jewellers. So, there goes the £16,000 that this may cost me.

I have ordered them to hold the million which the Civil List owes you for 1810 at the disposal of your man of business, in order to pay your debts.

You should find in the coffers of Malmaison twenty to twenty-five thousand pounds; you can take them to buy your plate and linen.

I have instructed them to make you a very fine porcelain service; they will take your commands in order that it may be a very fine one. Napoleon.

---

3. General Treasurer of the Crown.

No. 12.

To the Empress, at Malmaison

Wednesday, 6 p.m., 1810.

My Dear,—I see no objection to your receiving the King of Westphalia whenever you wish. The King and Queen of Bavaria will probably come to see you on Friday.

I long to come to Malmaison, but you must really show fortitude and self-restraint; the page on duty this morning told me that he saw you weeping.

I am going to dine quite alone.

Adieu, dear. Never doubt the depth of my feelings for you; you would be unjust and unfair if you did.

Napoleon.

No. 13.

To the Empress, at Malmaison

Saturday, 1 p.m., 1810.

My Dear,—Yesterday I saw Eugène, who told me that you gave a reception to the kings. I was at the concert till eight o'clock, and only dined, quite alone, at that hour.

I long to see you. If I do not come today, I will come after mass.

Adieu, dear. I hope to find you sensible and in good health. This weather should indeed make you put on flesh.

Napoleon.

January 9.—The clergy of Paris annul the religious marriage of Napoleon with Josephine (so *Biographie Universelle*, Michaud; Montgaillard gives January 18). Confirmed by the *Metropolitan Officialité*, January 12 (Pasquier). .

No. 14.

To the Empress, at Malmaison

Trianon, January 17, 1810.

My Dear,—D'Audenarde, whom I sent to you this morning, tells me that since you have been at Malmaison you have no longer any courage. Yet that place is full of our happy memories, which can and ought never to change, at least on my side.

I want badly to see you, but I must have some assurance that you are strong and not weak; I too am rather like you, and it makes me frightfully wretched.

Adieu, Josephine; goodnight. If you doubted me, you would be very ungrateful. Napoleon.

No. 15.
To the Empress, at Malmaison

January 20, 1810.

My Dear,—I send you the box that I promised you the day before yesterday—representing the Island of Lobau. I was rather tired yesterday. I work much, and do not go out.

Adieu, dear. Napoleon.

No. 16.
To the Empress, at Malmaison

Noon, Tuesday, 1810.

I hear that you are making yourself miserable; this is too bad. You have no confidence in me, and all the rumours that are being spread strike you; this is not knowing me, Josephine. I am much annoyed, and if I do not find you cheerful and contented, I shall scold you right well.

Adieu, dear. Napoleon.

No. 17.
To the Empress, at Malmaison

Sunday, 9 p.m., 1810.

My Dear,—I was very glad to see you the day before yesterday.

I hope to go to Malmaison during the week. I have had all your affairs looked after here, and ordered that everything be brought to the Elysée-Napoleon.

Please take care of yourself.

Adieu, dear. Napoleon.

No. 18.
To the Empress, at Malmaison

January 30, 1810.

My Dear,—Your letter to hand. I hope the walk you had yesterday, in order to show people your conservatories, has done you good.

I will gladly see you at the Elysée, and shall be very glad to see

148

you oftener, for you know how I love you.   Napoleon.

No. 19.
To the Empress, at Malmaison

Saturday , 6 p.m., 1810.

I told Eugène that you would rather give ear to the vulgar gossip of a great city than to what I told you; yet people should not be allowed to invent fictions to make you miserable.

I have had all your effects moved to the Elysée. You shall come to Paris at once; but be at ease and contented, and have full confidence in me.   Napoleon.

February 2.—Soult occupies Seville. The Junta takes refuge at Cadiz.

February 6.—Guadeloupe surrenders to the English.

February 7.—Convention of marriage between the Emperor Napoleon and the Archduchess Marie Louise.

No. 20.
To the Empress, at the Elyseé-Napoleon

February 19, 1810.

My Dear,—I have received your letter. I long to see you, but the reflections that you make may be true. It is, perhaps, not desirable that we should be under the same roof for the first year. Yet Bessières' country-house is too far off to go and return in one day; moreover I have rather a cold, and am not sure of being able to go there.

Adieu, dear.   Napoleon.

No. 21.
To the Empress, at the Elyseé-Napoleon

Friday, 6 p.m., 1810.

Savary, as soon as he arrived, brought me your letter; I am sorry to see you are unhappy. I am very glad that you saw nothing of the fire. I had fine weather at Rambouillet.

Hortense told me that you had some idea of coming to a dinner at Bessières, and of returning to Paris to sleep. I am sorry that you have not been able to manage it.

Adieu, dear. Be cheerful, and consider how much you please me thereby.   Napoleon.

No. 22.
To the Empress, at Malmaison

March 12, 1810.

My Dear,—I trust that you will be pleased with what I have done for Navarre. You must see from that how anxious I am to make myself agreeable to you.

Get ready to take possession of Navarre; you will go there on March 25, to pass the month of April.

Adieu, dear.   Napoleon.

April 1.—Civil marriage of Napoleon and Marie Louise. (Religious marriage, April 2.)

Series N

No. 1.

Letter of the Empress Josephine to the Emperor Napoleon.

Navarre, April 19, 1810.

Sire, I have received, by my son, the assurance that your Majesty consents to my return to Malmaison, and grants to me the advances asked for in order to make the *château* of Navarre habitable. This double favour, Sire, dispels to a great extent the uneasiness, nay, even the fears which your Majesty's long silence had inspired. I was afraid that I might be entirely banished from your memory; I see that I am not. I am therefore less wretched today, and even as happy as henceforward it will be possible for me to be.

I shall go at the end of the month to Malmaison, since your Majesty sees no objection to it. But I ought to tell you, Sire, that I should not so soon have taken advantage of the latitude which your Majesty left me in this respect had the house of Navarre not required, for my health's sake and for that of my household, repairs which are urgent. My idea is to stay at Malmaison a very short time; I shall soon leave it in order to go to the waters. But while I am at Malmaison, your Majesty may be sure that I shall live there as if I were a thousand leagues from Paris. I have made a great sacrifice, Sire, and every day I realise more its full extent. Yet that sacrifice will be, as it ought to be, a complete one on my part. Your Highness, amid your happiness, shall be troubled by no expression of my regret.

I shall pray unceasingly for your Majesty's happiness, perhaps even I shall pray that I may see you again; but your Majesty may be assured that I shall always respect our new relationship. I shall respect it in silence, relying on the attachment that you had to me formerly; I shall call for no new proof; I shall trust to everything from your justice and your heart.

I limit myself to asking from you one favour: it is, that you will deign to find a way of sometimes convincing both myself and my *entourage* that I have still a small place in your memory and a great place in your esteem and friendship. By this means, whatever happens, my sorrows will be mitigated without, as it seems to me, compromising that which is of permanent importance to me, the happiness of your Majesty.

Josephine.

No. 1A.
(Reply of the Emperor Napoleon to the preceding) To the Empress Josephine, at Navarre

Compiègne, April 21 , 1810.

My Dear,—I have yours of April 18th; it is written in a bad style. I am always the same; people like me do not change. I know not what Eugène has told you. I have not written to you because you have not written to me, and my sole desire is to fulfil your slightest inclination.

I see with pleasure that you are going to Malmaison and that you are contented; as for me, I shall be so likewise on hearing news from you and in giving you mine. I say no more about it until you have compared this letter with yours, and after that I will leave you to judge which of us two is the better friend.

Adieu, dear; keep well, and be just for your sake and mine.

Napoleon.

April 23rd.—Battle of Lerida. Suchet defeats Spaniards.

No. 2.
Reply of the Empress Josephine.

A thousand, thousand loving thanks for not having forgotten me. My son has just brought me your letter. With what impetuosity I read it, and yet I took a long time over it, for there was not a word which did not make me weep; but these tears were very pleasant ones. I have found my whole heart again—such as it will always be; there are affections which are life itself, and which can only end with it.

I was in despair to find my letter of the 19th had displeased you; I do not remember the exact expressions, but I know what torture I felt in writing it—the grief at having no news from you. I wrote you on my departure from Malmaison, and since then how often have I wished to write you! but I appreciated the causes of your silence and feared to be importunate with a letter. Yours has been the true balm for me. Be happy, be as much so as you deserve; it is my whole heart which speaks to you. You have also just given me my share of happiness, and a share which I value the most, for nothing can equal in my estimation a proof that you still remember me.

Adieu, dear; I again thank you as affectionately as I shall always love you.   Josephine.

No. 2A.
To the Empress Josephine, at the Château Navarre

Compiègne, April 28, 1810.

My Dear,—I have just received two letters from you. I am writing to Eugène. I have ordered that the marriage of Tascher with the Princess de la Leyen shall take place.

Tomorrow I shall go to Antwerp to see my fleet and to give orders about the works. I shall return on May 15th.

Eugène tells me that you wish to go to the waters; trouble yourself about nothing. Do not listen to the gossip of Paris; it is idle and far from knowing the real state of things. My affection for you does not change, and I long to know that you are happy and contented.   Napoleon.

No. 3.
To the Empress Josephine, at Malmaison

My Dear,—I have your letter. Eugène will give you tidings of my journey and of the Empress. I am very glad that you are going to the waters. I trust they may do you good.

I wish very much to see you. If you are at Malmaison at the end of the month, I will come to see you. I expect to be at St. Cloud on the 30th of the month. My health is very good . . . it only needs to hear that you are contented and well. Let me know in what name you intend to travel.

Never doubt the whole truth of my affection for you; it will last as long as I. You would be very unjust if you doubted it.

Napoleon.

July 1st.—Louis Bonaparte, King of Holland, abdicates in favour of his son.

No. 4.

To the Empress Josephine, at the waters of Aix, in Savoy

Rambouillet, July 8, 1810.

My Dear,—I have your letter of July 8th. You will have seen Eugène, and his presence will have done you good. I learn with pleasure that the waters are beneficial to you. The King of Holland has just abdicated the throne, while leaving the Regency, according to the Constitution, in the hands of the Queen. He has quitted Amsterdam and left the Grand Duke of Berg behind.

I have reunited Holland to France, which has, however, the advantage of setting the Queen at liberty, and that [1] unfortunate girl is coming to Paris with her son the Grand Duke of Berg that will make her perfectly happy.

My health is good. I have come here to hunt for a few days. I shall see you this autumn with pleasure. Never doubt my friendship; I never change.

Keep well, be cheerful, and believe in the truth of my attachment.

Napoleon.

July 9th.—Holland incorporated with the French Empire.

July 10th.—Ney takes Ciudad Rodrigo, after twenty-five days open trenches.

No. 5.

To the Empress Josephine, at the waters of Aix, in Savoy

St. Cloud, July 20, 1810.

My Dear,—I have received your letter of July 14th, and note with pleasure that the waters are doing you good, and that you like Geneva. I think that you are doing well to go there for a

---

1. So *Collection Didot*, followed by Aubenas. St. Amand has "*ton infortunée fille.*"

few weeks.

My health is fairly good. The conduct of the King of Holland has worried me.

Hortense is shortly coming to Paris. The Grand Duke of Berg is on his way; I expect him tomorrow.

Adieu, dear. Napoleon.

No. 6.
To the Empress Josephine, at the waters of Aix, in Savoy

Trianon, August 10, 1810.

Your letter to hand. I was pained to see what a risk you had run. For an inhabitant of the isles of the ocean to die in a lake would have been a fatality indeed!

The Queen is better, and I hope her health will be re-established. Her husband is in Bohemia, apparently not knowing what to do.

I am fairly well, and beg you to believe in my sincere attachment. Napoleon.

August 21st.—Swedes elect Marshal Bernadotte Crown Prince of Sweden.

August 27th.—Massena takes Almeida.

No. 7.
To the Empress Josephine, at the waters of Aix, in Savoy

St. Cloud, September 14, 1810.

My Dear,—I have your letter of September 9th. I learn with pleasure that you keep well. There is no longer the slightest doubt that the Empress has entered on the fourth month of her pregnancy; she is well, and is much attached to me. The young Princes Napoleon are very well; they are in the Pavilion d'Italie, in the Park of St. Cloud.

My health is fairly good. I wish to learn that you are happy and contented. I hear that one of your *entourage* has broken a leg while going on the glacier.

Adieu, dear. Never doubt the interest I take in you and the affection that I bear towards you.

Napoleon.

September 27th.—Battle of Busaco. Like Ebersburg, another of Massena's expensive and unnecessary frontal attacks. He loses 5000 men, but next day turns the position of Wellington, who continues to retire.

No. 8.
To the Empress, at Malmaison

Paris, this Friday.

My Dear,—Yours to hand. I am sorry to see that you have been ill; I fear it must be this bad weather.

Madame de la T—— is one of the most foolish women of the Faubourg. I have borne her cackle for a very long time; I am sick of it, and have ordered that she does not come again to Paris. There are five or six other old women that I equally wish to send away from Paris; they are spoiling the young ones by their follies.

I will name Madame de Makau Baroness since you wish it, and carry out your other commissions.

My health is pretty good. The conduct of B—— appears to me very ridiculous. I trust to hear that you are better.

Adieu, dear. Napoleon.

No. 9.
To the Empress Josephine, at Geneva

Fontainebleau, October 1, 1810.

I have received your letter. Hortense, whom I have seen, will have told you what I think. Go to see your son this winter; come back to the waters of Aix next year, or, still better, wait for the spring at Navarre. I would advise you to go to Navarre at once, if I did not fear you would get tired of it. In my view, the only suitable places for you this winter are either Milan or Navarre; after that, I approve of whatever you may do, for I do not wish to vex you in anything.

Adieu, dear. The Empress is as I told you in my last letter. I am naming Madame de Montesquieu governess of the Children of France. Be contented, and do not get excited; never doubt my affection for you. Napoleon.

October 6th.—Wellington reaches the lines of Torres Vedras.

November 9th.—Opening of St. Quentin Canal at Paris.

No. 10.

To the Empress Josephine, at the Navarre

Fontainebleau, November 14, 1810.

My Dear,—I have received your letter. Hortense has spoken to me about it. I note with pleasure that you are contented. I hope that you are not very tired of Navarre.

My health is very good. The Empress progresses satisfactorily. I will do the various things you ask regarding your household. Take care of your health, and never doubt my affection for you.   Napoleon.

No. 11.

To the Empress Josephine, at the Navarre

I have your letter. I see no objection to the marriage of Mackau with Wattier, if he wishes it; this general is a very brave man. I am in good health. I hope to have a son; I shall let you know immediately.

Adieu, dear. I am very glad that Madame d'Arberg [2] has told you things which please you. When you see me, you will find me with my old affection for you.   Napoleon.

December 3rd.—English take Mauritius.

---

2. Josephine's chief maid-of-honour.

Series O

1811

Nun steht das Reich gesichert, wie gegründet,
Nun fühlt er froh im Sohne sich gegründet.

Und sei durch Sie dies letze Glück beschieden—
Der alles wollen kann, will auch den Frieden.
—Goethe (*Ibro der Kaiserin von Frankreich Majestät*).

No. 1.
To the Empress Josephine, at the Navarre

Paris, January 8th, 1811.

I have your New Year's letter. I thank you for its contents. I note with pleasure that you are well and happy. I hear that there are more women than men at Navarre.

My health is excellent, though I have not been out for a fortnight. Eugène appears to have no fears about his wife; he gives you a grandson.

Adieu, dear; keep well.   Napoleon.

February 19th.—Soult defeats Spaniards at the Gébora, near Badajoz.

February 28th.—French occupy Duchy of Oldenburg, to complete the line of the North Sea blockade against England. This occupation embitters the Emperor of Russia and his family.

March 10th.—Mortier captures Badajoz after a siege of 54 days.

March 20th.—Birth of the King of Rome—"a pompous title buried in the tomb of the Ostrogoths."

No. 2.
To the Empress Josephine, at the Navarre

Paris, March 22nd, 1811.

My Dear,—I have your letter. I thank you for it.

My son is fat, and in excellent health. I trust he may continue to improve. He has my chest, my mouth, and my eyes. I hope he may fulfil his destiny. I am always well pleased with Eugène; he has never given me the least anxiety.

Napoleon.

April 4th.—Battle of Fuentes d'Onoro. Massena attacks English, and is repulsed.

June 18th.—Wellington raises siege of Badajoz, and retires on Portugal.

June 29th.—French storm Tarragona, whereupon Suchet created Marshal.

No. 3.
To the Empress Josephine, at Malmaison

Trianon, August 25th, 1811.

I have your letter. I see with pleasure that you are in good health. I have been for some days at Trianon. I expect to go to Compiègne. My health is very good.

Put some order into your affairs. Spend only £60,000, and save as much every year; that will make a reserve of £600,000 in ten years for your grandchildren. It is pleasant to be able to give them something, and be helpful to them. Instead of that, I hear you have debts, which would be really too bad. Look after your affairs, and don't give to everyone who wants to help himself. If you wish to please me, let me hear that you have accumulated a large fortune. Consider how ill I must think of you, if I know that you, with £125,000 a year, are in debt.

Adieu, dear; keep well.

Napoleon.

No. 4.
To the Empress, at Malmaison

Friday, 8 a.m., 1811.

I send to know how you are, for Hortense tells me you were in bed yesterday. I was annoyed with you about your debts. I do not wish you to have any; on the contrary, I wish you to put a million aside every year, to give to your grandchildren when they get married.

Nevertheless, never doubt my affection for you, and don't worry any more about the present embarrassment.

Adieu, dear. Send, me word that you are well. They say that you are as fat as a good Normandy farmeress.

Napoleon.

October 25th-26th.—Battle of Murviedro and capture of Sagunto: Blake and O'Donnell heavily defeated by Suchet.

December 20th.—Senatus Consultus puts 120,000 conscripts (born in 1792) at disposal of Government for 1812.

December 26th.—Suchet defeats Spanish, and crosses Guadalaviar.

Series P

1812

'Tis the same landscape which the modern Mars saw
Who march'd to Moscow, led by Fame, the siren!
To lose by one month's frost, some twenty years
Of conquest, and his guard of grenadiers.
—Byron (*Don Juan, canto* 10. *stanza* 58).

Montgaillard sums up his tirade against Napoleon for the Russian campaign by noting that it took the Romans ten years to conquer Gaul, while Napoleon "would not give two to the conquest of that vast desert of Scythia which forced Darius to flee, Alexander to draw back, Crassus to perish; where Julian terminated his career, where Valerian covered himself with shame, and which saw the disasters of Charles XII."

January 9th.—Suchet captures Valencia, 18,000 Spanish troops, and 400 cannon. The marshal is made Duke of Albuféra.

January 15th.—Imperial decree ordains 100,000 acres to be put under cultivation of beetroot, for the manufacture of indigenous sugar.

January 19th.—Taking of Ciudad Rodrigo by Wellington.

January 26th.—French, under General Friand, occupy Stralsund and Swedish Pomerania.

February 24th.—Treaty of alliance between France and Prussia; the latter to support France in case of a war with Russia.

March 13th.—Senatus Consultus divides the National Guards into three bans, to include all capable men not already in military service. They are not to serve outside France. A hundred cohorts, each 970 strong, of the first ban (men between 20 and 26), put at disposal of Government.

March 14th.—Treaty between France and Austria; reciprocal help, in need, of 30,000 men and 60 guns. The integrity of European Turkey mutually guaranteed.

March 26th.—Treaty between Russia and Sweden. Bernadotte is promised Norway by Alexander.

April 7th.—The English take Badajoz by assault. "The French General, Philippon, with but 3000 men, has been besieged thrice within thirteen months by armies of 50,000 men" (*Montgaillard*).

April 24th.—Alexander leaves St. Petersburg, to take command of his Grand Army.

May 9th.—Napoleon leaves Paris for Germany.

May 11th.—Assassination of English Prime Minister, Perceval.

May 17th-28th.—Napoleon at Dresden; joined there by the Emperor and Empress of Austria, and afresh "*parterre* of kings."

May 28th.—Treaty of Bucharest, between Turkey and Russia. The Pruth as boundary, and Servia restored to Turkey. This treaty, so fatal to Napoleon, and of which he only heard in October, was mainly the work of Stratford de Redcliffe, then aged twenty-five. Wellington, thinking the treaty his brother's work, speaks of it as "the most important service that ever fell to the lot of any individual to perform."

No. 1.

June 12th.—Suchet defeats an Anglo- Spanish army outside Tarragona.

To the Empress, at Malmaison

June 12th, 1812.

My Dear,—I shall always receive news from you with great interest.

The waters will, I hope, do you good, and I shall see you with much pleasure on your return.

Never doubt the interest I feel in you. I will arrange all the matters of which you speak.

Napoleon.

June 16th.—Lord Liverpool Prime Minister of England.

June 18th.—United States declares war against England concerning rights of neutrals.

June 19th.—The captive Pope (Pius VII.) brought to Fontainebleau.

No. 2.
To the Empress, at Malmaison

Gumbinnen, June 20th, 1812.

I have your letter of June 10th. I see no obstacle to your going to Milan, to be near the Vice-Reine. You will do well to go *incognito*. You will find it very hot.

My health is very good. Eugène is well, and is doing good work. Never doubt the interest I have in you, and my friendship.   Napoleon.

June 22nd.—Napoleon from his headquarters, Wilkowyszki, declares war against Russia. His army comprised 550,000 men and 1200 cannon, and he held sway at this epoch over 85,000,000 souls—half the then population of Europe.

June 24th.—French cross the Niemen, over 450,000 strong.[1] Of these 20,000 are Italians, 80,000 from Confederation of the Rhine, 30,000 Poles, 30,000 Austrians, and 20,000 Prussians. The Russian army numbers 360,000.

June 28th.—French enter Wilna, the old capital of Lithuania. Napoleon remains here till *July 16th*, establishing a provisional government, and leaving his Foreign Minister, Maret, there.

July 12th.—Americans invade Canada.

July 18th.—Treaty of peace between England and Sweden; and between Russia and the Spanish Regency at Cadiz.

July 22nd.—Battle of Salamanca (Arapiles). Marmont defeated by Wellington, and badly wounded. French lose nearly 8000 men and 5000 prisoners; English loss, 5200. The Spanish Regency had decided to submit to Joseph Bonaparte, but this battle deters them. French retire behind the Douro.

July 23rd.—Combat of Mohilow, on the Dneiper. Davoust defeats Bagration.

July 28th.—French enter Witepsk.

---

1 Averaged from early historians of the campaigns. Marbot gives the numbers 155,400 French and 175,000 Allies. Allowing for the secession of the Austrian and Prussian contingents and for 30,000 prisoners, he gives the actual French death-roll by February 1813 at 65,000. This is a minimum estimate.

August 1st.—Treaty of alliance between Great Britain and Russia. English fleet henceforward guards the Gulf of Riga. Combat of Obaiarzma, on the bank of the Drissa. Marshal Oudinot defeats Wittgenstein. Russians lose 5000 men and 14 guns.

August 9th—Battle of Brownstown (near Toronto). Americans defeated; surrender August 16th with 2500 men and 33 guns to General Brock.

August 12th—Wellington enters Madrid.

August 17th-18th—Battle and capture of Smolensk. Napoleon defeats Barclay de Tolly; Russians lose 12,000, French less than half.

August 18th.—Battle of Polotsk, fifty miles from Witepsk, down the Dwina. St. Cyr defeats Wittgenstein's much larger army, and takes 20 guns. (St. Cyr made marshal for this battle, August 27th.)

August 19th—Combat of Volontino-Cova, beyond Smolensk. Ney defeats Russians.

August 27th.—Norway guaranteed Sweden in lieu of Finland by Russia.

August 28th.—Interview at Abo, in Finland, between Alexander, Bernadotte, and Lord Cathcart (English ambassador). Decided that Sweden shall join the crusade against France, and that Moreau be imported from U.S.A. to command another army.

August 20th.—Viazma, burnt by Russians, entered by the French.

September 7th.—Battle of Borodino (*La Moskowa*). Nearly all the Russian generals are present: Barclay de Tolly, Beningsen, Bagration (who is killed), all under Kutusoff. Russians lose 30,000 men, French 20,000, including many generals who had survived all the campaigns of the Revolution. The French, hungry and soaked in rain, have no energy to pursue.

September 14th.—Occupation of Moscow; fired by emissaries of Rostopchin, its late governor. Of 4000 stone houses only 200 remain, of 8000 wooden ones 500. Over 20,000 sick and wounded burnt in their beds. Fire lasts till September 20th.

September 18th.—Russian Army of the Danube under Admiral Tschitchagow joins the Army of Reserve.

September 26th.—Russian troops from Finland disembark at Riga.

September 30th.—Napoleon finds a copy of Treaty of Bucharest at Moscow.

October 11th.—Admiral Tschitchagow with 36,000 men reaches Bresc, on the Bug, threatening the French communications with Warsaw.

October 17th-19th.—Second combat of Polotsk. Wittgenstein again defeated by St. Cyr, who it wounded.

October 18th.—Combat of Winkowo; Kutusoff defeats Murat. Americans defeated at Queenston Heights, on the Niagara, and lose 900 men.

October 19th—Commencement of the Retreat from Moscow.

October 22nd.—Burgos captured by Wellington.

October 23rd.—Conspiracy of Malet at Paris; Cambacérès to the rescue. Evacuation of Moscow by Mortier after forty days' occupation. The French army now retreating has only half its original strength, and the best cavalry regiments boast only 100 horses.

October 24th.—Battle of Malo-Jaroslavitz. Eugène with 17,000 men defeats Kutusoff with 60,000; but Napoleon finds the enemy too strong and too tenacious to risk the fertile Kaluga route.

November 3rd.—Battle of Wiazma. Rearguard action, in which Ney and Eugène are distinguished.

November 9th.—Napoleon reaches Smolensk and hears of Malet conspiracy.

November 14th.—Evacuation of Smolensk.

November 16th.—Russian Army (of the Danube) takes Minsk, and cuts off the French from the Niemen.

November 16th-19th—Combat of Krasnoi, twenty-five miles west of Smolensk. Kutusoff with 30,000 horse and 70,000 foot tries to stop the French, who have only 25,000 effective combatants. Magnificent fighting by Ney with his rearguard of 6000.

November 21st.—Russians seize at Borizow the bridges over the Beresina, which are

November 23rd.—Retaken by Oudinot.

November 26th-28th.—French cross the Beresina, but lose 20,000 prisoners and nearly all their cannon (150).

November 29th.—Napoleon writes Maret he has heard nothing of France or Spain for fifteen days.

December 3rd.—Twenty-ninth bulletin dated Malodeczna, fifty miles west of Borisow.

December 5th.—Napoleon reaches Smorgoni, and starts for France.

December 10th.—Murat, left in command, evacuates Wilna. French retreat in utter rout;"It is not General Kutusoff who routed the French, it is General Morosow" (the frost), said the Russians.

December 14th.—Napoleon reaches Dresden, and

December 18th.—Paris.

December 19th.—Evacuation of Kovno and passage of the Niemen.

December 20th.—Napoleon welcomed by the Senate in a speech by the naturalist Lacépède:"The absence of your Majesty, sire, is always a national calamity."

December 30th.—Defection of the Prussian General York and Convention of Taurogen, near Tilsit, between Russia and Prussia. This defection is the signal for the uprising of Germany from the Oder to the Rhine, from the Baltic to the Julienne Alps.

1813.

January 5th.—Königsberg occupied by the Russians.

January 13th.—Senatus Consultus calls up 250,000 conscripts.

January 22nd.—Americans defeated at Frenchtown, near Detroit, and lose 1200 men.

January 25th.—*Concordat* at Fontainebleau between Napoleon and Pope Pius VII., with advantageous terms for the Papacy. The Pope, however, soon breaks faith.

January 28th—Murat deserts the French army for Naples, and leaves Posen. "Your husband is very brave on the battlefield, but he is weaker than a woman or a monk when he is not face to face with an enemy. He has no moral courage" (Napoleon to his sister Caroline, January 24th, 1813. Brotonne, 1032). Replaced by Eugène (Napoleons letter dated January 22nd).

February 1st.—Proclamation of Louis XVIII. to the French people (dated London).

February 8th.—Warsaw surrenders to Russia.

February 10th.—Proclamation of Emperor Alexander calling on the people of Germany to shake off the yoke of "one man."

February 28th.—Sixth Continental Coalition against France. Treaty signed between Russia and Prussia at Kalisch.

March 3rd.—New treaty between England and Sweden at Stockholm: Sweden to receive a subsidy of a million sterling and the island of Guadaloupe in return for supporting the Coalition with 30,000 men.

March 4th.—*Cossacks* occupy Berlin. Madison inaugurated President U.S.A.

March 9th—Eugène removes his headquarters to Leipsic.

March 12th.—French evacuate Hamburg.

March 21st.—Russians and Prussians take new town of Dresden.

April 1st.—France declares war on Prussia.

April 10th.—Death of Lagrange, mathematician; greatly bemoaned by Napoleon, who considered his death as a "*presentiment*" (D'Abrants).

April 14th.—Swedish army lands in Germany.

April 15th.—Napoleon leaves Paris; arrives Erfurt (April 25th). Americans take Mobile.

April 16th.—Thorn (garrisoned by 900 Bavarians) surrenders to the Russians. Fort York (now Toronto) and

April 27th.—Upper Canada taken by the Americans.

May 1st.—Death of the Abbé Delille, poet. Opening of campaign. French forces scattered in Germany, 166,000 men; Allies' forces ready for action, 225,000 men. Marshal Bessières killed by a cannonball at Poserna.

May 2nd—Napoleon with 90,000 men defeats Prussians and Russians at Lutzen (Gross-Goerschen) with 110,000; French loss, 10,000. Battle won chiefly by French artillery. Emperor of Russia and King of Prussia present.

May 8th.—Napoleon and the French reoccupy Dresden.

May 18th.—Eugène reaches Milan, and enrols an Italian army 47,000 strong.

May 19th-21st.—Combats of Konigswartha, Bautzen, Hochkirch, Würschen. Napoleon defeats Prussians and Russians; French loss, 12,000; Allies, 20,000.

May 23rd.—Duroc (shot on May 22nd) dies. "Duroc," said the Emperor, "there is another life. It is there you will go to await me, and there we shall meet again someday."

May 27th.—Americans capture Fort George (Lake Ontario) and

May 29th.—Defeat English at Sackett's Harbour.

May 30th.—French re-enter Hamburg and

June 1st.—Occupy Breslau. British frigate *Shannon* captures *Chesapeake* in fifteen minutes outside Boston harbour.

June 4th.—Armistice of Plesswitz, between Napoleon and the Allies.

June 6th.—Americans (3500) surprised at Burlington Heights by 700 British.

June 15th.—Siege of Tarragona raised by Suchet; English re-embark, leaving their artillery. "If I had had two marshals such as Suchet, I should not only have conquered Spain, but I should have kept it" (Napoleon in Campan's *Memoirs*).

June 21st.—Battle of Vittoria; total rout of the French under Marshal Jourdan and King Joseph. In retreat the army is much more harassed by the guerillas than by the English.

June 23rd.—Admiral Cockburn defeated at Craney Island by Americans.

June 24th—Five hundred Americans surrender to two hundred Canadians at Beaver's Dams.

June 25th.—Combat of Tolosa. Foy stops the advance of the English right wing.

June 30th—Convention at Dresden. Napoleon accepts the mediation of Austria; armistice prolonged to August 10th.

July 1st.—Soult sent to take chief command in Spain.

July 10th—Alliance between France and Denmark.

July 12th.—Congress of Prague. Austria, Prussia, and Russia decide that Germany must be independent, and the French Empire bounded by the Rhine and the Alps; "but to reign over 36,000,000 men did not appear to Napoleon a sufficiently great destiny" (Montgaillard). Congress breaks up July 28th.

July 26th—Moreau arrives from U.S., and lands at Gothenburg.

July 31st.—Soult attacks Anglo-Spanish army near Roncesvalles in order to succour Pampeluna. Is repulsed, with loss of 8000 men.

August 12th.—Austria notifies its adhesion to the Allies.

August 15th.—Jomini, the Swiss tactician, turns traitor and escapes to the Allies. He advises them of Napoleon s plans to seize Berlin and relieve Dantzic [see letter to Ney, No. 19,714, 20,006, and especially 20,360 (August 12th) in *Correspondence*]. On August 16th Napoleon writes to Cambacérès:

"Jomini, Ney's chief of staff", has deserted. It is he who published some volumes on the campaigns and who has been in the pay of Russia for a long time. He has yielded to corruption. He is a soldier of little value, yet he is a writer who has grasped some of the sound principles of war"

August 17th.—Renewal of hostilities in Germany. Napoleon's army, 280,000, of whom half recruits who had never seen a battle; the Allies 520,000, excluding militia. In his counter-manifesto to Austria, dated Bautzen, Napoleon declares:

Austria, the enemy of France, and cloaking her ambition under the mask of a mediation, complicated everything. . . . But Austria, our avowed foe, is in a truer guise, and one perfectly obvious. Europe is therefore much nearer peace; there is one complication the less.

August 18th.—Suchet, having blown up fortifications of Tarragona, evacuates Valentia.

August 21st.—Opening of the campaign in Italy. Eugène, with 50,000 men, commands the Franco-Italian army.

August 23rd—Combats of Gross-Beeren and Ahrensdorf, near Berlin. Bernadotte defeats Oudinot with loss of 1 500 men and 20 guns. Berlin is preserved to the Allies. Oudinot replaced by Ney. Lauriston defeats Army of Silesia at Goldberg with heavy loss.

August 26th-27th.—Battle of Dresden. Napoleon marches a hundred miles in seventy hours to the rescue. With less than 100,000 men he defeats the Allied Army of 180,000 under Schwartzenberg, Wittgenstein, and Kleist. Austrians lose 20,000 prisoners and 60 guns. Moreau is mortally wounded (dies September 1st). Combat of the Katzbach, in Silesia. Blucher defeats Macdonald with heavy loss, who loses 10,000 to 12,000 men in his retreat.

August 30th.—Combat of Kulm. Vandamme enveloped in Bohemia, and surrenders with 12,000 men.

August 31st.—Combat of Irun. Soult attacks Wellington to save San Sebastian, but is repulsed. Graham storms San Sebastian.

September 6th—Combat of Dennewitz (near Berlin). Ney routed by Bulow and Bernadotte; loses his artillery, baggage, and 12,000 men.

September 10th.—Americans capture the English flotilla on Lake Erie.

September 12th.—Combat of Villafranca (near Barcelona). Suchet defeats English General Bentinck.

October 7th—Wellington crosses the Bidassoa into France.

It is on the frontier of France itself that ends the enterprise of Napoleon on Spain. The Spaniards have given the first conception of a people's war versus a war of professionals. For it would be a mistake to think that the battles of Salamanca (July 22nd, 1812) and Vittoria (June 21st, 1813) forced the French to abandon the Peninsula. . . . It was the daily losses, the destruction of man by man, the drops of French blood falling one by one, which in five years aggregated a death-roll of 150,000 men. As to the English, they appeared in this war only as they do in every world-crisis, to gather, in the midst of general desolation, the fruits of their policy, and to consolidate their plans of maritime despotism, of exclusive commerce—(Montgaillard).

October 15th.—Bavarian army secedes and joins the Austrians.

October 16th-19th.—Battles of Leipsic. Allied army 330,000 men (Schwartzenberg, Bernadotte, Blucher, Beningsen), Napoleon 175,000. Twenty-six battalions and ten squadrons of Saxon and Wurtemberg men leave Napoleon and turn their guns against the French. Napoleon is not defeated, but determines to retreat. The rearguard (20,000 men) and 200 cannon taken. Poniatowski drowned; Reynier and Lauriston captured.

October 20th.—Blucher made Field-Marshal.

October 23rd—French army reach Erfurt.

October 30th.—Combat of Hanau. Napoleon defeats Wrede with heavy loss.

October 31st.—Combat and capture of Bassano by Eugène. English capture Pampeluna.

November 2nd.—Napoleon arrives at Mayence (where typhus carries off 40,000 French) and is

November 9th.—At St. Cloud.

November 10th.—Wellington defeats Soult at St. Jean de Luz.

November 11th.—Surrender of Dresden by Gouvion St. Cyr; its French soldiers to return under parole to France. Austrians refuse to ratify the convention, and 1700 officers and 23,000 men remain prisoners of war.

November 14th.—Napoleon addresses the Senate: "All Europe marched with us a year ago; all Europe marches against us today. That is because the world's opinion is directed either by France or England"

November 15th—Eugène defeats Austrians at Caldiero. Senatus-Consultus puts 300,000 conscripts at disposal of government.

November 24th.—Capture of Amsterdam by Prussian General Bulow.

December 1st.—Allies declare at Frankfort that they are at war with the Emperor and not with France.

December 2nd.—Bulow occupies Utrecht. Holland secedes from the French Empire.

December 5th.—Capture of Lubeck by the Swedes, and surrender of Stettin (7000 prisoners), Zamosk (December 22nd), Modlin (December 25th), and Torgau (December 26th, with 10,000 men).

December 8th-13th.—Soult defends the passage of the Nive—costly to both sides. Murat (now hostile to Napoleon) enters Ancona.

December 9th-10th.—French evacuate Breda.

December 11th—Treaty of Valençay between Napoleon and his prisoner Ferdinand VII., who is to reign over Spain, but not to cede Minorca or Ceuta (now in their power) to the English.

December 15th.—Denmark secedes from French alliance.

December 21st.—Allies, 100,000 strong, cross the Rhine in ten divisions (Bale to Schaffhausen). Jomini is said to have contributed to this violation of Swiss territory.

December 24th.—Final evacuation of Holland by the French.

December 28th.—Austrians capture Ragusa.

December 31st—Napoleon, having trouble with his Commons, dissolves the *Corps Législatif*. Austrians capture Geneva. Blucher crosses the Rhine at Mannheim and Coblentz. Exclusive of *Landwehr* and levies *en masse*, there are now a million trained men in arms against Napoleon.

1814.

The Allied Powers having proclaimed that the Emperor Napoleon was the sole obstacle to the re-establishment of the Peace of Europe, the Emperor Napoleon, faithful to his oath, declares that he renounces, for himself and his heirs, the thrones of France and Italy, and that there is no personal sacrifice, even that of life itself, that he will not be ready to make for the sake of France.—(*Act of Abdication.*)

January 1st.—Capitulation of Danzic, which General Rapp had defended for nearly a year, having lost 20,000 (out of 30,000) men by fever. Russians, who had promised to send the French home, break faith, following the example of Schwartzenberg at Dresden.

January 2nd—Russians take Fort Louis (Lower Rhine); and

January 3rd.—Austrians Montbéliard; and Bavarians Colmar.

January 6th.—General York occupies Trèves. Convention between Murat and England and (January 11th) with Austria. Murat is to join Allies with 30,000 men.

January 7th.—Austrians occupy Vesoul.

January 8th.—French *Rentes* 5 *per cents*, at 47.50. Wurtemberg troops occupy Epinal.

January 10th.—General York reaches Forbach (on the Moselle).

January 15th.—*Cossacks* occupy Cologne.

January 16th.—Russians occupy Nancy.

January 19th.—Austrians occupy Dijon; Bavarians, Neufchateau. Murat's troops occupy Rome.

January 20th—Capture of Toul by the Russians; and of Chambéry by the Austrians.

January 21st.—Austrians occupy Chilons-sur-Saone. General York crosses the Meuse.

January 23rd.—Pope Pius VII. returns to Rome.

January 25th—General York and Army of Silesia established at St. Dizier and Joinville on the Marne. Austrians occupy Bar-sur-Aube. Napoleon leaves Paris; and:

January 26th—Reaches Châlons-sur- Marne; and

January 27th.—Retakes St. Dizier in person.

January 29th.—Combat of Brienne. Napoleon defeats Blucher.

February 1st—Battle of La Rothière, six miles north of Brienne. French, 40,000; Allies, 110,000. Drawn battle, but French retreat on Troyes; French evacuate Brussels.

February 4th.—Eugène retires upon the Mincio.

February 5th—Cortes disavow Napoleon's treaty of Valençay with Ferdinand VII. Opening of Congress of Châtillon. General York occupies Chalons-sur-Marne.

February 7th.—Allies seize Troyes.

February 8th.—Battle of the Mincio. Eugène with 30,000 conscripts defeats Austrians under Bellegarde with 50,000 veterans.

February 10th.—Combat of Champaubert. Napoleon defeats Russians.

February 11th.—Combat of Montmirail. Napoleon defeats Sacken. Russians occupy Nogent-sur-Seine; and

February 12th—Laon.

February 14th.—Napoleon routs Blucher at Vauchamp. His losses, 10,000 men; French loss, 600 men. In five days Napoleon has wiped out the five corps of the Army of Silesia, inflicting a loss of 25,000 men.

February 17th.—Combat near Nangis. Napoleon defeats Austro-Russians with loss of 10,000 men and 12 cannon.

February 18th.—Combat of Montereau. Prince Royal of Wurtemberg defeated with loss of 7000.

February 21st.—Comte d'Artois arrives at Vesoul.

February 22nd—Combat of Méry-sur-Seine. Sacken defeated by Boyer's Division, who fight in masks—it being Shrove Tuesday.

February 24th.—French re-enter Troyes.

February 27th.—Bulow captures La Fère with large stores. Battle of Orthes (Pyrenees), Wellington with 70,000 defeats Soult entrenched with 38,000. Foy badly wounded.

February 27th-28th—Combats of Bar and Ferté-sur-Aube. Marshals Oudinot and Macdonald forced to retire on the Seine.

March 1st.—Treaty of Chaumont Allies against Napoleon.

March 2nd.—Bulow takes Soissons.

March 4th.—Macdonald evacuates Troyes.

March 7th.—Battle of Craonne between Napoleon (30,000 men)

and Sacken (100,000). Indecisive.

March 9th—English driven from Berg-op-Zoom.

March 9th-10th.—Combat under Laon: *depôt* of Allied army. Napoleon fails to capture it.

March 12th.—Duc d'Angoulême arrives at Bordeaux. This town is the first to declare for the Bourbons, and to welcome him as Louis XVIII.

March 13th.—Ferdinand VII. set at liberty.

March 14th—Napoleon retakes Rheims from the Russians.

March 15th.—Rupture of Treaty of Châtillon.

March 20th—Battle of Tarbes. Wellington defeats French.

March 20th-21st—Battle of Arcis-sur-Aube. Indecisive.

March 21st.—Austrians enter Lyons. Augereau retires on Valence. Had Eugène joined him with his 40,000 men he might have saved France after Vauchamp.

March 25th—Combat of Fère-Champenoise. Marmont and Mortier defeated with loss of 9000 men.

March 26th.—Combat of St. Dizier. Napoleon defeats Russians, and starts to save Paris.

March 29th.—Allies outside Paris. Napoleon at Troyes (125 miles off).

March 30th.—Battle of Paris. The Emperor's orders disobeyed. Heavy cannon from Cherbourg left outside Paris, also 20,000 men. Clarke deserts to the Allies. Joseph runs away, leaving Marmont permission to capitulate. After losing 5000 men (and Allies 8000) Marmont evacuates Paris and retires. Napoleon reaches Fontainebleau in the evening, and hears the bad news.

March 31st.—Emperor of Russia, King of Prussia, and 36,000 men enter Paris. Stocks and shares advance. Emperor Alexander states, "The Allied Sovereigns will treat no longer with Napoleon Bonaparte, nor any of his family."

April 1st.—Senate, with Talleyrand as President, institute a Provisional Government.

April 2nd.—Provisional Government address the army: "You are no longer the soldiers of Napoleon; the Senate and the whole of France absolve you from your oaths." They also declare Napoleon deposed from the throne, and his family from the succession.

April 4th—Napoleon signs a declaration of abdication in favour of his son, but after two days' deliberation, and Mormont's defection, Alexander insists on an absolute abdication.

April 5th—Convention of Chevilly. Marmont agrees to join the Provisional Government, and disband his army under promise that Allies will guarantee life and liberty to Napoleon Bonaparte. Funds on March 29th at 45, now at 63.75.

April 6th.—New Constitution decreed by the Senate. The National Guard ordered to wear the White Cockade in lieu of the Tricolour.

April 10th—Battle of Toulouse. Hotly contested; almost a defeat for Wellington.

April 11th.—Treaty of Paris between Napoleon and Allies (Austria, Russia, and Prussia). Isle of Elba reserved for Napoleon and his family, with a revenue of £200,000; the Duchies of Parma and Placentia for Marie Louise and her son. England accedes to this Treaty. Act of Abdication of the Emperor Napoleon.

April 12th.—Count d'Artois enters Paris.

April 16th—Convention between Eugène and Austrian General Bellegarde. Emperor of Austria sees Marie Louise at the little Trianon, and decides upon his daughter's return to Vienna.

April 18th.—Armistice of Soult and Wellington.

April 20th.—Napoleon leaves Fontainebleau, and bids *adieu* to his Old Guard:

> Do not mourn over my fate; if I have determined to survive, it is in order still to dedicate myself to your glory; I wish to write about the great things we have done together

April 24th.—Louis XVIII. lands at Calais, and

May 3rd—Enters Paris.

May 4th.—Napoleon reaches Elba.

May 29th.—Death of Josephine, aged 51.

May 30th.—Peace of Paris,

Notes

The Italian Campaigns, 1796-97
Series A
(The numbers correspond to the numbers of the Letters.)
No. 1.

Bonaparte made Commander-in-Chief of the Army of Italy.—Marmont's account of how this came to pass is probably substantially correct, as he has less interest in distorting the facts than any other writer as well fitted for the task. The winter had rolled by in the midst of pleasures—*soirées* at the Luxembourg, dinners of Madame Tallien, "nor," he adds, "were we hard to please." "The Directory often conversed with General Bonaparte about the army of Italy, whose general—Schérer—was always representing the position as difficult, and never ceasing to ask for help in men, victuals, and money. General Bonaparte showed, in many concise observations, that all that was superfluous. He strongly blamed the little advantage taken from the victory at Loano, and asserted that, even yet, all that could be put right. Thus a sort of controversy was maintained between Schérer and the Directory, counselled and inspired by Bonaparte." At last when Bonaparte drew up plans—afterwards followed—for the invasion of Piedmont, Schérer replied roughly that he who had drawn up the plan of campaign had better come and execute it. They took him at his word, and Bonaparte was named General-in-Chief of the army of Italy (vol. 1. 93).

"*7 a.m.*"—Probably written early in March. Leaving Paris on March 11th, Napoleon writes Letourneur, President of the Directory, of his marriage with the "*citoyenne* Tascher Beauharnais," and tells him that he has already asked Barras to inform them of the fact. "The confidence which the Directory has shown me under all circumstances makes it my duty to keep it advised of all my actions. It is a new link

JOSEPHINE BEAUHARNAIS
CIRCA 1795

which binds me to the fatherland; it is one more proof of my fixed determination to find safety only in the Republic."[1]

No. 2.

"Our good Ossian"—The Italian translation of Ossian by Cesarotti was a masterpiece; better, in fact, than the original. He was a friend of Macpherson, and had learnt English in order to translate his work. Cesarotti lived till an advanced age, and was sought out in his retirement in order to receive honours and pensions from the Emperor Napoleon.

"Our good Ossian" speaks, like Homer, of the joy of grief.

No. 4.

"Chauvet is dead"—Chauvet is first mentioned in Napoleon's correspondence in a letter to his brother Joseph, August 9, 1795. Mdme. Junot, *Memoirs*, 1. 138, tells us that Bonaparte was very fond of him, and that he was a man of gentle manners and very ordinary conversation. She declares that Bonaparte had been a suitor for the hand of her mother shortly before his marriage with Josephine, and that because the former rejected him, the general had refused a favour to her son; this had caused a quarrel which Chauvet had in vain tried to settle. On March 27th Bonaparte had written Chauvet from Nice that every day that he delayed joining him, "takes away from my operations one chance of probability for their success."

No. 5.

St. Amand notes that Bonaparte begins to suspect his wife in this letter, while the previous ones, especially that of April 3rd, show perfect confidence. Napoleon is on the eve of a serious battle, and has only just put his forces into fighting trim. On the previous day (April 6th) he wrote to the Directory that the movement against Genoa, of which he does not approve, has brought the enemy out of their winter quarters almost before he has had time to make ready. "The army is in a state of alarming destitution; I have still great difficulties to surmount, but they are surmountable: misery has excused want of discipline, and without discipline never a victory. I hope to have all in good trim shortly—there are signs already; in a few days we shall be fighting. The Sardinian army consists of 50,000 foot, and 5000 horse; I have only 45,000 men at my disposal, all told. Chauvet, the

---

1. No. 89 of Napoleon III.'s *Correspondence of Napoleon I.*, vol. 1., the last letter signed Buonaparte; after March 24 we only find Bonaparte.

commissary-general, died at Genoa: it is a heavy loss to the army, he was active and enterprising."

Two days later Napoleon, still at Albenga, reports that he has found Royalist traitors in the army, and complains that the Treasury had not sent the promised pay for the men, "but in spite of all, we shall advance." Massena, eleven years older than his new commander-in-chief, had received him coldly, but soon became his right-hand man, always genial, and full of good ideas. Massena's men are ill with too much salt meat, they have hardly any shoes, but, as in 1800,[2] he has never a doubt that Bonaparte will make a good campaign, and determines to loyally support him. Poor Laharpe, so soon to die, is a man of a different stamp—one of those, doubtless, of whom Bonaparte thinks when he writes to Josephine, "Men worry me." The Swiss, in fact, was a chronic grumbler, but a first-rate fighting man, even when his men were using their last cartridges.

"The lovers of nineteen"—The allusion is lost. Aubenas, who reproduces two or three of these letters, makes a comment to this sentence, *"Nous n'avons pu trouver un nom à mettre sous cette fantasque imagination"* (vol. 1. 317).

"My brother" viz. Joseph.—He and Junot reached Paris in five days, and had a great ovation. Carnot, at a dinner-party, showed Napoleon's portrait next to his heart, because "I foresee he will be the saviour of France, and I wish him to know that he has at the Directory only admirers and friends."

No. 6.

Unalterably good. "C'est Joseph peint d'un seul trait."—Aubenas (vol. 1. 320).

"If you want a place for anyone, you can send him here. I will give him one"—Bonaparte was beginning to feel firm in the saddle, while at Paris Josephine was treated like a princess. Under date April 25th, Letourneur, as one of the Directory, writes him, "A vast career opens itself before you; the Directory has measured the whole extent of it." They little knew! The letter concludes by expressing confidence that their general will never be reproached with the shameful repose of Capua.

In a further letter, bearing the same date, Letourneur insists on a full and accurate account of the battles being sent, as they will be nec-

---

2. Compelled to surrender Genoa, before Marengo takes place, he swears to the Austrian general he will be back there in fourteen days, and keeps his word.

essary "for the history of the triumphs of the Republic." In a private letter to the Directory (No. 220, vol. 1. of the *Correspondence*, 1858), dated Carru, April 24th, Bonaparte tells them that when he returns to camp, worn-out, he has to work all night to put matters straight, and repress pillage. "Soldiery without bread work themselves into an excess of frenzy which makes one blush to be a man." [3] . . . "I intend to make terrible examples. I shall restore order, or cease to command these brigands. The campaign is not yet decided. The enemy is desperate, numerous, and fights well. He knows I am in want of everything, and trusts entirely to time; but I trust entirely to the good genius of the Republic, to the bravery of the soldiers, to the harmony of the officers, and even to the confidence they repose in me."

No. 7.

Aubenas goes into ecstasies over this letter, "the longest, most eloquent, and most impassioned of the whole series" (vol. 1. 322).

June 15.—Here occurs the first gap in the correspondence, but his letters to the Directory between this date and the last letter to Josephine extant (April 24) are full of interest, including his conscientious disobedience at Cherasco, and the aura of his destiny to *ride the whirlwind and direct the storm* which first inspired him after Lodi. On April 28th was signed the armistice of Cherasco, by which his rear was secured by three strong fortresses. [4]

He writes the Directory that Piedmont is at their mercy, and that in making the armistice into a definite peace he trusts they will not forget the little island of Saint-Pierre, which will be more useful in the future than Corsica and Sardinia combined. He looks upon northern Italy as practically conquered, and speaks of invading Bavaria through the Tyrol. "Prodigious" is practically the verdict of the Directory, and later of Jomini. "My columns are marching; Beaulieu flees. I hope to catch him. I shall impose a contribution of some millions on the Duke

---

3. Two days later he evidently feels this letter too severe, and writes: "All goes well. Pillage is less pronounced. This first thirst of an army destitute of everything is quenched. The poor fellows are excusable; after having sighed for three years at the top of the Alps, they arrive in the Promised Land, and wish to taste of it."

4. Bingham, with his customary ill-nature, remarks that Bonaparte, "in spite of the orders of the Directory, took upon himself to sign the armistice." These orders, dated March 6th, were intended for a novice, and no longer applicable to the conqueror of two armies, and which a Despatch on the way, dated April 25th, already modified. Jomini admits the wisdom of this advantageous peace, which secured Nice and Savoy to France, and gave her all the chief mountain-passes leading into Italy.

LE GÉNÉRAL EN CHEF
DE L'ARMÉE D'ITALIE,

of Parma: he will sue for peace: don't be in a hurry, so that I may have time to make him also contribute to the cost of the campaign, by replenishing our stores and rehorsing our wagons at his expense."

Bonaparte suggests that Genoa should pay fifteen millions indemnity for the frigates and vessels taken in the port. Certain risks had to be run in invading Lombardy, owing to want of horse artillery, but at Cherasco he secured artillery and horses. When writing to the Directory for a dozen companies, he tells them not to entrust the execution of this measure "to the men of the bureaus, for it takes them ten days to forward an order." Writing to Carnot on the same day he states he is marching against Beaulieu, who has 26,000 foot out of 38,000 at commencement of campaign. Napoleon's force is 28,000, but he has less cavalry. On May 1st, in a letter dated Acqui to Citizen Faipoult, he asks for particulars of the pictures, statues, &c., of Milan, Parma, Placentia, Modena, and Bologna. On the same day Massena writes that his men are needing shoes. On May 6th Bonaparte announces the capture of Tortona, "a very fine fortress, which cost the King of Sardinia over fifteen millions," while Cherasco has furnished him with twenty-eight guns. Meanwhile Massena has taken possession of Alessandria, with all its stores.

On May 9th Napoleon writes to Carnot:

We have at last crossed the Po. The second campaign is begun; Beaulieu . . . has fool-hardiness but no genius. One more victory, and Italy is ours.

A clever commissary-general is all he needs, and his men are growing fat—with good meat and good wine. He sends to Paris twenty old masters, with fine examples of Correggio and Michael-Angelo. It is pleasant to find Napoleon's confidence in Carnot, in view of Barras' insinuations that the latter had cared only for Moreau—his type of Xenophon.

In this very letter Napoleon writes Carnot:

I owe you my special thanks for the care that you have kindly given to my wife; I recommend her to you, she is a sincere patriot, and I love her to distraction.

He is sending "a dozen millions" to France, and hopes that some of it will be useful to the army of the Rhine. Meanwhile, and two days before Napoleon's letter to Carnot just mentioned, the latter, on behalf of the Directory, suggests the division of his command with the old Alsatian General Kellermann. The Directory's idea of a gilded pill seems to be a prodigiously long letter. It is one of those heartbreaking effusions that, even to this day, emanate from board-rooms, to the dismay and disgust of their recipients. After plastering him with sickening sophistries as to his "sweetest recompense," it gives the utterly unnecessary monition, "March! no fatal repose, there are still laurels to gather!"

Nevertheless, his plan of ending the war by an advance through the Tyrol strikes them as too risky. He is to conquer the Milanais, and then divide his army with Kellermann, who is to guard the conquered province, while he goes south to Naples and Rome. As an implied excuse for not sending adequate reinforcements, Carnot adds, "The exaggerated rumours that you have skilfully disseminated as to the numbers of the French troops in Italy, will augment the fear of our enemies and almost double your means of action."

The Milanais is to be heavily mulcted, but he is to be prudent. If Rome makes advances, his first demand should be that the Pope may order immediate public prayers for the prosperity and success of the French Republic! The sending of old masters to France to adorn her National Galleries seems to have been entirely a conception of Napoleon's. He has given sufficiently good reasons, from a patriotic point of view; for money is soon spent, but a masterpiece may encourage Art among his countrymen a generation later. The plunderers of the Parthenon of 1800 could not henceforward throw stones at him in this respect. But his real object was to win the people of Paris by thus sending them Glory personified in unique works of genius.

The Directory, already jealous of his fame, endeavour to neutralise the effect of his initiative by hearty concurrence, and write, "Italy has been illumined and enriched by their possession, but the time is now come when their reign should pass to France to stablish and beautify that of Liberty." The despatch adds somewhat naively that the effects of the vandalism committed during their own Republican orgies would be obliterated by this glorious campaign, which should "join to the splendour of military trophies the charm of beneficent and restful arts." The Directory ends by inviting him to choose one or two artists to select the most valuable pictures and other masterpieces.

Meanwhile, the Directory's supineness in pushing on the war on the Rhine is enabling the Austrians to send large reinforcements against Napoleon. Bonaparte, who has recently suffered (Jomini, vol. 8. 113) from Kellermann's tardiness in sending reinforcements at an important moment, replies to the letters of May 7th a week later, and writes direct to Citizen Carnot from Lodi, as well as to the Executive Directory.

On the receipt of the Directory's letter of the 7th your wishes were fulfilled, and the Milanais is ours. I shall shortly march, to carry out your intentions, on Leghorn and Rome; all that will soon be done. I am writing the Directory relatively to their idea of dividing the army. I swear that I have no thought beyond the interest of my country. Moreover, you will always find me straight (*dans la ligne droit*). . . . As it might happen that this letter to the Directory may be badly construed, and since you have assured me of your friendship, I take this opportunity of addressing you, begging you to make what use of it your prudence and attachment for me may suggest. . . . Kellermann will command the army as well as I, for no one is more convinced than I am that the victories are due to the courage and pluck of the army; but I think joining Kellermann and myself in Italy is to lose everything. I cannot serve willingly with a man who considers himself the first general in Europe; and, besides, I believe one bad general is better than two good ones.

War is like government: it is an affair of tact. To be of any use, I must enjoy the same confidence that you testified to me in Paris. Where I make war, here or there, is a matter of indifference. To serve my country, to deserve from posterity a page in our history, to give the Government proofs of my attachment and devotion—that is the sum of my ambition. But I am very anxious not to lose in a week the fatigues, anxieties, and dangers of two months, and to find myself fettered. I began with a certain amount of fame; I wish to continue worthy of you.

To the Directory he writes that the expeditions to Leghorn, Rome, and Naples are small affairs, but to be safely conducted must have one general in command.

I have made the campaign without consulting a soul; I should have done no good if I had had to share my views with another. I have gained some advantages over superior forces, and in utter want of everything, because, certain of your confidence, my marches have been as quick as my thoughts.

He foretells disaster if he is shackled with another general. "Everyone has his own method of making war. General Kellermann has more experience, and will do it better than I; but both together will do it very badly."

With Barras he knew eloquence was useless, and therefore bribed him with a million *francs*. On May 10th was gained the terrible battle of the Bridge of Lodi, where he won promotion from his soldiers, and became their "little corporal," and where he told Las Cases that he "was struck with the possibility of becoming famous. It was then that the first spark of my ambition was kindled."

On entering Milan he told Marmont, "Fortune has smiled on me today, only because I despise her favours; she is a woman, and the more she does for me, the more I shall exact from her. In our day no one has originated anything great; it is for me to give the example."

On May 15th, thirty-five days after the commencement of the campaign, he entered Milan, under a triumphal arch and amid the acclamations of the populace. On the previous evening he was guilty of what Dr. Johnson would have considered a fitting herald of his spoliation of picture-galleries—the perpetration of a pun. At a dinner-table the hostess observed that his youth was remarkable in so great a conqueror, whereat he replied, "Truly, madam, I am not very old at present—barely twenty-seven—but in less than twenty-four hours I shall count many more, for I shall have attained Milan" (*mille ans*).

On May 22nd he returned to Lodi, but heard immediately that Lombardy in general, and Pavia in particular, was in open revolt. He makes a terrible example of Pavia, shooting its chief citizens, and, for the only time, giving up a town to three hours' pillage. The Directory congratulates him on these severe measures: "The laws of war and the safety of the army render them legitimate in such circumstances." He writes them that had the blood of a single Frenchman been spilt, he would have erected a column on the ruins of Pavia, on which should have been inscribed, "Here was the town of Pavia."

On May 21st, Carnot replies to the letter from Lodi:

> You appear desirous, citizen general, of continuing to conduct the whole series of military operations in Italy, at the actual seat of war. The Directory has carefully considered your proposition, and the confidence that they place in your talents and republican zeal has decided this question in the affirmative. . . . The rest of the military operations towards the Austrian frontier and round Mantua are absolutely dependent on your success against Beaulieu. The Directory feels how difficult it would be to direct them from Paris. It leaves to you in this respect the greatest latitude, while recommending the most extreme pru-

dence. Its intention is, however, that the army shall cross into the Tyrol only after the expedition to the south of Italy."

This was a complete victory for Bonaparte (Bingham calls it the Directory's "abject apology"), and, as Scott points out, he now "obtained an ascendency which he took admirable care not to relinquish; and it became the sole task of the Directory, so far as Italy was concerned, to study phrases for intimating their approbation of the young general's measures.

He had forged a sword for France, and he now won her heart by gilding it. On May 16th the Directory had asked him to supply Kellermann with money for the army of the Alps, and by May 22nd he is able to write that six or eight million *francs* in gold, silver, ingots, or jewels is lying at their disposal with one of the best bankers in Genoa, being superfluous to the needs of the army. "If you wish it, I can have a million sent to Bale for the army of the Rhine." He has already helped Kellermann, and paid his men. He also announces a further million requisitioned from Modena. "As it has neither fortresses nor muskets, I could not ask for them."

Henceforth he lubricates the manifold wheels of French policy with Italian gold, and gains thereby the approbation and gratitude of the French armies and people. Meanwhile he does not neglect those who might bear him a grudge. To Kellermann and to all the Directors he sends splendid chargers. From Parma he has the five best pictures chosen for Paris—the Saint Jerome and the Madonna della Scodella, both by Correggio; the Preaching of St. John in the Desert, a Paul Veronese, and a Van Dyck, besides fine examples of Raphael, Caracci, &c.

The Directory is anxious that he shall chastise the English at Leghorn, as the fate of Corsica is somewhat dependent on it, whose loss "will make London tremble." They secretly dread a war in the Tyrol, forgetting that Bonaparte is a specialist in mountain fighting, educated under Paoli. They remind him that he has not sent the plans of his battles. "You ought not to lack draughtsmen in Italy. Eh! what are your young engineer officers doing?"

On May 31st Carnot writes to urge him to press the siege of Mantua, reasserting that the reinforcements which Beaulieu has received will not take from that army its sense of inferiority, and that ten battalions of Hoche's army are on the way. It approves and confirms the "generous fraternity" with which Bonaparte offers a million *francs* to the armies on the Rhine.

On June 7th he tells the Directory that Rome is about to fulminate a bull against the French Royalists, but that he thinks the expedition to Naples should be deferred, and also a quarrel with Venice—at least till he has beaten his other enemies; it is not expedient to tackle everyone at once. On June 6th he thanks Carnot for a kind letter, adding that the best reward to sweeten labour and perils is the esteem of the few men one really admires. He fears the hot weather for his men: "we shall soon be in July, when every march will cost us 200 sick."

The same day he writes General Clarke that all is flourishing, but that the dog-star is coming on at a gallop, and that there is no remedy against its malign influence. "Luckless beings that we are! Our position with nature is merely observation, without control." He holds that the only safe way to end the campaign without being beaten is not to go to the south of Italy. On the 9th he thanks Kellermann for the troops he sends, and their excellent discipline. On the 11th—always as anxious to help his generals as himself—he urges the Directory to press the Swiss Government to refund La Harpe's property to his children.

"*Presentiment of ill*"—Marmont tells us what this was. The glass of his wife's portrait, which he always carried with him, was found to be broken. Turning frightfully pale, he said to Marmont, "My wife is either very ill, or unfaithful." She left Paris June 24th.

Marmont says:

Once at Milan, General Bonaparte was very happy, for at that time he lived only for his wife.... Never love more pure, more true, more exclusive, has possessed the heart of any man.

No. 8.

Between June 15th and the renewal of Josephine's correspondence a glance at the intervening dates will show that Bonaparte and his army were not wasting time. The treaty with Rome was a masterpiece, as in addition to money and works of art, he obtained the port of Ancona, siege-guns with which to bombard Mantua, and best of all, a letter from the Pope to the faithful of France, recommending submission to the new government there. In consideration of this, and possibly yielding to the religious sentiments of Josephine, he spared Rome his presence—the only capital which he abstained from entering, when he had, as in the present case, the opportunity. It was not, however, until February 1797 that the Pope fulfilled his obligations under this Treaty, and then under new compulsion.

Fortuné.—Josephine's dog (see note to Letter 2, Series B).

Series B

No. 1.

July 6, Sortie from Mantua of the Austrians.—According to Jomini the French on this occasion were not successful (vol. 8 162). In one of his several letters to the Directory on this date is seen Bonaparte's anxiety for reinforcements; the enemy has already 67,000 men against his available 40,000. Meanwhile he is helping the Corsicans to throw off the British yoke, and believes that the French possession of Leghorn will enable the French to gain that island without firing a shot.

No. 2.

Marmirolo.—On July 12th he writes to the Directory from Verona that for some days he and the enemy have been watching each other. "Woe to him who makes a false move." He indicates that he is about to make a *coup de main* on Mantua, with 300 men dressed in Austrian uniforms. He is by no means certain of success, which "depends entirely on luck—either on a dog [5] or a goose." He complains of much sickness among his men round Mantua, owing to the heat and *miasmata* from the marshes, but so far no deaths. He will be ready to make Venice disgorge a few millions shortly, if the Directory make a quarrel in the interim.

On the 13th he was with Josephine, as he writes from Milan, but leaves on the 14th, and on the 17th is preparing a *coup de main* with 800 grenadiers, which, as we see from the next letter, fails.

Fortuné.—Arnault tells an anecdote of this lap-dog, which in 1794, in the days of the Terror, had been used as a bearer of secret despatches between Josephine in prison and the governess of her children outside the grille. Henceforward Josephine would never be parted from it. One day in June 1797 the dog was lying on the same couch as its mistress, and Bonaparte, accosting Arnault and pointing to the dog with his finger, said, "You see that dog there. He is my rival. He was in possession of *Madame's* bed when I married her. I wished to make him get out—vain hope! I was told I must resign myself to sleep elsewhere, or consent to share with him. That was sufficiently exasperating, but it was a question of taking or leaving, and I resigned myself. The favourite was less accommodating than I. I bear the proof of it in this leg."

Not content with barking at everyone, he bit not only men but other dogs, and was finally killed by a mastiff, much to Bonaparte's

---

5 Murat, says Marmont, who hated him, was the culprit here.

secret satisfaction; for, as St. Amand adds, "he could easily win battles, accomplish miracles, make or unmake principalities, but could not show a dog the door."

No. 3.

"The village of Virgil"—Michelet (*Jusqu'au 18 Brumaire*) thinks that here he got the idea of the Fête of Virgil, established a few months later. In engravings of the hero of Italy we see him near the tomb of Virgil, his brows shaded by a laurel crown.

No. 4.

Achille.—Murat. He had been appointed one of Bonaparte's *aides-de-camp* February 29th, made General of Brigade after the Battle of Lodi (May 10th); is sent to Paris after Junot with nine trophies, and arrives there first. He flirts there outrageously with Josephine, but does not escort her back to her husband.

No. 5.

"Will o' the wisp" i.e. *l'ardent.*—This word, according to Ménage, was given by the Sieur de St. Germain to those lively young sparks who, about the year 1634, used to meet at the house of Mr. Marsh (M. de Marest), who was one of them.

No. 6.

The needs of the army.—Difficulties were accumulating, and Napoleon was, as he admits at St. Helena, seriously alarmed. Wurmser's force proves to be large, Piedmont is angry with the Republic and ready to rise, and Venice and Rome would willingly follow its example; the English have taken Porto-Ferrajo, and their skilful minister, Windham, is sowing the seeds of discord at Naples. Although on July 20th he has written a friend in Corsica that "all smiles on the Republic," he writes Saliceti, another brother Corsican, very differently on August 1st.

> Fortune appears to oppose us at present. . . . I have raised the siege of Mantua; I am at Brescia with nearly all my army. I shall take the first opportunely of fighting a battle with the enemy which will decide the fate of Italy—if I'm beaten, I shall retire on the Adda; if I win, I shall not stop in the marshes of Mantua. . . . Let the citadels of Milan, Tortona, Alessandria, and Pavia be provisioned. . . . We are all very tired; I have ridden five horses to death.

Reading between the lines of this letter to Josephine, it is evident that he thinks she will be safer with him than at Milan—Wurmser having the option of advancing *via* Brescia on Milan, and cutting off the French communications. The Marshal's fatal mistake was in using only half his army for the purpose.

This raising of the siege of Mantua (July 31st) was heart-rending work for Bonaparte, but, as Jomini shows, he had no artillery horses, and it was better to lose the siege train, consisting of guns taken from the enemy, than to jeopardise the whole army. Wurmser had begun his campaign successfully by defeating Massena, and pushing back Sauret at Salo.

"The Austrians," wrote Massena, "are drunk with brandy, and fight furiously," while his men are famished and can only hang on by their teeth. Bonaparte calls his first war council, and thinks for a moment of retreat, but Augereau insists on fighting, which is successfully accomplished while Wurmser is basking himself among the captured artillery outside Mantua. Bonaparte had been perfectly honest in telling the Directory his difficulties, and sends his brother Louis to the Directory for that purpose on the eve of battle. He is complimented in a letter from the Directory dated August 12th—a letter probably the more genuine as they had just received a further despatch announcing a victory.

On August 3rd Bonaparte won a battle at Lonato, and the next day Augereau gained great laurels at Castiglione; in later years the Emperor often incited Augereau by referring to those "fine days of Castiglione."

Between July 20th and August 12th the French army took 15,000 prisoners, 70 guns, and wounded or killed 25,000, with little more than half the forces of the Austrians. Bonaparte gives his losses at 7000, exclusive of the 15,000 sick he has in hospital; from July 3ist to August 6th he never changed his boots, or lay down in a bed. Nevertheless, Jomini thinks that he showed less vigour in the execution of his plans than in the earlier part of the campaign; but, as an opinion *per contra*, we may note that the French grenadiers made their "little Corporal" *Sergeant* at Castiglione.

Doubtless the proximity of his wife at the commencement (July 31st) made him more careful, and therefore less intrepid. On August 18th he wrote Kellermann with an urgent request for troops. On August 17th Colonel Graham, after hinting at the frightful excesses committed by the Austrians in their retreat, adds in a postscript "From generals to subalterns the universal language of the army is that we must make peace, as we do not know how to make war." [6]

On August 13th Bonaparte sent to the Directory his opinion of most of his generals, in order to show that he required some better ones. Some of his criticisms are interesting:

Berthier—"Talents, activity, courage, character; he has them all."

Augereau—"Much character, courage, firmness, activity; is accustomed to war, beloved by the soldiers, lucky in his operations."

Massena—"Active, indefatigable, has boldness, grasp, and promptitude in making his decisions."

Serrurier—"Fights like a soldier, takes no responsibility; determined, has not much opinion of his troops, is often ailing."

Despinois—"Flabby, inactive, slack, has not the genius for war, is not liked by the soldiers, does not fight with his head; has nevertheless good, sound political principles: would do well to command in the interior."

Sauret—"A good, very good soldier, not sufficiently enlightened to be a general; unlucky."

Of eight more he has little good to say, but the Directory in acknowledging his letter of August 23rd remarks that he has forgotten several officers, and especially the Irish general Kilmaine.

About the same time Colonel Graham (Lord Lynedoch) was writing to the British Government from Trent that the Austrians, despite their defeats, were "undoubtedly brave fine troops, and an able chief would put all to rights in a little time." [7] On August 18th he adds "When the wonderful activity, energy, and attention that prevail in the French service, from the commander-in-chief downward, are compared to the indecision, indifference, and indolence universal here, the success of their rash but skilful manoeuvres is not surprising."

No. 7.

Brescia.—Napoleon was here on July 27th, meeting Josephine about the date arranged (July 25th), and she returned with him. On July 29th they were nearly captured by an Austrian ambuscade near Ceronione, and Josephine wept with fright. "Wurmser," said Napoleon, embracing her, "shall pay dearly for those tears." She accompanies him to Castel Nova, and sees a skirmish at Verona; but the sight of wounded men makes her leave the army, and, finding it impossible

---

6. J. H. Rose in *Eng. Hist. Review*, January 1899.

7. See Essay by J. H. Rose in *Eng. Hist. Review*, January 1899.

to reach Brescia, she flees *via* Ferrara and Bologna to Lucca. She leaves the French army in dire straits and awaits news anxiously, while the Senate of Lucca presents her with the oil kept exclusively for royalty. Thence she goes *via* Florence to Milan.

By August 7th the Austrian army was broken and in full retreat, and Bonaparte conducts his correspondence from Brescia from August 11th to 18th. On the 25th he is at Milan, where he meets his wife after her long pilgrimage, and spends four days. By August 30th he is again at Brescia, and reminds her that he left her "vexed, annoyed, and not well." From a letter to her aunt, Madame de Renaudin, at this time, quoted by Aubenas, we can see her real feelings:

> I am fêted wherever I go; all the princes of Italy give me fêtes, even the Grand Duke of Tuscany, brother of the Emperor. Ah, well, I prefer being a private individual in France. I care not for honours bestowed in this country. I get sadly bored. My health has undoubtedly a great deal to do with making me unhappy; I am often out of sorts. If happiness could assure health, I ought to be in the best of health. I have the most amiable husband imaginable. I have no time to long for anything. My wishes are his. He is all day long in adoration before me, as if I were a divinity; there could not possibly be a better husband. M. Serbelloni will tell you how he loves me. He often writes to my children; he loves them dearly. He is sending Hortense, by M. Serbelloni, a lovely repeater, jewelled and enamelled; to Eugène a splendid gold watch.

No. 9.

"*I hope we shall get into Trent by the 5th*"—He entered the city on that day. In his pursuit of Wurmser, he and his army cover sixty miles in two days, through the terrific Val Saguna and Brenta gorges, brushing aside opposition by the way.

No. 12.

"*One of these nights the doors will be burst open with a bang*"—Apparently within two or three days, for Bonaparte is at Milan on September 21st, and stays with his wife till October 12th.

On October 1st he writes to the Directory that his total forces are only 27,900; and that the Austrians, within six weeks, will have 50,000. He asks for 26,000 more men to end the war satisfactorily: "If the preservation of Italy is dear to you, citizen directors, send me help."

On the 8th they reply with the promise of 10,000 to 12,000, to which he replies (October 11th) that if 10,000 have started only 5000 will reach him. The Directory at this time are very poverty stricken, and ask him once more to pay Kellermann's Army of the Alps, as being "to some extent part of that which you command." This must have been "nuts and wine" for the general who was to have been superseded by Kellermann a few months earlier.

On October 1st they advise him that Wurmser's name is on the list of emigrants, and that if the Marshal will surrender Mantua at once he need not be sent to Paris for trial. If, however, Bonaparte thinks that this knowledge will make the old Marshal more desperate, he is not to be told. Bonaparte, of course, does not send the message. For some time these letters had been signed by the President Lareveillere Lépeaux, but on September 19th there was a charming letter from Carnot:

> Although accustomed to unprecedented deeds on your part, our hopes have been surpassed by the victory of Bassano. What glory is yours, immortal Bonaparte! Moreau was about to effect a juncture with you when that wretched *reculade* of Jourdan upset all our plans. Do not forget that immediately the armies go into winter quarters on the Rhine the Austrians will have forces available to help Wurmser.

At Milan Bonaparte advises the Directory that he is dealing with unpunished "*fripponeries* "in the commissariat department. Here he receives from young Kellermann, afterwards the hero of Marengo, a *précis* of the condition of the Brescia fever-hospitals, dated October 6th:

> A wretched mattress, dirty and full of vermin, a coarse sheet to each bed, rarely washed, no counterpanes, much dilatoriness, such is the spectacle that the fever-hospitals of Brescia present; it is heart-rending. The soldiers justly complain that, having conquered opulent Italy at the cost of their life-blood, they might, without enjoying comforts, at least find the help and attention which their situation demands. Bread and rice are the only passable foods, but the meat is hard. I beg that the general-in-chief will immediately give attention to his companions in glory, who wish for restored health only that they may gather fresh laurels.

Thus Bonaparte had his Bloemfontein, and perhaps his Burdett-Coutts.

On October 12th he tells the Directory that Mantua will not fall till February—the exact date of its capitulation. One is tempted to wonder if Napoleon was human enough to have inserted one little paragraph of his despatch of October 12th from Milan with one eye on its perusal by his wife, as it contains a veiled sneer at Hoche's exploits:

Send me rather generals of brigade than generals of division. All that comes to us from La Vendée is unaccustomed to war on a large scale; we have the same reproach against the troops, but they are well-hardened.

On the same day he shows them that all the marvels of his six months' campaign have cost the French Government only £440,000 (eleven million *francs*). He pleads, however, for special auditors to have charge of the accounts. Napoleon had not only made war support war, but had sent twenty million *francs* requisitioned in Italy to the Republic. On October 12th he leaves Milan for Modena, where he remains from the 14th to the 18th, is at Bologna on the 19th, and Ferrara from the 19th to the 22nd, reaching Verona on the 24th.

Jomini has well pointed out that Napoleon's conception of making two or three large Italian republics in place of many small ones minimised the power of the Pope, and also that of Austria, by abolishing its feudal rigours.

By this time Bonaparte is heartily sick of the war. On October 2nd he writes direct to the Emperor of Germany:

Europe wants peace. This disastrous war has lasted too long;

And on the 16th to Marshal Wurmser:

The siege of Mantua, sir, is more disastrous than two campaigns.

His weariness is tempered with policy, as Alvinzi was *en route*, and the French reinforcements had not arrived, not even the 10,000 promised in May.

No. 13.

"*Corsica is ours*"—At St. Helena he told his generals, "The King of England wore the Corsican crown only two years. This whim cost the British treasury five millions sterling. John Bull's riches could not have been worse employed."

He writes to the Directory on the same day:

The expulsion of the English from the Mediterranean has considerable influence on the success of our military operations in Italy. We can exact more onerous conditions from Naples, which will have the greatest moral effect on the minds of the Italians, assures our communications, and makes Naples tremble as far as Sicily.

On October 25th he writes:

Wurmser is at his last gasp; he is short of wine, meat, and forage; he is eating his horses, and has 15,000 sick. In fifty days Mantua will either be taken or delivered.

No. 14.

Verona.—Bonaparte had made a long stay at Verona, to November 4th, waiting reinforcements which never came. On November 5th he writes to the Directory:

All the troops of the Directory arrive post-haste at an alarming rate, and we—we are left to ourselves. Fine promises and a few driblets of men are all we have received;

And on November 13th he writes again:

Perchance we are on the eve of losing Italy. None of the expected reinforcements have arrived. . . . I am doing my duty, the officers and men are doing theirs; my heart is breaking, but my conscience is at rest. Help—send me help! . . . I despair of preventing the relief of Mantua, which in a week would have been ours. The wounded are the pick of the army; all our superior officers, all our picked generals are *hors de combat*; those who have come to me are so incompetent, and they have not the soldiers' confidence. The army of Italy, reduced to a handful of men, is exhausted. The heroes of Lodi, Millesimo, Castiglione, and Bassano have died for their country, or are in hospital; [8] to the corps remain only their reputation and their glory. Joubert, Lannes, Lanusse, Victor, Murat, Chabot, Dupuy, Rampon, Pijon, Menard, Chabran, and St. Hilaire are wounded. . . . In a few days we shall make a last effort. Had I received the 83rd, 3500 strong, and of good repute in the army, I would have answered for everything. Perhaps in a few days 40,000 will not suffice.

The reason for this unwonted pessimism was the state of his troops. His brother Louis reported that Vaubois' men had no shoes and were almost naked, in the midst of snow and mountains; that desertions

8. With fevers caught in the rice-swamps of Lombardy.

were taking place of soldiers with bare and bleeding feet, who told the enemy the plans and conditions of their army. Finally Vaubois bungles, through not knowing the ground, and is put under the orders of Massena, while two of his half-brigades are severely censured by Napoleon in person for their cowardice.

No. 15.

"*Once more I breathe freely.*"—Thrice had Napoleon been foiled, as much by the weather and his shoeless soldiers as by numbers (40,000 Austrians to his 28,000), and his position was well-nigh hopeless on November 14th. He trusts Verona to 3000 men, and the blockade of Mantua to Kilmaine, and the defence of Rivoli to Vaubois—the weakest link in the chain—and determines to manoeuvre by the Lower Adige upon the Austrian communications. He gets forty-eight hours' start, and wins Arcola; in 1814 he deserved equal success, but bad luck and treachery turned the scale. The battle of Arcola lasted seventy- two hours, and for forty-eight hours was in favour of the Austrians. Pending the arrival of the promised reinforcements, the battle was bought too dear, and weakened Bonaparte more than the Austrians, who received new troops almost daily. He replaced Vaubois by Joubert.

No. 18.

"*The 29th.*"—But he is at Milan from November 27th to December 16th. Most people know, from some print or other, the picture by Gros of Bonaparte, flag in hand, leading his men across the murderous bridge of Arcola. It was during this visit to Milan that his portrait was taken, and Lavalette has preserved for us the domestic rather than the dignified manner of the sitting accorded. He refused to give a fixed time, and the artist was in despair, until Josephine came to his aid by taking her husband on her knees every morning after breakfast, and keeping him there a short time. Lavalette assisted at three of these sittings—apparently to remove the bashful embarrassment of the young painter. St. Amand suggests that Gros taking the portrait of Bonaparte at Milan, just after Arcola, would, especially under such novel conditions, prove a fitting theme for our artists today!

From December 16th to 21st Bonaparte is at Verona, whence he returns to Milan. There is perhaps a veiled innuendo in Barras' letter of December 30th. Clarke had advised the Directory that Alvinzi was planning an attack, which Barras mentions, but adds: "Your return to Milan shows that you consider another attack in favour of Wurmser unlikely, or, at least, not imminent." He is at Milan till January 7th, whence he goes to Bologna, the city which, he says, "of all the Italian cities has constantly shown the greatest energy and the most considerable share of real information."

No. 20.

General Brune.—This incident fixes the date of this letter to be 23 *Nivôse* (January 12), and not 23 *Messidor* (July 11), as hitherto published in the French editions of this letter. On January 12, 1797, he wrote General Clarke from Verona (No. 1375 of the *Correspondence*) almost an exact duplicate of this letter—a very rare coincidence in the epistles of Napoleon.

> Scarcely set out from Roverbella, I learnt that the enemy had appeared at Verona. Massena made his dispositions, which have been very successful; we have made 600 prisoners, and we have taken three pieces of cannon. General Brune has had seven bullets in his clothes, without having been touched by one of them; this is what it is to be lucky. We have had only ten men killed, and a hundred wounded.

Bonaparte had left Bologna on January 10, reaching Verona *via* Roverbella on the 12th.

No. 21.

February 3rd.—"*I wrote you this morning.*"—This and probably other letters describing Rivoli, La Favorite, and the imminent fall of Mantua, are missing. In summing up the campaign Thiers declares that in ten months 55,000 French (all told, including reinforcements) had beaten more than 200,000 Austrians, taken 80,000 of them prisoners, killed and wounded 20,000. They had fought twelve pitched battles, and sixty actions. These figures are probably as much above the mark as those of Napoleon's detractors are below it.

One does not know which to admire most, Bonaparte's absence from Marshal Wurmser's humiliation, or his abstention from entering Rome as a conqueror. The first was the act of a perfect gentleman, worthy of the best traditions of chivalry, the second was the very quintessence of far-seeing sagacity, not "baulking the end half-won, for an instant dole of praise." As he told Mdme. de Rémusat at Passeriano, "I conquered the Pope better by not going to Rome than if I had burnt his capital." Scott has compared his treatment of Wurmser to that of the Black Prince with his royal prisoner, King John of France. Wurmser was an Alsatian on the list of *émigrés*, and Bonaparte gave the

Marshal his life by sending him back to Austria, a fact which Wurmser requited by warning Bonaparte of a conspiracy to poison him[9] in
Romagna, which Napoleon thinks would otherwise have been successful.

No. 24.

"*Perhaps I shall make peace with the Pope*"—On February 12th the
Pope had written to "his dear son, General Bonaparte," to depute
plenipotentiaries for a peace, and ends by assuring him "of our highest esteem," and concluding with the paternal apostolic benediction.
Meanwhile Napoleon, instead of sacking Faenza, has just invoked the
monks and priests to follow the precepts of the Gospel.

No. 25.

"*The unlimited power you hold over me.*"—There seems no question that during the Italian campaigns he was absolutely faithful to
Josephine, although there was scarcely a beauty in Milan who did not
aspire to please him and to conquer him. In his fidelity there was, says
St. Amand, much love and a little calculation. As Napoleon has said
himself, his position was delicate in the extreme; he commanded old
generals; every one of his movements was jealously watched; his cir-
cumspection was extreme. His fortune lay in his wisdom. He would
have to forget himself for one hour, and how many of his victories
depended upon no more! The celebrated singer, La Grassini, who had
all Italy at her feet, cared only for the young general who would not
at that time vouchsafe her a glance.

SERIES C

THE CAMPAIGN OF MARENGO, 1800

Elected to the joint consulate by the events of the 18th *Brumaire*
(November 9), 1799, Napoleon spent the first Christmas Day after his
return from Egypt in writing personal letters to the King of England
and Emperor of Austria, with a view to peace. He asks King George
how it is that the two most enlightened nations of Europe do not realise that peace is the chief need as well as the chief glory ... and concludes by asserting that the fate of all civilised nations is bound up in
the conclusion of a war "which embraces the entire world." His efforts
fail in both cases. On December 27th he makes the *Moniteur* the sole
official journal. On February 7th, 1800, he orders ten days' military

---

9 With *aqua tofana*, says Marmont

mourning for the death of Washington—that "great man who, like the French, had fought for equality and liberty."

On April 22nd he urges Moreau to begin his campaign with the army of the Rhine, an order reiterated on April 24th through Carnot, again made Minister of War. A diversion to save the army of Italy was now imperative. On May 5th he congratulated Moreau on the battle of Stockach, but informs him that Massena's position is critical, shut up in Genoa, and with food only till May 25th. He advises Massena the same day that he leaves Paris that night to join the Army of Reserve, that the cherished child of victory must hold out as long as possible, at least until May 30th. At Geneva he met M. Necker. On May 14th he writes General Mortier, commandant of Paris, to keep that city quiet, as he will have still to be away a few days longer, which he trusts "will not be indifferent to M. de Mélas."

No. 3.

This letter was written from Ivrea, May 29th, 1800. On the 30th Napoleon is at Vercelli, on June 1st at Novara, and on June 2nd in Milan. Eugène served under Murat at the passage of the Ticino, May 31st.

M.'s; probably *"Maman," i.e.* his mother.

Cherries.—This fruit had already tender associations. Las Cases tells us that when Napoleon was only sixteen he met at Valence Mademoiselle du Colombier, who was not insensible to his merits. It was the first love of both. . . .

> "We were the most innocent creatures imaginable," the Emperor used to say; "we contrived little meetings together. I well remember one which took place on a midsummer morning, just as daylight began to dawn. It will scarcely be believed that all our happiness consisted in eating cherries together" (vol. 1. 81, 1836).

No. 4.

Milan.—He arrived here on June 2nd, and met with a great reception. In his bulletin of June 5th we find him assisting at an improvised concert. It ends, somewhat quaintly for a bulletin, as follows: "Italian music has a charm ever new. The celebrated singers, Billington,[10] La Grassini, and Marchesi are expected at Milan. They say they are about

---

10. On reaching London a few months later Mistress Billington was engaged simultaneously by Drury Lane and Covent Garden, and during the following year harvested £10,000 from these two engagements.

to start for Paris to give concerts there." According to M. Frédéric Masson, this Paris visit masked ulterior motives, and was arranged at a *déjeûner* on the same day, where La Grassini, Napoleon, and Berthier breakfasted together. Henceforward to Marengo Napoleon spends every spare day listening to the marvellous songstress, and as at Eylau, seven years later, runs great risks by admitting Venus into the camp of Mars.

At St. Helena he declares that from June 3rd to 8th he was busy "receiving deputations, and showing himself to people assembled from all parts of Lombardy to see their liberator." The Austrians had declared that he had died in Egypt. The date of No. 4 should probably be June 9th, on which day the rain was very heavy. He reached Stradella the next day.

SERIES D

No. 1.

The date is doubtless 27 *Messidor* (July 16), and the fete alluded to that of July 14. The following day Napoleon signed the *Concordat* with the Pope, which paved the way for the restoration of the Roman Catholic religion in France (September 11).

The blister.—On July 7 he quaintly writes Talleyrand: "They have put a second blister on my arm, which prevented me giving audience yesterday. Time of sickness is an opportune moment for coming to terms with the priests."

Some plants.—No trait in Josephine's character is more characteristic than her love of flowers not the selfish love of a mere collector,[11] but the bountiful joy of one who wishes to share her treasures. Malmaison had become the "veritable Jardin des Plantes" of the epoch,[12] far better than its Paris namesake in those days. The splendid hothouses, constructed by M. Thibaut, had been modelled on those of Kew, and enabled Josephine to collect exotics from every clime, and especially from her beloved Martinique. No jewel was so precious to her as a rare and beautiful flower. The Minister of Marine never forgot to instruct the deep-sea captains to bring back floral tributes from the far-off tropics.

---

11. She was, however, no mere amateur, and knew, says Mile. d'Avrillon, the names of all her plants, the family to which they belonged, their native soil, and special properties.

12. *Rueil, le château de Richelieu et la Malmaison*, by Jacquin and Duesberg, p. 130; in Aubenas' *Joséphine*, vol. 1.

These often fell, together with the ships, into the hands of the British sea-dogs, but the Prince Regent always had them sent on from London, and thus rendered, says Aubenas, "the gallant homage of a courtly enemy to the charming tastes and to the popularity already acquired by this universally beloved woman." Her curator, M. Aimé Bonpland, was an accomplished naturalist, who had been with Humboldt in America, and brought thence 6000 new plants. On his return in 1804 he was nominated by Josephine manager of the gardens of Malmaison and Navarre.

In the splendid work, *Le Jardin de la Malmaison,* in three volumes, are plates, with descriptions of 184 plants, mostly new, collected there from Egypt, Arabia, the United States, the Antilles, Mexico, Madeira, the Cape of Good Hope, Mauritius, the East Indies, New Caledonia, Australia, and China. To Josephine we owe the Camellia, and the Catalpa, from the flora of Peru, whilst her maiden name (La Pagerie) was perpetuated by Messrs. Pavon and Ruiz in the Lapageria.

If the weather is as bad.—As we shall see later, Bourrienne was invaluable to Josephine's court for his histrionic powers, and he seems to have been a prime favourite. On the present occasion he received the following *Account of the Journey to Plombières. To the Inhabitants of Malmaison,*—probably the work of Count Rapp, touched up by Hortense (Bourrienne's *Napoleon,* vol. 2. 85. Bentley, 1836):—

The whole party left Malmaison in tears, which brought on such dreadful headaches that all the amiable company were quite overcome by the idea of the journey. Madame Bonaparte, *mère,* supported the fatigues of this memorable day with the greatest courage; but Madame Bonaparte, *consulesse,* did not show any. The two young ladies who sat in the *dormeuse,* Mademoiselle Hortense and Madame Lavalette, were rival candidates for a bottle of Eau de Cologne; and every now and then the amiable M. Rapp made the carriage stop for the comfort of his poor little sick heart, which overflowed with bile; in fact, he was obliged to take to bed on arriving at Epernay, while the rest of the amiable party tried to drown their sorrows in champagne.

The second day was more fortunate on the score of health and spirits, but provisions were wanting, and great were the sufferings of the stomach. The travellers lived on in the hope of a good supper at Toul, but despair was at its height when on arriving there they found only a wretched inn, and nothing in it. We saw some odd-looking folks there, which indemnified us a little for spinach dressed with lamp-oil, and red asparagus fried with curdled milk. Who would not have been amused to see the Malmaison gourmands seated at a table so shockingly served!

In no record of history is there to be found a day passed in distress so dreadful as that on which we arrived at Plombières. On departing from Toul we intended to breakfast at Nancy, for every stomach had been empty for two days, but the civil and military authorities came out to meet us, and prevented us from executing our plan. We continued our route, wasting away, so that you might see us growing thinner every moment. To complete our misfortune, the *dormeuse*, which seemed to have taken a fancy to embark on the Moselle for Metz, barely escaped an overturn. But at Plombières we have been well compensated for this unlucky journey, for on our arrival we were received with all kinds of rejoicings. The town was illuminated, the cannon fired, and the faces of handsome women at all the windows gave us reason to hope that we shall bear our absence from Malmaison with the less regret.

With the exception of some anecdotes, which we reserve for chit-chat on our return, you have here a correct account of our journey, which we, the undersigned, hereby certify.

Josephine Bonaparte.

Beauharnais Lavalette.

Hortense Beauharnais.

Rapp.

Bonaparte, Mère.

The company ask pardon for the blots.

21 *Messidor* (July 10).

It is requested that the person who receives this journal will show it to all who take an interest in the fair travellers.

At this time Hortense was madly in love with Napoleon's favourite general, Duroc, who, however, loved his master more, and preferred not to interfere with his projects, especially as a marriage with Hortense would mean separation from Napoleon. Hortense and Bourrienne were both excellent billiard players, and the latter used this opportunity to carry letters from Hortense to her lukewarm lover.

Malmaison, without you, is too dreary.—Although Madame la Grassini had been specially summoned to sing at the Fête de la Concorde the day before.

No. 2.

This is the third pilgrimage Josephine has made, under the doctor's orders, to Plombières; but the longed-for heir will have to be sought for elsewhere, by fair means or foul. Lucien, who as Spanish Ambassador had vainly spent the previous year in arranging the divorce and remarriage of Napoleon to a daughter of the King of Spain, suggests adultery at Plombières, or a "warming-pan conspiracy," as the last alternatives. [13] Josephine complains to Napoleon of his brother's "poisonous" suggestions, and Lucien is again disgraced. In a few months an heir is found in Hortense's first-born, Napoleon Charles, born October 10.

The fat Eugène had come partly to be near his sister in her mother's absence, and partly to receive his colonelcy. Josephine is wretched to be absent, and writes to Hortense (June 16):—

> I am utterly wretched, my dear Hortense, to be separated from you, and my mind is as sick as my body. I feel that I was not born, my dear child, for so much grandeur. . . . By now Eugène should be with you; that thought consoles me.

Aubenas has found in the Tascher archives a charming letter from Josephine to her mother in Martinique, announcing how soon she may hope to find herself a great-grandmother.

No. 3.

Your letter has come.—Possibly the one to Hortense quoted above, as Josephine was not fond of writing many letters.

Injured whilst shooting a boar.—Constant was not aware of this occurrence, and was therefore somewhat incredulous of Las Cases (vol. 1. 289). The account in the "Memorial of St. Helena "is as follows:-
"Another time, while hunting the wild boar at Marly, all his suite were put to flight; it was like the rout of an army. The Emperor, with Soult and Berthier,[5] maintained their ground against three enormous boars.

---

13. Lucien declares that Napoleon said to his wife, in his presence and that of Joseph, "Imitate Livia, and you will find me Augustus."—(Jung, vol. 2. 206.) Lucien evidently suspects an occult sinister allusion here, but Napoleon is only alluding to the succession devolving on the first child of their joint families. Lucien refused Hortense, but Louis was more amenable to his brother's wishes. On her triumphal entry into Muhlberg (November 1805), the Empress reads on a column a hundred feet high—"*Josephinae, Galliarum Augustae.*"

5. Made Grand Huntsman in 1804.

'We killed all three, but I received a hurt from my adversary, and nearly lost this finger,' said the Emperor, pointing to the third finger of his left hand, which indeed bore the mark of a severe wound. c But the most laughable circumstance of all was to see the multitude of men, surrounded by their dogs, screening themselves behind the three heroes, and calling out lustily "Save the Emperor![14] save the Emperor! "while not one advanced to my assistance"'(vol. 2. 202. Colburn, 1836).

The Barber of Seville.—This was their best piece, and spectators (except Lucien) agree that in it the little theatre at Malmaison and its actors were unsurpassed in Paris. Bourrienne as Bartholo, Hortense as Rosina, carried off the palm. According to the Duchesse d'Abrantès, Wednesday was the usual day of representation, when the First Consul was wont to ask forty persons to dinner, and a hundred and fifty for the evening. As the Duchess had reason to know, Bonaparte was the severest of critics. "Lauriston made a noble lover," says the Duchess—"rather heavy" being Bourrienne's more professional comment. Eugène, says Méneval, excelled in footman's parts.[15] Michot, from the Theatre Français, was stage manager; and Bonaparte provided what Constant has called "the Malmaison Troupe," with their dresses and a collection of dramas. He was always spurring them on to more ambitious flights, and by complimenting Bourrienne on his prodigious memory, would stimulate him to learn the longest parts. Lucien, who refused to act, declares that Bonaparte quoted the saying of Louis XVI. concerning Marie Antoinette and her company, that the performances "were royally badly played." Junot, however, even in these days played the part of a drunkard only too well (Jung, vol. 2. 256).

No. 4.

The Sèvres Manufactory.—After his visit, he wrote Duroc: "This morning I gave, in the form of gratuity, a week's wages to the workmen of the Sèvres manufactory. Have the amount given to the director. It should not exceed a thousand *écus.*"

No. 5.

Your lover, who is tired of being alone.—So much so that he got up at five o'clock in the morning to read his letters in a young bride's bedchamber. The story is brightly told by the lady in question, Madame

---

14. An anachronism; he was at this time First Consul.
15. An euphuistic way of saying he could not learn longer ones. In war time Napoleon had to insist on Eugène keeping his letters with him and constantly re-reading them.

d'Abrantès (vol. 2. ch. 19). A few days before the Marly hunt, mentioned in No. 3, the young wife of seventeen, whom Bonaparte had known from infancy, and whose mother (Madame Permon) he had wished to marry, found the First Consul seated by her bedside with a thick packet of letters, which he was carefully opening and making marginal notes upon. At six he went off singing, pinching the lady's foot through the bed-clothes as he went. The next day the same thing happened, and the third day she locked herself in, and prevented her maid from finding the key.

In vain—the unwelcome visitor fetched a master-key. As a last resource, she wheedled her husband, General Junot, into breaking orders and spending the night with her; and the next day (June 22) Bonaparte came in to proclaim the hunting morning, but by her side found his old comrade of Toulon, fast asleep. The latter dreamily but good-humouredly asked, "Why, General, what are you doing in a lady's chamber at this hour? "and the former replied, "I came to awake Madame Junot for the chase, but I find her provided with an alarum still earlier than myself. I might scold, for you are contraband here, M. Junot."

He then withdrew, after offering Junot a horse for the hunt. The husband jumped up, exclaiming, "Faith! that is an amiable man! What goodness! Instead of scolding, instead of sending me sneaking back to my duty in Paris! Confess, my Laura, that he is not only an admirable being, but above the sphere of human nature."

Laura, however, was still dubious. Later in the day she was taken to task by the First Consul, who was astounded when she told him that his action might compromise her. "I shall never forget," she says, "Napoleon's expression of countenance at this moment; it displayed a rapid succession of emotions, none of them evil." Josephine heard of the affair, and was jealous for some little time to come.

General Ney.—Bonaparte had instructed Josephine to find him a nice wife, and she had chosen Mlle. Agläe-Louise Auguié, the intimate friend and schoolfellow of Hortense, and daughter of a former *Receveur-Général des Finances*. To the latter Ney goes fortified with a charming letter from Josephine, dated May 30—the month which the *Encyclopaedia Britannica* has erroneously given for that of the marriage, which seems to have taken place at the end of July (*Biographie Universelle, Michaud*, vol. 30). Napoleon (who stood godfather to all the children of his generals) and Hortense were sponsors for the first-born of this union, Napoleon Joseph, born May 8, 1803. The Duchess d'Abrantès describes her first meeting with Madame Ney at the Boulogne fête of August 15, 1802.

Her simplicity and timidity "were the more attractive inasmuch as they formed a contrast to most of the ladies by whom she was surrounded at the court of France. . . . The softness and benevolence of Madame Ney's smile, together with the intelligent expression of her large dark eyes, rendered her a very beautiful woman, and her lively manners and accomplishments enhanced her personal graces" (vol. 3. 31). The brave way in which she bore her husband's execution won the admiration of Napoleon, who at St. Helena coupled her with Mdme. de Lavalette and Mdme. Labedoyère.

SERIES E

No. 1.

Madame.—Napoleon became Emperor on May 18th, and this was the first letter to his wife since Imperial etiquette had become *de rigueur*, and the first letter to Josephine signed Napoleon. Méneval gives a somewhat amusing description of the fine gradations of instructions he received on this head from his master. This would seem to be a reason for this uncommon form of salutation; but, *per contra*, Las Cases (vol. 1. 276) mentions some so-called letters beginning *Madame et chère épouse*, which Napoleon declares to be spurious.

Pont de Briquet, a little village about a mile from Boulogne. On his first visit to the latter he was met by a deputation of farmers, of whom one read out the following address:

> General, here we are, twenty farmers, and we offer you a score of big, sturdy lads, who are, and always shall be, at your service. Take them along with you, General; they will help you to give England a good thrashing. As for ourselves, we have another duty to fulfil: with our arms we will till the ground, so that bread be not wanting to the brave fellows who are destined to destroy the English.

Napoleon thanked the honest yeomen, and determined to make the only habitable dwelling there his headquarters. The place is called from the foundations of bricks found there—the remains of one of Caesar's camps.

The wind having considerably freshened.—Constant tells a good story of the Emperor's obstinacy, but also of his bravery, a few days later. Napoleon had ordered a review of his ships, which Admiral Bruix had ignored, seeing a storm imminent. Napoleon sends off Bruix to Holland in disgrace, and orders the review to take place; but when, amid the wild storm, he sees "more than twenty gunboats run aground," and no succour vouchsafed to the drowning men, he springs into the nearest lifeboat, crying, "We must save them somehow." A wave breaks over the boat; he is drenched and nearly carried overboard, losing the hat he had worn at Marengo. Such pluck begets enthusiasm; but, in spite of all they could do, two hundred lives were lost. This is Constant's version; probably his loss is exaggerated. The Emperor, writing Talleyrand on August 1st, speaks only of three or four ships lost, and *"une quinzaine d'hommes."*

No. 2.

The waters.—Mile. d'Avrillon describes them and their effect—the sulphur baths giving *erysipelas* to people in poor health. Corvisart had accompanied the Empress, to superintend their effect, which was as usual *nil.*

All the vexations.—Constant (vol. 1. 230, &c., 1896) is of use to explain what these were—having obtained possession of a diary of the tour by one of Josephine's ladies-in-waiting, which had fallen into Napoleon's hands. In the first place, the roads (where there were any[16]) were frightful, especially in the Ardennes forest, and the diary for August 1st concludes by stating "that some of the carriages were so battered that they had to be bound together with ropes. One ought not to expect women to travel about like a lot of dragoons." The writer of the diary, however, preferred to stay in the carriage, and let Josephine and the rest get wet feet, thinking the risk she ran the least.

Another vexation to Josephine was the published report of her gift to the Mayoress of Rheims of a malachite medallion set in brilliants, and of her saying as she did so, "It is the colour of Hope." Although she had really used this expression, it was the last thing she would like to see in print, taking into consideration the reason for her yearly peregrinations to Plombières, and now to Aix, and their invariable inefficiency. Under the date August 14th, the writer of the diary gives a severe criticism of Josephine.

> She is exactly like a ten-year-old child—good-natured, frivolous, impressionable; in tears at one moment, and comforted the next.... She has just wit enough not to be an utter idiot. Ig-

---

16. The Emperor had himself planned the Itinerary, and had mistaken a projected road for a completed one, between Rethel and Marche

norant—as are most Creoles—she has learned nothing, or next to nothing, except by conversation; but, having passed her life in good society, she has got good manners, grace, and a mastery of that sort of jargon which, in society, sometimes passes for wit. Social events constitute the canvas which she embroiders, which she arranges, and which give her a subject for conversation. She is witty for quite a whole quarter of an hour every day. . . . Her diffidence is charming . . . her temper very sweet and even; it is impossible not to be fond of her. I fear that . . . this need of unbosoming, of communicating all her thoughts and impressions, of telling all that passes between herself and the Emperor, keeps the latter from taking her into his confidence. . . . She told me this morning that, during all the years she had spent with him, never once had she seen him let himself go.

Eugène has started for Blois,—where he became the head of the electoral college of Loir et Cher, having just been made Colonel-General of the *Chasseurs* by Napoleon. The Beauharnais family were originally natives of Blois.

No. 3.

Aix-la-Chapelle.—In this, the first Imperial pilgrimage to take the waters, great preparations had been made, forty-seven horses bought at an average cost of £60 apiece; and eight carriages, which are not dear at £1000 for the lot, with £400 additional for harness and fittings.

At Aix they had fox-hunting and hare-coursing so called, but probably the final tragedy was consummated with a gun. Lord Rosebery reminds us that at St. Helena the Emperor actually shot a cow! They explored coal mines, and examined all the local manufactories, including the relics of Charlemagne—of which great warrior and statesman Josephine refused an arm, as having a still more puissant one ever at hand for her protection.

When tidings come that the Emperor will arrive on September 2, and prolong their stay from Paris, there is general lamentation among Josephine's womenkind, especially on the part of that perennial wet blanket and busybody, Madame de Larochefoucauld, who will make herself a still greater nuisance at Mayence two years later.

No. 4.

During the past week.—As a matter of fact he only reached Ostend on April 12th from Boulogne, having left Dunkirk on the 11th.

The day after tomorrow.—This fête was the distribution of the Legion of Honour at Boulogne and a review of 80,000 men. The decorations were enshrined in the helmet of Bertrand du Guesclin, which in its turn was supported on the shield of the Chevalier Bayard.

Hortense arrived at Boulogne, with her son, and the Prince and Princess Murat, a few days later, and saw the Emperor. Josephine received a letter from Hortense soon after Napoleon joined her (September 2nd), to which she replied on September 8th. "The Emperor has read your letter; he has been rather vexed not to hear from you occasionally. He would not doubt your kind heart if he knew it as well as I, but appearances are against you. Since he can think you are neglecting him, lose no time in repairing the wrongs which are not real," for "Bonaparte loves you like his own child, which adds much to my affection for him."

I am very well satisfied . . . with the flotillas.—The descent upon England was to have taken place in September, when the death of Admiral Latouche-Tréville at Toulon, August 19th, altered all Napoleon's plans. Just about this time also *Fulton* submitted his steamship invention to Bonaparte. The latter, however, had recently been heavily mulcted in other valueless discoveries, and refers Fulton to the savants of the Institute, who report it chimerical and impracticable. The fate of England probably lay in the balance at this moment, more than in 1588 or 1798.

Napoleon and Josephine leave Aix for Cologne on September 12, and it is now the ladies' turn to institute a hunt—the "real chamois hunt"; for each country inn swarms with this pestilence that walketh in darkness, and which, alas! is no respecter of persons.

No. 5.

Two points are noteworthy in this letter—(1) that like No. I of this series (see note thereto) it commences *Madame and dear Wife*; and (2) it is signed Bonaparte and not Napoleon, which somewhat militates against its authenticity.

Arras, August 29th.—Early on this day he had been at St. Cloud. On the 30th he writes Cambacérès from Arras that he is "satisfied with the spirit of this department." On the same day he writes thence to the King of Prussia and Fouché. To his Minister of Police he writes: "That detestable journal, *Le Citoyen François*, seems only to wish to wallow in blood. For eight days running we have been entertained with nothing but the Saint Bartholomew. Who on earth is the editor (*rédacteur*) of this paper? With what gusto this wretch relishes the crimes and misfortunes of our fathers! My intention is that you should put a stop to it. Have the editor (*directeur*) of this paper changed, or suppress it." On Friday he is at Mons (writing interesting letters respecting the removal of church ruins), and reaches his wife on the Sunday (September 2nd) as his letter foreshadowed.

I am rather impatient to see you.—The past few months had been an anxious time for Josephine. Talleyrand (who, having insulted her in 1799, thought her his enemy) was scheming for her divorce, and wished Napoleon to marry the Princess Wilhelmina of Baden, and thus cement an alliance with Bavaria and Russia (Constant, vol. 1. 240). The Bonaparte family were very anxious that Josephine should not be crowned. Napoleon had too great a contempt for the weaknesses of average human nature to expect much honesty from Talleyrand. But he was not as yet case-hardened to ingratitude, and was always highly sensitive to caricature and hostile criticism.

Talleyrand had been the main cause of the death of the Duc d'Enghien, and was now trying to show that he had wished to prevent it; but possibly the crowning offence was contained in a lady's diary, that fell into the emperor's hands, where Talleyrand is said to have called his master "a regular little Nero" in his system of espionage. The diary in question is in Constant's *Memoirs*, vol. 1., and this letter helps to fix the error in the dates, probably caused by confusion between the Revolutionary and Gregorian Calendars.

No. 6.

T.—This may be Talleyrand, whom Mdme. de Rémusat in a letter to her husband (September 21st) at Aix, hinted to be on bad terms with the Emperor—a fact confirmed and explained by Méneval. It may also have been Tallien, who returned to France in 1802, where he had been divorced from his unfaithful wife.

B.—Doubtlessly Bourrienne, who was in disgrace with Napoleon, and who was always trying to impose on Josephine's good nature. No sooner had Napoleon left for Boulogne on July 14th than his former secretary inflicts himself on the wife at Malmaison.

Napoleon joins Josephine at St. Cloud on or before October 13th, where preparations are already being made for the Coronation by the Pope—the first ceremony of the kind for eight centuries.

No. 1.

To Josephine.—She was at Plombières from August 2 to September 10, but no letter is available for the period, neither to Hortense nor from Napoleon.

Strasburg.—She is in the former Episcopal Palace, at the foot of the cathedral.

Stuttgard.—He is driven over from Ludwigsburg on October 4th, and hears the German opera of *Don Juan.*

I am well placed.—On the same day Napoleon writes his brother Joseph that he has already won two great victories—(1) by having no sick or deserters, but many new conscripts; and (2) because the Badenese army and those of Bavaria and Wurtemberg had joined him, and all Germany well disposed.

No. 2.

Louisburg.—Ludwigsburg.

In a few days.—To Talleyrand he wrote from Strasburg on September 27: "Within a fortnight we shall see several things."

A new bride.—This letter, in the collection of his *Correspondence ordered by Napoleon III.,* concludes at this point.

Electress.—The Princess Charlotte-Auguste-Mathilde (1766-1828), daughter of George III., our Princess Royal, who married Frederick I. Napoleon says she is "not well treated by the Elector, to whom, nevertheless, she seems much attached" (Brotonne, No. 111). She was equally pleased with Napoleon, and wrote home how astonished she was to find him so polite and agreeable a person.

No. 3.

I have assisted at a marriage.—The bride was the Princess of Saxe-Hildburghhausen, who was marrying the second son of the Elector.

No. 5.

Written at Augsburg. On October 15th he reaches the abbey of Elchingen, which is situated on a height, from whence a wide view is obtained, and establishes his headquarters there.

No. 6.

Spent the whole of today indoors.—This is also mentioned in his Seventh Bulletin (dated the same day), which adds, "But repose is not compatible with the direction of this immense army."

Vicenza.—Massena did not, however, reach this place till November 3rd. The French editions have *Vienna*, but *Vicenza* is evidently meant.

No. 7.

He is still at Elchingen, but at Augsburg the next day. On the 21st he issues a decree to his army that *Vendémiaire*,[17] of which this was the last day but one, should be counted as a campaign for pensions and military services.

Elchingen.—Méneval speaks of this village "rising in an amphitheatre above the Danube, surrounded by walled gardens, and houses rising one above the other." From it Napoleon saw the city of Ulm below, commanded by his cannon. Marshal Ney won his title of Duke of Elchingen by capturing it on October 14th, and fully deserved it. The Emperor used to leave the abbey every morning to go to the camp before Ulm, where he used to spend the day, and sometimes the night. The rain was so heavy that, until a plank was found, Napoleon sat in a tent with his feet in water (Savary, vol. 2. 196).

Such a catastrophe.—At Ulm General Mack, with eight field-marshals, seven lieutenant-generals, and 33,000 men surrender. Napoleon had despised Mack even in 1800, when he told Bourrienne at Malmaison, "Mack is a man of the lowest mediocrity I ever saw in my life; he is full of self-sufficiency and conceit, and believes himself equal to anything. He has no talent. I should like to see him some day opposed to one of our good generals; we should then see fine work. He is a boaster, and that is all. He is really one of the most silly men existing, and besides all that, he is unlucky" (vol. 1 304). Napoleon stipulated for Mack's life in one of the articles of the Treaty of Presburg.

No. 9.

Munich.—Napoleon arrived here on October 24th.

Lemarois.—A trusty *aide-de-camp*, who had witnessed Napoleon's civil marriage in March 1796, at 10 p.m.

I was grieved.—They had no news from October 12th to 21st in Paris, where they learnt daily that Strasburg was in the same predicament. Mdme. de Rémusat, at Paris, was equally anxious, and such women, in the Emperor's absence, tended by their presence or even by their correspondence to increase the alarms of Josephine.

Amuse yourself.—M. Masson (*Josephine, Imperatrice et Reine*, p. 424)

---

17. The first month of the Republican calendar.

has an interesting note of how she used to attend lodge at the Orient in Strasburg, to preside at a *"loge d'adoption sous la direction de Madame de Dietrich, grand maîtresse titulaire."*

Talleyrand has come.—He was urgently needed to help in the correspondence with the King of Prussia (concerning the French violation of his Anspach territory), with whom Napoleon's relations were becoming more strained.

No. 10.

We are always in forests.—Baron Lejeune, with his artist's eye, describes his impressions of the Amstetten forest as he travelled through it with Murat the following morning (November 4th):

> Those of us who came from the south of Europe had never before realised how beautiful Nature can be in the winter. In this particular instance everything was robed in the most gleaming attire; the silvery rime softening the rich colours of the decaying oak leaves, and the sombre vegetation of the pines. The frozen drapery, combined with the mist, in which everything was more or less enveloped, gave a soft, mysterious charm to the surrounding objects, producing a most beautiful picture. Lit up by the sunshine, thousands of long icicles, such as those which sometimes droop from our fountains and waterwheels, hung like shining lustres from the trees. Never did ballroom shine with so many diamonds; the long branches of the oaks, pines, and other forest trees were weighed down by the masses of hoar-frost, while the snow converted their summits into rounded roofs, forming beneath them grottoes resembling those of the Pyrenean mountains, with their shining stalactites and graceful columns (vol. 1 24).

My enemies.—Later in the day Napoleon writes from Lambach to the Emperor of Austria a pacific letter, which contains the paragraph:

> My ambition is wholly concentrated on the reestablishment of my commerce and of my marine, and England grievously opposes itself to both.

No. 11.

Written from Lintz, the capital of Upper Austria, where Napoleon was on the 4th.

No. 12.

Napoleon took up his abode at the palace of Schoenbrunn on the

14th, and proves his "two-o'clock-in-the-morning courage" by passing through Vienna at that time the following morning.

No. 13.

They owe everything to you.—Aubenas quotes this, and remarks (vol. 2. 326): "No one had pride in France more than Napoleon, stronger even than his conviction of her superiority in the presence of other contemporary sovereigns and courts. He wishes that in Germany, where she will meet families with all the pride and sometimes all the haughtiness of their ancestry, Josephine will not forget that she is Empress of the French, superior to those who are about to receive her, and who owe full respect and homage to her."

No. 14.

Austerlitz.—Never was a victory more needful; but never was the Emperor more confident. Savary says that it would take a volume to contain all that emanated from his mind during that twenty-four hours (December 1-2). Nor was it confined to military considerations. General Ségur describes how he spent his evening meal with his marshals, discussing with Junot the last new tragedy (*Les Templiers*, by Raynouard), and from it to Racine, Corneille, and the fatalism of our ancestors.

December 2nd was a veritable Black Monday for the Coalition in general, and for Russia in particular, where Monday is always looked upon as an unlucky day. Their forebodings increased when, on the eve of the battle, the Emperor Alexander was thrown from his horse (Czartoriski, vol. 2 106).

No. 17.

A long time since I had news of you.—Josephine was always a bad correspondent, but at this juncture was reading that stilted but sensational romance—*Caleb Williams*; "or hearing the *Achilles* of Paër, or the *Romeo and Juliet* of Zingarelli in the intervals of her imperial progress through Germany. M. Masson, not often too indulgent to Josephine, thinks her conduct excusable at this period—paying and receiving visits, dressing and redressing, always in gala costume, and without a moment's solitude.

No. 19.

I await events.—A phrase usually attributed to Talleyrand in 1815. However, the Treaty of Presburg was soon signed (December 2nd), and the same day Napoleon met the Archduke Charles at Stamersdorf, a meeting arranged from mutual esteem. Napoleon had an unswerving admiration for this past and future foe, and said to Madame d'Abrantès, "That man has a soul, a golden heart."[18] Napoleon, however, did not wish to discuss politics, and only arranged for an interview of two hours, "one of which," he wrote Talleyrand, "will be employed in dining, the other in talking war and in mutual protestations."

I, for my party am sufficiently busy.—No part of Napoleon's career is more wonderful than the way in which he conducts the affairs of France and of Europe from a hostile capital. This was his first experience of the kind, and perhaps the easiest, although Prussian diplomacy had needed very delicate and astute handling. But when Napoleon determined, without even consulting his wife, to cement political alliances by matrimonial ones with his and her relatives, he was treading on somewhat new and difficult ground. First and foremost, he wanted a princess for his ideal young man, Josephine's son Eugène, and he preferred Auguste, the daughter of the King of Bavaria, to the offered Austrian Archduchess.

But the young Hereditary Prince of Baden was in love and accepted by his beautiful cousin Auguste; so, to compensate him for his loss, the handsome and vivacious Stephanie Beauharnais, fresh from Madame Campan's finishing touches, was sent for. For his brother Jerome a bride is found by Napoleon in the daughter of the King of Wurtemberg. Baden, Bavaria, and Wurtemberg were too much indebted to France for the spoils they were getting from Austria to object, provided the ladies and their mammas were agreeable; but the conqueror of Austerlitz found this part the most difficult, and had to be so attentive to the Queen of Bavaria that Josephine was jealous.

However, all the matches came off, and still more remarkable, all turned out happily, a fact which certainly redounds to Napoleon's credit as a match-maker. On December 31st, at 1.45 a.m., he entered Munich by torchlight and under a triumphal arch. His chamberlain, M. de Thiard, assured him that if he left Munich the marriage with Eugène would fall through, and he agrees to stay, although he declared that his absence, which accentuated the Bank crisis, is costing him 1,500,000 *francs* a day.

The marriage took place on January 14th, four days after Eugène arrived at Munich and three days after that young Bayard had been bereft of his cherished moustache. Henceforth the bridegroom is called "*Mon fils*" in Napoleon's correspondence, and in the contract

18. *Memoirs*, vol. 2. 165.

of marriage Napoleon-Eugène de France. The Emperor and Empress reached the Tuileries on January 27th. The marriage of Stephanie was even more difficult to manage, for, as St. Amand points out, the Prince of Baden had for brothers-in-law the Emperor of Russia, the King of Sweden, and the King of Bavaria—two of whom at least were friends of England. Josephine had once an uncle-in-law, the Count Beauharnais, whose wife Fanny was a well-known literary character of the time, but ot whom the poet Lebrun made the epigram—

Elle fait son visage, et ne fait pas ses vers.

Stephanie was the grand-daughter of this couple, and as Grand-Duchess of Baden was beloved and respected, and lived on until 1860.

Series G

No. 1.

Napoleon left St. Cloud with Josephine on September 25th, and had reached Mayence on the 28th, where his Foot Guard were awaiting him. He left Mayence on October 1st, and reached Wurzburg the next day, whence this letter was written, just before starting for Bamberg. Josephine was installed in the Teutonic palace at Mayence.

Princess of Baden, Stephanie Beauharnais. (For her marriage, see note, end of Series F.)

Hortense was by no means happy with her husband at the best of times, and she cordially hated Holland. She was said to be very frightened of Napoleon, but (like most people) could easily influence her mother. Napoleon's letter to her of this date (October 5th) is certainly not a severe one:—

I have received yours of September 14th. I am sending to the Chief Justice in order to accord pardon to the individual in whom you are interested. Your news always gives me pleasure. I trust you will keep well, and never doubt my great friendship for you.

The Grand Duke, i.e. of Wurzburg. The castle where Napoleon was staying seemed to him sufficiently strong to be armed and provisioned, and he made a great *depôt* in the city. "Volumes," says Méneval, "would not suffice to describe the multitude of his military and administrative measures here, and the precautions which he took against even the most improbable hazards of war."

Florence.—Probably September 1796, when Napoleon was hard

pressed, and Josephine had to fetch a compass from Verona to regain Milan, and thus evade Wurmser's troops.

No. 2.

Bamberg.—Arriving at Bamberg on the 6th, Napoleon issued a proclamation to his army which concluded—

Let the Prussian army experience the same fate that it experienced fourteen years ago. Let it learn that, if it is easy to acquire increase of territory and power by means of the friendship of the great people, their enmity, which can be provoked only by the abandonment of all spirit of wisdom and sense, is more terrible than the tempests of the ocean.

Eugène.—Napoleon wrote him on the 5th, and twice on the 7th, on which date we have *eighteen* letters in the *Correspondence.*

Her husband.—The Hereditary Grand Duke of Baden, to whom Napoleon had written from Mayence on September 30th, accepting his services, and fixing the rendezvous at Bamberg for October 4th or 5th.

On this day Napoleon invaded Prussian territory by entering Bayreuth, having preceded by one day the date of their ultimatum—a rhapsody of twenty pages, which Napoleon in his First Bulletin compares to "one of those which the English Cabinet pay their literary men £500 *per annum* to write." It is in this Bulletin where he describes the Queen of Prussia (dressed as an Amazon, in the uniform of her regiment of dragoons, and writing twenty letters a day) to be like Armida in her frenzy, setting fire to her own palace.

No. 3.

By this time the Prussian army is already in a tight corner, with its back on the Rhine, which, as Napoleon says in his Third Bulletin written on this day, is "*assez bizarre,* from which very important events should ensue." On the previous day he concludes a letter to Talleyrand—

One cannot conceive how the Duke of Brunswick, to whom one allows some talent, can direct the operations of this army in so ridiculous a manner.

Erfurt.—Here endless discussions, but, as Napoleon says in his bulletin of this day—

Consternation is at Erfurt, . . . but while they deliberate, the French army is marching. . . . Still the wishes of the King of

Prussia have been executed; he wished that by October 8th the French army should have evacuated the territory of the Confederation which *has* been evacuated, but in place of repassing the Rhine, it has passed the Saal.

If she wants to see a battle.—*Queen Louise*, great-grandmother of the present Emperor William, and in 1806 aged thirty. St. Amand says that "when she rode on horseback before her troops, with her helmet of polished steel, shaded by a plume, her gleaming golden *cuirass*, her tunic of cloth of silver, her red buskins with golden spurs," she resembled, as the bulletin said, one of the heroines of Tasso. She hated France, and especially Napoleon, as the child of the French Revolution.

No. 4.

I nearly captured him and the Queen.—They escaped only by an hour, Napoleon writes Berthier. Blucher aided their escape by telling a French General about an imaginary armistice, which the latter was severely reprimanded by Napoleon for believing.

No battle was more beautifully worked out than the battle of Jena—Davoust performing specially well his move in the combinations by which the Prussian army was hopelessly entangled, as Mack at Ulm a year before. Bernadotte alone, and as usual, gave cause for dissatisfaction. He had a personal hatred for his chief, caused by the knowledge that his wife (Desirée Clary) had never ceased to regret that she had missed her opportunity of being the wife of Napoleon. Bernadotte, therefore, was loath to give initial impetus to the victories of the French Emperor, though, when success was no longer doubtful, he would prove that it was not want of capacity but want of will that had kept him back. He was the Talleyrand of the camp, and had an equal aptitude for fishing in troubled waters.

I have bivouacked.—Whether the issue of a battle was decisive, or, as at Eylau, only partially so, Napoleon never shunned the disagreeable part of battle—the tending of the wounded and the burial of the dead. Savary tells us that at Jena, as at Austerlitz, the Emperor rode round the field of battle, alighting from his horse with a little brandy flask (constantly refilled), putting his hand to each unconscious soldier's breast, and when he found unexpected life, giving way to a joy "impossible to describe" (vol. 2 184). Méneval also speaks of his performing this "pious duty, in the fulfilment of which nothing was allowed to stand in his way."

No. 5.

Fatigues, bivouacs . . . have made me fat.—The Austerlitz campaign had the same effect. See a remarkable letter to Count Miot de Melito on January 30th, 1806:

> The campaign I have just terminated, the movement, the excitement have made me stout. I believe that if all the kings of Europe were to coalesce against me I should have a ridiculous paunch.

And it was so!

The *great M. Napoleon*, aged four, and the younger, aged two, are with Hortense and their grandmother at Mayence, where a Court had assembled, including most of the wives of Napoleon's generals, burning for news. A lookout had been placed by the Empress some two miles on the main-road beyond Mayence, whence sight of a courier was signalled in advance.

No. 7.

Potsdam.—As a reward for Auerstadt, Napoleon orders Davoust and his famous Third Corps to be the first to enter Berlin the following day.

No. 8.

Written from Berlin, where he is from October 28th to November 25th.

You do nothing but cry.—Josephine spent her evenings gauging futurity with a card-pack, and although it announced Jena and Auerstadt before the messenger, it may possibly, thinks M. Masson, have been less propitious for the future—and behind all was the sinister portion of the *spae*-wife's prophecy still unfulfilled.

No. 9A.

Madame Tallien had been in her time, especially in the years 1795-99, one of the most beautiful and witty women in France. Madame d'Abrantès calls her the Venus of the Capitol; and Lucien Bonaparte speaks of the court of the voluptuous Director, Barras, where the beautiful Tallien was the veritable Calypso. The people, however, could not forget her second husband, Tallien, from whom she was divorced in 1802 (having had three children born while he was in Egypt, 1798-1802); and whilst they called Josephine "*Notre Dame des Victoires*," they called Madame Tallien "*Notre Dame de Septembre*,"

The latter was, however, celebrated both for her beauty and her intrigues;[19] and when, in 1799, Bonaparte seized supreme power the fair lady[20] invaded Barras in his bath to inform him of it; but found her indolent Ulysses only capable of ejaculating, "What can be done? that man has taken us all in!" Napoleon probably remembered this, and may refer to her rather than to the Queen of Prussia in the next letter, where he makes severe strictures on intriguing women. Moreover, Napoleon in his early campaigns had played a ridiculous part in some of Gillray's most indecent cartoons, where Mmes. Tallien and Josephine took with Barras the leading roles; and as Madame Tallien was not considered respectable in 1796, she was hardly a fit friend for the Empress of the French ten years later.

In the interval this lady, divorced a second time, had married the Prince de Chimay (Caraman). Napoleon knew also that she had been the mistress of Ouvrard, the banker, who in his Spanish speculations a few months earlier had involved the Bank of France to the tune of four millions sterling, and forced Napoleon to make a premature peace after Austerlitz. The Emperor had returned at white heat to Paris, and wished he could build a gallows for Ouvrard high enough for him to be on view throughout France. Madame Tallien's own father, M. de Cabarrus, was a French banker in Spain, and probably in close relation with Ouvrard.

No. 10.
Written from Berlin.

The bad things I say about women.—Napoleon looked upon this as a woman's war, and his temper occasionally gets the mastery of him. No war had ever been so distasteful to him or so personal. Prussia, whose alliance he had been courting for nearly ten years, was now worthless to him, and all because of petticoat government at Berlin. In the Fifteenth Bulletin (dated Wittenburg, October 23rd) he states that the Queen had accused her husband of cowardice in order to bring about the war. But it is doubtless the Sixteenth Bulletin (dated Potsdam, October 25th) to which Josephine refers, and which refers to the oath of alliance of the Emperor Alexander and the King of Prussia in the death chamber of Frederick the Great.

---

19. Bouillet, *Dictionnaire Universelle,* &c.
20. "The Queen of that Court was the fair Madame Tallien. All that imagination can conceive will scarcely approach the reality; beautiful after the antique fashion, she had at once grace and dignity; without being endowed with a superior wit, she possessed the art of making the best of it, and won people's hearts by her great kindness."—*Memoirs of Marmont,* vol. 1. 5 p. 887.

It is from this moment that the Queen quitted the care of her domestic concerns and the serious occupations of the toilet in order to meddle with the affairs of State.

He refers to a Berlin caricature of the scene which was at the time in all the shops, "exciting even the laughter of clodhoppers." The handsome Emperor of Russia was portrayed, by his side the Queen, and on his other side the King of Prussia with his hand raised above the tomb of the Great Frederick; the Queen herself, draped in a shawl nearly as the London engravings represent Lady Hamilton, pressing her hand on her heart, and apparently gazing upon the Emperor of Russia." In the Eighteenth Bulletin (October 26th) it is said the Prussian people did not want war, that a handful of women and young officers had alone made this "*tapage*," and that the Queen, "formerly a timid and modest woman looking after her domestic concerns," had become turbulent and warlike, and had "conducted the monarchy within a few days to the brink of the precipice."

As the Queen of Prussia was a beautiful woman, she has had nearly as many partisans as Mary Stuart or Marie Antoinette, but with far less cause. Napoleon, who was the incarnation of practical common sense, saw in her the first cause of the war, and considered that so far as verbal flagellation could punish her, she should have it. He had neither time nor sympathy for the "Please you, do not hurt us" attitude of a bellicose new woman, who, as Imogen or Ida, have played with edged tools from the time of Shakespeare to that of Sullivan.

As an antidote, however, to his severe words against women he put, perhaps somewhat ostentatiously, the Princess d'Hatzfeld episode in his Twenty-second Bulletin (Berlin, October 29th). A year later (November 26th, 1807), when his Old Guard return to Paris and free performances are given at all the theatres, there is the *Triumph of Trajan* at the Opera, where Trajan, burning with his own hand the papers enclosing the secrets of a conspiracy, is a somewhat skilful allusion to the present episode.

No. 11.

Magdeburg had surrendered on November 8th, with 20 generals, 800 officers and 22,000 men, 800 pieces of cannon, and immense stores.

Lubeck.—This capitulation was that of Blucher, who had escaped after Jena through a rather dishonourable ruse. It had taken three army corps to hem him in.

No. 13.

Written from Berlin, but not included in the *Correspondence*.

Madame L——, i.e. Madame de la Rochefoucauld, a third or fourth cousin (by her first marriage) of Josephine, and her chief lady of honour. She was an incorrigible Royalist, and hated Napoleon; but as she had been useful at the Tuileries in establishing the Court, Napoleon, as usual, could not make up his mind to cause her dismissal. In 1806, however, she made Josephine miserable and Mayence unbearable. She foretold that the Prussians would win every battle, and even after Jena she (to use an expression of M. Masson), "continued her music on the sly" (*en sourdine*). See Letters 19 and 26 of this Series.

No. 17.

December 2, the anniversary of Austerlitz (1805) and of Napoleon's coronation (1804). He now announces to his soldiers the Polish campaign.

No. 18.

Not in the *Correspondence*.

Jealousy.—If Josephine's letters and conduct had been a little more worthy of her position, she might have saved herself. Madame Walewski, who had not yet appeared on the scene.

No. 19.

Desir de femme est un feu qui dèvore.—The quotation is given in Jung's *Memoirs of Lucien* (vol. 2. 62). "*Ce qu'une femme desire est un feu qui consume, celui d'une reine un vulcane qui dévore.*"

No. 23.

I am dependent on events.—He says the same at St. Helena. "Throughout my whole reign I was the keystone of an edifice entirely new, and resting on the most slender foundations. Its duration depended on the issue of my battles. I was never, in truth, master of my own movements; I was never at my own disposal."

No. 26.

The fair ones of Great Poland.—If Berthier and other regular correspondents of Josephine were like Savary in their enthusiasm, no wonder the Mayence coterie began to stir up jealousy. Here is the description of the Duke of Rovigo (vol. 2 17):

The stay at Warsaw had for us something of witchery; even with regard to amusements it was practically the same life as at Paris: the Emperor had his concert twice a week, at the end of which he held a reception, where many of the leading people met. A great number of ladies from the best families were admired alike for the brilliancy of their beauty, and for their wonderful amiability.

One may rightly say that the Polish ladies inspired with jealousy the charming women of every other civilised clime. They united, for the most part, to the manners of good society a fund of information which is not commonly found even among Frenchwomen, and is very far above anything we see in towns, where the custom of meeting in public has become a necessity. It seemed to us that the Polish ladies, compelled to spend the greater part of the year in their country-houses, applied themselves there to reading as well as to the cultivation of their talents, and it was thus that in the chief towns, where they went to pass the winter, they appeared successful over all their rivals.

St. Amand says:

In the intoxication of their enthusiasm and admiration, the most beautiful among them—and Poland is the country of beauty—lavished on him, like sirens, their most seducing smiles.

Josephine was right to be jealous, for, as the artist Baron Lejeune adds, *"They were, moreover, as graceful as the Creole women so often are."*

A wretched barn, reached over still more wretched roads. The Emperor and his horse had nearly been lost in the mud, and Marshal Duroc had a shoulder put out by his carriage being upset.

Such things become common property.—So was another event, much to Josephine's chagrin. On this date Napoleon heard of a son (Léon) born to him by Eléanore, a former schoolfellow of Madame Murat. M. Masson thinks this event epoch-making in the life of Napoleon. "Henceforth the charm is broken, and the Emperor assured of having an heir of his own blood."

No. 27.

Warsaw, January 3.—On his way from Pultusk on January 1, he had received a Polish ovation at Bronie, where he first met Madame Walewski. The whole story is well told by M. Masson in *Napoleon et les Femmes*; but here we must content ourselves with the mere facts, and first, for the sake of comparison, cite his love-letters to the lady in question:—

(1.) "I have seen only you, I have admired only you, I desire only you. A very prompt answer to calm the impatient ardour of N."

(2.) "Have I displeased you? I have still the right to hope the contrary. Have I been mistaken? Your eagerness diminishes, while mine augments. You take away my rest! Oh, give a little joy, a little happiness to a poor heart all ready to worship you. Is it so difficult to get a reply? You owe me one.—N."

(3.) "There are moments when too high rank is a burden, and that is what I feel. How can I satisfy the needs of a heart hopelessly in love, which would fling itself at your feet, and which finds itself stopped by the weight of lofty considerations paralysing the most lively desires? Oh, if you would! Only you could remove the obstacles that lie between us. My friend Duroc will clear the way. Oh, come! come! All your wishes shall be gratified. Your native land will be dearer to me when you have had pity on my poor heart.—N."

(4.) "Marie, my sweet Marie! My first thought is for you, my first desire to see you again. You will come again, will you not? You promised me to do so. If not, the eagle will fly to you. I shall see you at dinner, a friend tells me. Deign, then, to accept this bouquet; let it become a mysterious link which shall establish between us a secret union in the midst of the crowd surrounding us. Exposed to the glances of the crowd, we shall still understand each other. When my hand presses my heart, you will know that it is full of thoughts of you; and in answer you will press closer your bouquet. Love me, my bonny Marie, and never let your hand leave your bouquet.—N."

In this letter, in which he has substituted *tu* for *vous*, there is more passion than we have seen since 1796. The fair lady now leaves her decrepit old husband, nearly fifty years her senior, and takes up her abode in Finckenstein Castle, for nearly two months of the interval between Eylau and Friedland.

"In order," says Pasquier, "that nothing should be lacking to characterise the calm state of his mind and the security of his position, it was soon known that he had seen fit to enjoy a pleasurable relaxation by calling to him a Polish gentlewoman of excellent birth, with whom he had contracted a *liaison* while passing through Warsaw, and who, as a consequence of this journey, had the honour of bearing him a son."

Repudiated by her husband, she came to Paris, where she was very kindly treated by Josephine, who, having once seen her, found in her no rival, but an enthusiastic patriot, "sacrificed to Plutus," as Napoleon told Lucien at Mantua a few months later, adding that "her soul was as beautiful as her face."

No. 28.

Be cheerful—gai.—This adjective is a favourite one in letters to his wife, and dates from 1796.

No. 29.

Roads unsafe and detestable.—The French troops used to say that the four following words constituted the whole language of the Poles: *Kleba? Niema. Vota? Sara.* ("Some bread? There is none. Some water? We will go and fetch it.")

Napoleon one day passed by a column of infantry suffering the greatest privations on account of the mud, which prevented the arrival of provisions. "*Papa, kleba?*" exclaimed a soldier.

"*Niema,*" replied the Emperor. The whole column burst into a fit of laughter; they asked for nothing more. Baron Lejeune, Constant, and Méneval have variants of the same story.

No. 35.

Written from Warsaw, and omitted from the *Correspondence.*

I hope that you are at Paris.—Madame Junot hints that her husband, as Governor of Paris, was being sounded by Bonaparte's sister, Murat's wife (with whom Junot was in love), if he would make Murat Napoleon's successor, in lieu of Eugène, if the Emperor were killed. If Napoleon had an inkling of this, he would wish Josephine to be on the spot.

T.—Is probably Tallien, who had misconducted himself in Egypt. Madame Junot met him at Madrid, but she and others had not forgotten the September massacres. "The wretch! how did he drag on his loathsome existence?" she exclaims.

No.36.

Paris.—Josephine arrived here January 31st; Queen Hortense going to the Hague and the Princess Stephanie to Mannheim.

No. 38.

Probably written from Arensdorf, on the eve of the battle of Eylau (February 9th), on which day a great ball took place in Paris, given by the Minister of Marine.

No. 39.

Eylau.—The battle of Preussich-Eylau was splendidly fought on both sides, but the Russian general, Beningsen, had all the luck.

(1) His *Cossacks* capture Napoleon's letter to Bernadotte, which enables him to escape all Napoleon's plans, which otherwise would have destroyed half the Russian army.

(2) A snowstorm in the middle of the day in the faces of the French ruins Augereau's corps and saves the Russians from a total rout.

(3) The arrival of a Prussian army corps, under General Lestocq, robbed Davoust of his glorious victory on the right, and much of the ground gained—including the village of Kuschnitten.

(4) The night came on just in time to save the rest of the Russian army, and to prevent Ney taking any decisive part in the battle. Bernadotte, as usual, failed to march to the sound of the guns, but, as Napoleon's orders to do so were captured by *Cossacks*, he might have had an excuse rather better than usual, had not General Hautpoult,[21] in touch both with him and Napoleon, advised him of his own orders and an imminent battle. Under such circumstances, no general save the Prince of Ponte-Corvo, says Bignon, would have remained inactive, "but it was the destiny of this marshal to have a role apart in all the great battles fought by the Emperor. His conduct was at least strange at Jena, it will not be less so, in 1809, at Wagram." The forces, according to Matthieu Dumas (*Précis des Evenements Militaires*, volume 18), were approximately 65,000 French against 80,000 allies[22]—the latter in a strong chosen position. Napoleon saved 1500, the wreckage of Augereau's[23] corps, that went astray in the blizzard (costing the French more than half their loss in the two days' fight), by a charge of his Horse Guard, but his Foot Guard never fired a shot. The allies lost 5000 to 6000 dead and 20,000 wounded. Napoleon told Montholon that his loss at

---

21. This brave general was mortally wounded in the cavalry charge which saved the battle, and the friends of Bernadotte assert that the message was never given—an assertion more credible if the future king's record had been better on other occasions.
22. Alison says 75,000 allies, 85,000 French, but admits allies had 100 more cannon.
23. Augereau, says Méneval, went out of his mind during this battle, and had to be sent back to France.

Eylau was 18,000, which probably included 2000 dead, and 15,000 to 16,000 wounded and prisoners.

As the French remained masters of the field of battle, the slightly wounded were evidently not counted by Napoleon, who in his bulletin gives 1900 dead and 5700 wounded. The list of wounded inmates of the hospital a month later, March 8th, totalled only 4600, which astonished Napoleon, who sent back for a recount. On receipt of this he wrote Daru (March 15):

> From your advices to hand, I see we are not far out of count. There were at the battle of Eylau 4000 or 5000 wounded, and 1000 in the combats preceding the battle.

No. 40.

Corbineau.—Mlle. d'Avrillon (vol. 2. 101) tells how, in haste to join his regiment at Paris, Corbineau had asked for a seat in her carriage from St. Cloud. She was delighted, as he was a charming man, "with no side on like Lauriston and Lemarois." He had just been made general, and said, "Either I will get killed or deserve the favour which the Emperor has granted me. *M'selle*, you shall hear me spoken of; if I am not killed I will perform some startling deed."

Dahlmann.—General Nicholas Dahlmann, commanding the chasseurs of the guard, was killed in the charge on the Russian infantry which saved the battle. On April 22nd Napoleon wrote Vice-Admiral Decrés to have three frigates put on the stocks to be called Dahlmann, Corbineau, and Hautpoul, and in each captain's cabin a marble inscription recounting their brave deeds.

No. 41.

Young Tascher.—The third of Josephine's *cousins-germain* of that name. He was afterwards *aide-de-camp* of Prince Eugène, and later *major-domo* of the Empress Eugenie.

No. 42.

After this letter St. Amand declares that Napoleon's letters to his wife become "cold, short, banal, absolutely insignificant." "They consisted of a few remarks about the rain or the fine weather, and always the same refrain—the invitation to be cheerful ... Napoleon, occupied elsewhere, wrote no longer to his legitimate wife, but as a duty, as paying a debt of conscience." He was occupied, indeed, but barely as the author supposes. It is Bingham (vol. 2. 281) who reminds us that in the first three months of 1807 we have 1715 letters and despatches preserved of his work during that period, while he often rode forty leagues a day, and had instructed his librarian to send him by each morning's courier two or three new books from Paris. Aubenas is more just than St. Amand.

If his style is no longer that of the First Consul, still less of the General of Italy, he was solicitous, punctilious, attentive, affectionate even although laconic, in that correspondence (with Josephine) which, in the midst of his much greater preoccupations, seems for him as much a pleasure as a duty.

No.43.

I am still at Eylau.—It took Napoleon and his army eight days to bury the dead and remove the wounded. Lejeune says:

His whole time was given up now to seeing that the wounded received proper care, and he insisted on the Russians being as well treated as the French. (vol. 1. 48).

The Emperor wrote Daru that if more surgeons had been on the spot he could have saved at least 200 lives; although, to look at the surgical instruments used on these fields, and now preserved in the museum of Les Invalides, it is wonderful that the men survived operations with such ghastly implements of torture. A few days later Napoleon tells Daru on no account to begrudge money for medicines, and especially for quinine.

This country is covered with dead and wounded.—

"Napoleon," says Dumas (vol. 1. 18, 41), "having given order that the succour to the wounded on both sides might be multiplied, rode over the field of battle, which all eye-witnesses agree to have been the most horrible field of carnage which war has ever offered. In a space of less than a square league, the ground covered with snow, and the frozen lakes, were heaped up with 10,000 dead, and 3000 to 4000 dead horses, *débris* of artillery, arms of all kinds, cannonballs, and shells. Six thousand Russians, expiring of their wounds, and of hunger and thirst, were left abandoned to the generosity of the conqueror."

No. 50.

Osterode.—"A wretched village, where I shall pass a considerable time." Owing to the messenger to Bernadotte being captured by Cossacks, the Emperor, if not surprised at Eylau on the second day, found at least all his own intentions anticipated. He could not risk the same misfortune again, and at Osterode all his army were within easy hailing distance, "within two marches at most" (Dumas). Savary speaks of him there, "working, eating, giving audience, and sleeping—all in the same room," alone keeping head against the storm of his marshals, who wished him to retire across the Vistula.

He remained over five weeks at Osterode, and more than two months at Finckenstein Castle, interesting himself in the affairs of Teheran and Monte Video, offering prizes for discoveries in electricity and medicine, giving advice as to the most scientific modes of teaching history and geography, while objecting to the creation of poet-laureates or Caesarians whose exaggerated praises would be sure to awaken the ridicule of the French people, even if it attained its object of finding a place of emolument for poets. Bignon says (vol. 6. 227):

> From Osterode or from Finckenstein he supervised, as from Paris or St. Cloud, the needs of France; he sought means to alleviate the hindrances to commerce, discussed the best ways to encourage literature and art, corresponded with all his ministers, and while awaiting the renewal of the fray, having a war of figures with his Chancellor of Exchequer.

It is not as good as the great city.—The day before he had written his brother Joseph that neither his officers nor his staff had taken their clothes off for two months; that he had not taken his boots off for a fortnight; that the wounded had to be moved 120 miles in sledges, in the open air; that bread was unprocurable; that the Emperor had been living for weeks upon potatoes, and the officers upon mere meat. "After having destroyed the Prussian monarchy, we are fighting against the remnant of the Prussians, against Russians, Cossacks, and Kalmucks, those roving tribes of the north, who formerly invaded the Roman Empire."

I have ordered what you wish for Malmaison.—About this time he also gave orders for what afterwards became the Bourse and the Madeleine, and gave hints for a new journal (March 7th), whose "criticism should be enlightened, well-intentioned, impartial, and robbed of that noxious brutality which characterises the discussions of existing journals, and which is so at variance with the true sentiments of the nation."

No. 54.

Minerva. In a letter of March 7th Josephine writes to Hortense:

> A few days ago I saw a frightful accident at the Opera. The actress who represented Minerva in the ballet of *Ulysses* fell

twenty feet and broke her arm. As she is poor, and has a family to support, I have sent her fifty *louis*.

This was probably the ballet, *The Return of Ulysses*, a subject given by Napoleon to Fouché as a suitable subject for representation. In the same letter Josephine writes:

All the private letters I have received agree in saying that the Emperor was very much exposed at the battle of Eylau. I get news of him very often, sometimes two letters a day, but that does not replace him.

This special danger at Eylau is told by Las Cases, who heard it from Bertrand. Napoleon was on foot, with only a few officers of his staff; a column of four to five thousand Russians came almost in contact with him. Berthier instantly ordered up the horses. The Emperor gave him a reproachful look; then sent orders to a battalion of his guard to advance, which was a good way behind, and standing still. As the Russians advanced he repeated several times, "What audacity, what audacity!" At the sight of his Grenadiers of the Guard the Russians stopped short. It was high time for them to do so, as Bertrand said. The Emperor had never stirred; all who surrounded him had been much alarmed.

No. 55.

"It is the first and only time," says Aubenas, "that, in these two volumes of letters (*Collection Didot*), Napoleon says *vous* to his wife. But his vexation does not last more than a few lines, and this short letter ends, '*Tout à toi?*' Not content with this softening, and convinced how grieved Josephine will be at this language of cold etiquette, he writes to her the same day, at ten o'clock at night, before going to bed, a second letter in his old style, which ends, '*Mille et mille amitiés.*'"

It is a later letter (March 25th) which ends as described, but No. 56 is, nevertheless, a kind letter.

No. 56.

Dupuis.—Former principal of the Brienne Military School. Napoleon, always solicitous for the happiness of those whom he had known in his youth, had made Dupuis his own librarian at Malmaison. His brother, who died in 1809, was the learned Egyptologist.

No. 58.

M. de T——, i.e. M. de Thiard. In *Lettres Inedites de Napoleon I.* (Brotonne), No. 176, to Talleyrand, March 22nd, the Emperor writes:

I have had M. de Thiard effaced from the list of officers. I have sent him away, after having testified all my displeasure, and told him to stay on his estate. He is a man without military honour and civic fidelity. . . . My intention is that he shall also be struck off from the number of my chamberlains. I have been poignantly grieved at such black ingratitude, but I think myself fortunate to have found out such a wicked man in time.

De Thiard seems to have been corresponding with the enemy from Warsaw.

No. 60.

Marshal Bessières.—His *château* of Grignon, now destroyed, was one of the most beautiful of Provence. Madame de Sevigné lived and was buried in the town of Grignon.

No. 63.

This was printed April 24th in the French editions, but April 14th is evidently the correct date.

No. 67.

"*Sweet, pouting, and capricious*"—Aubenas speaks of these lines "in the style of the Italian period, which seemed in fact to calm the fears of the Empress."

No. 68.

Madame ——. His own sister, Madame Murat, afterwards Queen of Naples. See note to Letter 35 for her influence over Junot. The latter was severely reprimanded by Napoleon on his return and banished from Paris.

Why, for example, does the Grand Duchess occupy your boxes at the theatres? Why does she go thither in your carriage? Hey! M. Junot! you are surprised that I am so well acquainted with your affairs and those of that little fool, Madame Murat?— (*Memoirs of the Duchess d'Abrantès*, vol. 3. 328.)

Measles.—As the poor child was ill four days, it was probably laryngitis from which he died—an ailment hardly distinguishable from croup, and one of the commonest *sequelae* of measles. He died on May 5th.

The best account is the *Memoirs of Stanislaus Giraudin.* They had applied leeches to the child's chest, and had finally recourse to some English powders of unknown composition, which caused a rally, followed by the final collapse. King Louis said the child's death was caused by the Dutch damp climate, which was bad for his own health. Josephine hastens to join her daughter, but breaks down at Lacken, where Hortense, more dead than alive, joins her, and returns to Paris with her.

No. 69.

I trust I may hear you have been rational in your sorrow.—As a matter of fact he had heard the opposite, for the following day (May 15th) he writes to his brother Jerome:

Napoleon died in three days at the Hague; I know not if the King has advised you of it. This event gives me the more pain insomuch as his father and mother are not rational, and are giving themselves up to all the transports of their grief.

To Fouché he writes three days later:

I have been very much afflicted by the misfortune which has befallen me. I had hoped for a more brilliant destiny for that poor child;

And on May 20th,

I have felt the loss of the little Napoleon very acutely. I would have wished that his father and mother should have received from their temperament as much courage as I for knowing how to bear all the ills of life. But they are younger, and have reflected less on the frailty of our worldly possessions.

It is typical of Napoleon that the only man to whom, as far as we know, he unbosomed his sorrow should be one of his early friends, even though that friend should be the false and faithless Fouché, who requited his confidence later by vile and baseless allegations respecting the parentage of this very child. In one respect only did Napoleon resemble David in his supposititious sin, which was, that when the child was dead, he had neither time nor temperament to waste in futile regrets. As he said on another occasion, if his wife had died during the Austerlitz Campaign it would not have delayed his operations a quarter of an hour. But he considers practical succour to the living as the most fitting memorial to the dead, and writes on June 4th to De Champagny:

Twenty years ago a malady called croup showed itself in the north of Europe. Some years ago it spread into France. I require you to offer a prize of £500 (12,000 *francs*), to be given to the doctor who writes the best essay on this malady and its mode of treatment.

Commenting on this letter Bignon (vol. 6. p. 262) adds,

It is, however, fortunate when, on the eve of battles, warlike princes are pondering over ways of preserving the population of their states.

No. 71.

May 20th.—On this date he writes Hortense:

My daughter, all the news I get from the Hague tells me that you are not rational. However legitimate your grief, it must have limits: never impair your health; seek distractions, and know that life is strewn with so many rocks, and may be the source of so many miseries, that death is not the greatest of all.—Your affectionate father,   Napoleon.

No. 74.

I am vexed with Hortense.—The same day he encloses with this a letter to Hortense.

My daughter, you have not written me a line during your great and righteous grief. You have forgotten everything, as if you had nothing more to lose. They say you care no longer for any one, that you are callous about everything; I note the truth of it by your silence. This is not well, Hortense, it is not what you promised me. Your son was everything for you. Are your mother and myself nothing? Had I been at Malmaison I should have shared your grief, but I should have wished you at the same time to turn to your best friends. Good-bye, my daughter, be cheerful; it is necessary to be resigned; keep well, in order to fulfil all your duties. My wife is utterly miserable about your condition; do not increase her sorrow.—Your affectionate father,   Napoleon.

Hortense had been on such bad terms with her husband for several months past that Napoleon evidently thinks it wiser not to allude to him, although he had written Louis a very strong letter on his treatment of his wife two months earlier (see letter 12,294 of the *Corre-*

spondence, April 4th). There is, however, a temporary reunion between husband and wife in their common sorrow.

No. 78.

Friedland.—On this day he wrote a further letter to the Queen of Holland (No. 12,761 of the *Correspondence*):

> My daughter, I have your letter dated Orleans. Your grief pains me, but I should like you to possess more courage; to live is to suffer, and the true man is always fighting for mastery over himself. I do not like to see you unjust towards the little Napoleon Louis, and towards all your friends. Your mother and I had hoped to be more to you than we are.

She had been sent to take the waters of Cauterets, and had left her child Napoleon Louis (who died at Forli, 1831) with Josephine, who writes to her daughter (June 11th):

> He amuses me much; he is so gentle. I find he has all the ways of that poor child that we mourn.

And a few days later:

> There remains to you a husband, an interesting child, and a mother whose love you know.

Josephine had with women the same tact that her husband had with men, but the Bonaparte family, with all its good qualities, strained the tact and tempers of both to the utmost.

No. 79.

Tilsit.—Referring to Napoleon and Alexander at Tilsit, Michaud says:

> Both full of wiles and devices, they affected nevertheless the most perfect sentiments of generosity, which at the bottom they scarcely dreamed of practising. Reunited, they were the masters of the world, but such a union seemed impossible; they would rather share it among themselves. Allies and rivals, friends and enemies, all were sacrificed; henceforth there were to be only two powers, that of the East and that of the West. Bonaparte at this time actually ruled from the Niemen to the Straits of Gibraltar, from the North Sea to the base of the Italian Peninsula.

No. 1.

Milan.—Magnificent public works were set on foot by Napoleon at Milan, and the Cathedral daily adorned with fresh marvels of sculpture. Arriving here on the morning of the 22nd, Napoleon goes first to hear the *Tè Deum* at the Cathedral, then to see Eugène's wife at the Monza Palace; in the evening to the La Scala Theatre, and finishes the day (to use an Irishism) by working most of the night.

Mont Cenis.—"The roads of the Simplon and Mont Cenis were kept in the finest order, and daily attracted fresh crowds of strangers to the Italian plains." So says Alison, but on the present occasion Napoleon was overtaken by a storm which put his life in danger. He was fortunate enough to reach a cave in which he took refuge. This cave appeared to him, as he afterwards said, "a cave of diamonds "(Méneval).

Eugène.—The writer in *Biog. Univ.* (art. Josephine) says:

During a journey that Napoleon made in Italy (November 1807) he wished, while loading Eugène with favours, to prepare his mind for his mother's divorce. The Decree of Milan, by which, in default of male and legitimate children[24] of *the direct line*, he adopted Eugène for his son and his successor to the throne of Italy, gave to those who knew how to read the secret thoughts of the Emperor in his patent acts the proof that he had excluded him from all inheritance in the Imperial Crown of France, and that he dreamed seriously of a new alliance himself.

No. 2.

Venice.—The Venetians gave Napoleon a wonderful ovation—many nobles spending a year's income on the fêtes. "Innumerable gondolas glittering with a thousand colours and resounding with the harmony of instruments, escorted the barges which bore, together with the master of the world, the Viceroy and the Vice-Queen of Italy, the King and Queen of Bavaria, the Princess of Lucca, the King of Naples (Joseph, who stayed six days with his brother), the Grand Duke of Berg, the Prince of Neufchâtel, and the greater part of the generals of the old army of Italy" (Thiers). While at Venice Napoleon was in easy touch with the Porte, of which he doubtless made full use, while, *per contra*, he was expected to give Greece her independence.

---

24. The Decree itself says "*nos enfants et descendants males, legitimes et naturels.*"

November 30th.—Leaving Milan, Napoleon came straight through Brescia to Verona, where he supped with the King and Queen of Bavaria. The next morning he started for Vicenza through avenues of vine-encircled poplars and broad yellow wheat-fields which "lay all golden in the sunlight and the breeze "(Constant). The Emperor went to the theatre at Vicenza, and left again at 2 a.m. Spending the night at Stra, he met the Venetian authorities early the next morning at Fusina.

No. 3.

Udine.—He is here on the 12th, and then hastens to meet his brother Lucien at Mantua—the main but secret object of his journey to Italy. It is *most* difficult to gauge the details—was it a political or a conjugal question that made the interview a failure? Madame D'Abrantès, voicing the rumours of the day, thinks the former; Lucien, writing *Memoirs* for his wife and children, declares it to be the latter.

Napoleon was prepared to legalise the children of his first wife, and marry the eldest to Prince Ferdinand, the heir to the Spanish crown; but Lucien considers the Bourbons to be enemies of France and of the Bonapartes. These *Memoirs* of Lucien are not perhaps very trustworthy, especially where his prejudices overlap his memory or his judgement, but always instructive and very readable. When the account of this interview was written (early in 1812), Lucien was an English prisoner, furious that his brother has just refused to exchange him for "some English Lords." Speaking of Josephine, the Emperor tells him that in spite of her reputation for good-nature, she is more malicious than generally supposed, although for her husband "she has no nails"; but he adds that rumours of impending divorce have made life between them very constrained.

"Only imagine," continued the Emperor, "that wife of mine weeps every time she has indigestion, because she says she thinks herself poisoned by those who wish me to marry someone else. It is perfectly hateful." He said that Joseph also thought of a divorce, as his wife gave him only daughters, and that the three brothers might be remarried on the same day. The Emperor regretted not having taken the Princess Augusta, daughter of his "best friend, the King of Bavaria," for himself, instead of for Eugène, who did not know how to appreciate her and was unfaithful. He was convinced that Russia by invading India would overthrow England, and that his own soldiers were ready to follow him to the antipodes.

He ends by offering Lucien his choice of thrones—Naples, Italy, "the brightest jewel of my Imperial crown," or Spain[25] (Madame D'Abrantès adds *Prussia*), if he will give way about Madame Jouberthon and her children. *"Tout pour Lucien divorcé, rien pour Lucien sans divorcé."* When Napoleon finds his brother obdurate he makes Eugène Prince of Venice, and his eldest daughter Princess of Bologna, with a large appanage. Lucien is in fresh disgrace within less than three months of the Mantuan interview, for on March 11, 1808, Napoleon writes brother Joseph,

> Lucien is misconducting himself at Rome . . . and is more Roman than the Pope himself. His conduct has been scandalous; he is my open enemy, and that of France. . . . I will not permit a Frenchman, and one of my own brothers, to be the first to conspire and act against me, with a rabble of priests.

I may soon be in Paris.—After leaving Milan he visits the fortifications at Alessandria, and is met by a torchlight procession at Marengo. Letters for two days (December 27-28th) are dated Turin, although Constant says he did not stop there. Crossing Mont Cenis on December 30th he reaches the Tuileries on the evening of New Year's Day (1808).

SERIES I

No. 1.

Bayonne is half-way between Paris and Madrid, nearly 600 miles from each. Napoleon arrived here April 15th, and left July 21st, returning with Josephine *via* Pau, Tarbes, Auch, Montauban, Agen, Bordeaux, Rochefort, Nantes. Everywhere he received a hearty welcome, even, and especially, in La Vendée. He arrives at Paris August 14th, hearing on August 3rd at Bordeaux of (what he calls) the "horrible catastrophe" of General Dupont at Baylen.

No. 2.

A country-house.—The Château of Marrac. Marbot had stayed there in 1803 with Augereau. Bausset informs us that this *château* had been built either for the Infanta Marie Victoire engaged to Louis XV., or for the Dowager Queen of Charles II., "the bewitched," when she was packed off from Madrid to Bayonne (see Hume's *Spain*, 1479-1788).

---

25. On October 11th Prince Ferdinand had written Napoleon for "the honour of allying himself to a Princess of his august family"; and Lucien's eldest daughter was Napoleon's only choice.

Everything is still most primitive.—Nevertheless he enjoyed the *parn-pernuque* which was danced before the *château* by seven men and ten maidens, gaily dressed—the women armed with tambourines and the men with *castanets*. Saint-Amand speaks of thirteen performers (seven men and six maidens) chosen from the leading families of the town, to render what for time immemorial had been considered fit homage for the most illustrious persons.

No. 3.

Prince of the Asturias.—The Emperor had received him at the chateau of Marrac, paid him all the honours due to royalty, while evading the word "Majesty," and insisting the same day on his giving up all claim to the Crown of Spain. Constant says he was heavy of gait, and rarely spoke.

The Queen.—A woman of violent passions. The Prince of the Asturias had designs on his mother's life, while the Queen openly begged Napoleon to put the Prince to death. On May 9th Napoleon writes Talleyrand to prepare to take charge of Ferdinand at Valençay, adding that if the latter were "to become attached to some pretty woman, whom we are sure of, it would be no disadvantage." A new experience for a Montmorency to become the keeper of a Bourbon, rather than his Constable. Pasquier, with his usual Malvolian decorum, gives fuller details. Napoleon, he says:

> enumerates with care (to Talleyrand) all the precautions that are to be taken to prevent his escape, and even goes so far as to busy himself with the distractions which may be permitted him. And, be it noted, the principal one thrown in his way was given him by a young person who lived at the time under M. De Talleyrand's roof. This liaison, of which Ferdinand soon became distrustful, did not last as long as it was desired to.

No. 4.

A son has been born.—By a plebiscite of the year 12. (1804-5), the children of Louis and Hortense were to be the heirs of Napoleon, and in conformity with this the child born on April 20th at 17 Rue Lafitte (now the residence of the Turkish Ambassador), was inscribed on the register of the Civil List destined for princes of the blood. His two elder brothers had not been so honoured, but in due course the King of Rome was entered thereon. Had Louis accepted the Crown of Spain which Napoleon had in vain offered to him, and of which Hortense would have made an ideal Queen, the chances are that Napoleon would never have divorced Josephine. St. Amand shows at length that the future Napoleon III. is truly the child of Louis, and neither of Admiral Verhuell nor of the Duke Decazès.

Louis and Hortense in the present case are sufficiently agreed to insist that the father's name be preserved by the child, who is called Charles Louis Napoleon, and not Charles Napoleon, which was the Emperor's first choice. In either case the name of the croup-stricken firstborn had been preserved. On April 23rd Josephine had already two letters from Cambacres respecting mother and child, and on this day the Empress writes her daughter:

I know that Napoleon is consoled for not having a sister.

Arrive on the 27th.—Josephine, always wishful to humour her husband's love of punctuality, duly arrived on the day fixed, and took up her abode with her husband in the *château* of Marrac. Ferdinand wrote to his uncle in Madrid to beware of the cursed Frenchmen, telling him also that Josephine had been badly received at Bayonne. The letter was intercepted, and Napoleon wrote Murat that the writer was a liar, a fool, and a hypocrite. The Emperor, in fact, never trusted the Prince henceforward. Bausset, who translated the letter, tells how the Emperor could scarcely believe that the Prince would use so strong an adjective, but was convinced on seeing the word *maldittos*, which he remarked was almost the Italian—*maledetto*.

SERIES J

Leaving St. Cloud September 22nd, Napoleon is at Metz on the 23rd, at Kaiserlautern on the 24th, where he sends a message to the Empress in a letter to Cambacérès, and on the 27th is at Erfurt On the 28th the Emperors of France and Russia sign a Convention of Alliance. Napoleon leaves Erfurt October 14th (the anniversary of Jena), travels *incognito*, and arrives St. Cloud October 18th.

No. 1.

I have rather a cold.—Napoleon had insisted on going to explore a new road he had ordered between Metz and Mayence, and which no one had ventured to say was not complete. The road was so bad that the carriage of the *mâitre des requêtes*, who had been summoned to account for the faulty work, was precipitated a hundred feet down a ravine near Kaiserlautern.

I am pleased with the Emperor and everyone here.—Which included what he had promised Talma for his audience—a *parterre* of kings.

Besides the two Emperors, the King of Prussia was represented by his brother Prince William, Austria by General Vincent, and there were also the Kings of Saxony, Bavaria, Wurtemberg, Westphalia, and Naples, the Prince Primate, the Princes of Anhalt, Coburg, Saxe-Weimar, Darmstadt, Baden, and Nassau. Talleyrand, Champagny, Maret, Duroc, Berthier, and Caulaincourt, with Generals Oudinot, Soult, and Lauriston accompanied Napoleon. Literature was represented by Goethe, Wieland, Müller; and feminine attractions by the Duchess of Saxe-Weimar and the wily Princess of Tour and Taxis, sister of the Queen of Prussia. Pasquier and others have proved that at Erfurt Talleyrand did far more harm than good to his master's cause, and in fact intended to do so.

On his arrival he spent his first evening with the Princess of Tour and Taxis, in order to meet the Emperor Alexander, and said: "Sire . . . It is for you to save Europe, and the only way of attaining this object is by resisting Napoleon. The French people are civilised, their Emperor is not: the sovereign of Russia is civilised, his people are not. It is therefore for the sovereign of Russia to be the ally of the French people,"—of whom Talleyrand declared himself to be the representative. By squaring Alexander this transcendental (unfrocked) Vicar of Bray, "with an oar in every boat," is once more hedging, or, to use his own phrase, guaranteeing the future, and at the same time securing the daughter of the Duchess of Courland for his nephew, Edmond de Périgord. "The Arch-apostate" carried his treason so far as to advise Alexander of Napoleon's ulterior views, and thus enabled the former to forestall them—no easy matter in conversations with Napoleon "lasting whole days" (see Letter No. 3, this Series). Talleyrand had also a grievance. He had been replaced as Foreign Minister by Champagny. He had accepted the surrender of his portfolio gladly, as now, becoming Vice-Grand Elector, he ranked with Cambacérès and Maret. But when he found that Napoleon, who liked to have credit for his own diplomacy, seldom consulted him, or allowed Champagny to do so, jealousy and ill-will naturally resulted.

No. 2.

Shooting over the battlefield of Jena.—The presence of the Emperor Alexander on this occasion was considered a great affront to his recent ally, the King of Prussia, and is severely commented on by Von Moltke in one of his Essays. In fairness to Alexander, we must remember that their host, the Duke of Saxe-Weimar, had married his sister. Von Moltke, by the way, speaks of *hares* forming the sport in question, but

Savary of a second battle of Jena fought against the *partridges*. The fact seems to be that all kinds of game, including stags and deer, were driven by the beaters to the royal sportsmen in their huts, and the Emperor Alexander, albeit short-sighted, succeeded in killing a stag, at eight feet distance, *at the first shot.*

The Weimar ball.—This followed the Jena shoot, and the dancing lasted all night. The Russian courtiers were scandalised at their Emperor dancing, but while he was present the dancing was conventional enough, consisting of promenading two and two to the strains of a Polish march. "Imperial Waltz, imported from the Rhine," was already the rage in Germany, and Napoleon, in order to be more worthy of his Austrian princess, tried next year to master this new science of tactics, but after a trial with the Princess Stephanie, the lady declared that her pupil should always give lessons, and never receive them. He was rather more successful at billiards, pursued under the same praiseworthy incentive.

A few trifling ailments.—Mainly a fearful nightmare; a new experience, in which he imagines his vitals torn out by a bear. "Significant of much!" As when also the Russian Emperor finds himself without a sword and accepts that of Napoleon as a gift: and when, on the last night, the latter orders his comedians to play "Bajazet,"—little thinking the appointed Tamerlane was by his side.

No. 3.

I am pleased with Alexander.—For the time being Josephine had most reason to be pleased with Alexander, who failed to secure his sister's hand for Napoleon.

He ought to be with me.—He might have been, had not Napoleon purposely evaded the Eastern Question. On this subject Savary writes (vol. 2. 297):—

Since Tilsit, Napoleon had sounded the personal views of his ambassador at Constantinople, General Sebastiani, as to this proposition of the Emperor of Russia (*i.e.* the partition of Turkey). This ambassador was utterly opposed to this project, and in a long report that he sent to the Emperor on his return from Constantinople, he demonstrated to him that it was absolutely necessary for France never to consent to the dismemberment of the Turkish Empire; the Emperor Napoleon adopted his views.

And these Talleyrand knew. The whirligig of time brings about its revenges, and in less than fifty years Lord Palmerston had to seek an alliance with France and the house of Napoleon in order to maintain the fixed policy that sent Napoleon I. to Moscow and to St. Helena.

"Alexander, with justice," says Alison, "looked upon Constantinople as the back-door of his empire, and was earnest that its key should be placed in his hands."

"Alexander," Napoleon told O'Meara, "wanted to get Constantinople, which I would not allow, as it would have destroyed the equilibrium of power in Europe. I reflected that France would gain Egypt, Syria, and the islands, which would have been nothing in comparison with what Russia would have obtained. I considered that the barbarians of the north were already too powerful, and probably in the course of time would overwhelm all Europe, as I now think they will. Austria already trembles: Russia and Prussia united, Austria falls, and England cannot prevent it."

Erfurt is the meridian of Napoleon's first thirteen years (1796-1808)—each more glorious; henceforward (1809-1821) ever faster he "rolls, darkling, down the torrent of his fate."

SERIES K

No. 5.
Written from Aranda.

No. 6.
Written from the Imperial Camp outside Madrid. Neither Napoleon[26] nor Joseph entered the capital, but King Joseph took up his abode at the Prado, the castle of the Kings of Spain, two miles away; while the Emperor was generally at Chamartin, some five miles distant. He had arrived on the heights surrounding Madrid on his Coronation Day (December 2nd), and does not fail to remind his soldiers and his people of this auspicious coincidence. The bulletin concludes with a tirade against England, whose conduct is "shameful," but her troops "well disciplined and superb." It declares that Spain has been treated by them as they have treated Holland, Sardinia, Austria, Russia, and Sweden. "They foment war everywhere; they distribute weapons like poison; but they shed their blood only for their direct and personal interests."

Parisian weather of the last fortnight in May.—In his bulletin of the

---

26. Napoleon visited Madrid and its Palais Royal *incognito*, and (like Vienna) by night (Bausset).

13th, he says:

> Never has such a month of December been known in this country; one would think it the beginning of spring. But ten days later all was changed, and the storm of Guadarrama undoubtedly saved Moore and the English army.

"Was it then decreed," groans Thiers, "that we, who were always successful against combined Europe, should on no single occasion prevail against those implacable foes?"

No. 8.

Other letters of this date are headed Madrid.

Kourakin.—Alexander Kourakin was the new Russian Ambassador at Paris, removed thence from Vienna to please Napoleon, and to replace Tolstoi, who, according to Savary, was always quarrelling with French officers on military points, but who could hardly be so narrow-minded a novice on these points as his namesake of today. This matter had been arranged at Erfurt.

No. 9.

The English appear to have received reinforcements.—Imagine a Transvaal with a population of ten millions, and one has a fair idea of the French difficulties in Spain, even without Portugal. The Spaniards could not fight a scientific battle like Jena or Friedland, but they were incomparable at guerrilla warfare. The *Memoirs* of Barons Marbot and Lejeune have well demonstrated this. The latter, an accomplished linguist, sent to locate Moore's army, found that to pass as an Englishman the magic words "*Damn it,*" won him complete success.

No. 10.

Benavente.—Here they found 600 horses, which had been hamstrung by the English.

The English flee panic-stricken.—The next day Napoleon writes Fouché to have songs written, and caricatures made of them, which are also to be translated into German and Italian, and circulated in Germany and Italy.

The weather is very bad.—Including 18 degrees of frost. Savary says they had never felt the cold so severe in Poland and that they ran a risk of being buried in the snow. The Emperor had to march on foot and was very much tired.

"On these occasions," adds Savary, "the Emperor was not self-

244

ish, as people would have us believe … he shared his supper [27] and his fire with all who accompanied him: he went so far as to make those eat whom he saw in need of it."

Napier gives other details:

Napoleon, on December 22nd, has 50,000 men at the foot of the Guadarrama. A deep snow choked the passes of the Sierra, and after twelve hours' toil the advanced guards were still on the wrong side: the general commanding reported the road impracticable, but Napoleon, dismounting, placed himself at the head of the column, and amidst storms of hail and driving snow, led his soldiers over the mountain.

At the passage of the Esla Moore escapes Napoleon by twelve hours. Marbot, as usual, gives picturesque details. Officers and men marched with locked arms, the Emperor between Lannes and Duroc. Half-way up, the marshals and generals, who wore jack-boots, could go no further. Napoleon, however, got hoisted on to a gun, and bestrode it: the marshals and generals did the same, and in this grotesque order they reached, after four hours' toil, the convent at the summit.

Lefebvre.—As they neared Benavente the slush became frightful, and the artillery could not keep pace. General Lefebvre- Desnouette went forward, with the horse regiment of the Guard, forded the Esla with four squadrons, was outnumbered by the English (3000 to 300), but he and sixty (Lejeune, who escaped, says a hundred) of his *chasseurs* were captured. He was brought in great triumph to Sir John Moore.

"That general," says Thiers, "possessed the courtesy characteristic of all great nations; he received with the greatest respect the brilliant general who commanded Napoleon's light cavalry, seated him at his table, and presented him with a magnificent Indian sabre."

No. 11.

Probably written from Astorga, where he arrived on January 1st, having brought 50,000 men two hundred miles in ten days.

Your letters.—These probably, and others received by a courier, decided him to let Soult follow the English to Corunna—especially as he knew that transports were awaiting the enemy there. He himself prepares to return, for Fouché and Talleyrand are in league, the slim and slippery Metternich is ambassador at Paris, Austria is arming, and

---

27. With Lejeune on one occasion.

the whole political horizon, apparently bright at Erfurt, completely overcast. Murat, balked of the Crown of Spain, is now hoping for that of France if Napoleon is killed or assassinated. It is Talleyrand and Fouché who have decided on Murat, and on the ultimate overthrow of the Beauharnais.

Unfortunately for their plans Eugène is apprised by Lavalette, and an incriminating letter to Murat captured and sent post-haste to Napoleon. This, says Pasquier, undoubtedly hastened the Emperor's return. Ignoring the complicity of Fouché, the whole weight of his anger falls on Talleyrand, who loses the post of High Chamberlain, which he had enjoyed since 1804. For half-an-hour this "arch-apostate," as Lord Rosebery calls him, receives a torrent of invectives.

> You are a thief, a coward, a man without honour; you do not believe in God; you have all your life been a traitor to your duties; you have deceived and betrayed everybody: nothing is sacred to you; you would sell your own father. I have loaded you down with gifts, and there is nothing that you would not undertake against me. Thus, for the past ten months, you have been shameless enough, because you supposed, rightly or wrongly, that my affairs in Spain were going astray, to say to all who would listen to you that you always blamed my undertaking there, whereas it was yourself who first put it into my head, and who persistently urged it. And that man, *that unfortunate* (he was thus designating the Duc d'Enghien), by whom was I advised of the place of his residence? Who drove me to deal cruelly with him? What then are you aiming at? What do you wish for? What do you hope? Do you dare to say? You deserve that I should smash you like a wine-glass. I can do it, but I despise you too much to take the trouble.

This we are assured by the impartial Pasquier, who heard it from an ear-witness, and second-hand from Talleyrand, is an abstract of what Napoleon said, and to which the ex-Bishop made no reply.

No. 12.

The English are in utter rout.—Still little but dead men and horses fell into his hands. Savary adds the interesting fact that all the (800) dead cavalry horses had a foot missing, which the English had to show their officers to prove that they had not sold their horses. Scott, on barely sufficient evidence perhaps, states, "The very treasure-chests of the army were thrown away and abandoned. There was never so complete an example of a disastrous retreat." The fact seems to have been that the soldiership was bad, but Moore's generalship excellent. Napier writes:

> No wild horde of Tartars ever fell with more license upon their rich effeminate neighbours than did the English troops upon the Spanish towns taken by storm.

What could be expected of such men in retreat, when even Lord Melville had just said in extenuation of our army that the worst men make the best soldiers?

Nos. 13 and 14.

Written at Valladolid. Here he received a deputation asking that his brother may reside in Madrid, to which he agrees, and awaits its arrangement before setting out for Paris.

At Valladolid he met De Pradt, whom he mistrusted; but who, like Talleyrand, always amused him. In the present case the *Abbé* told him that "the Spaniards would never thank him for interfering in their behalf, and that they were like Sganarelle in the farce, who quarrelled with a stranger for interfering with her husband when he was beating her" (Scott's "Napoleon").

He leaves Valladolid January 17th, and is in Paris on January 24th. He rode the first seventy miles, to Burgos, in five and a half hours, stopping only to change horses.[28] Well might Savary say, "Never had a sovereign ridden at such a speed."

Eugène has a daughter.—The Princess Eugnie-Hortense, born December 23rd at Milan; married the hereditary Prince of Hohenzollern Hechingen.

They are foolish in Paris—if not worse. Talleyrand, Fouché, and others were forming what amounted to a conspiracy, and the Empress herself, wittingly or unwittingly, had served as their tool. For the first time she answers a deputation of the *Corps Législatif*, who come to congratulate her on her husband's victories, and says that doubtless his Majesty would be very sensible of the homage of an assembly *which represents the nation*. Napoleon sees in this remark a germ of aggression on behalf of his House of Commons, more especially when emphasised by 125 blackballs against a Government Bill. He takes the effective but somewhat severe step of contradicting his wife in the *Moniteur*, or rather declaring that the Empress knew the laws too well not to know that the Emperor was the chief representative of the

---

28. *Biographie Universelle*. Michaud says ponies.

People, then the Senate, and last the *Corps Législatif.*

It would be a wild and even criminal assertion to try to represent the nation before the Emperor.

All through the first half of 1809 another dangerous plot, of which the centre was the Princess of Tour and Taxis, had its threads far and wide. Many of Soult's generals were implicated, and in communication with the English, preventing their commander getting news of Wellesley's movements (Napier). When they find Soult cannot be traduced, they lend a willing ear to stirring up strife between the Emperor and Soult, by suggesting that the latter should be made King of Portugal. Madame d'Abrantès, who heard in 1814 that the idea had found favour with English statesmen, thinks such a step would have seriously injured Napoleon (vol. 4. 53).

SERIES L
1809.

The dangers surrounding Napoleon were immense. The Austrian army, 320,000 strong (with her *Landwehr*, 544,000 men) and 800 cannon, had never been so great, never so fitted for war. Prussia was already seething with secret societies, of which as yet the only formidable one was the Tugendbund, whose headquarters were Konigsburg, and whose chief members were Stein, Stadion, Blucher, Jahn. Perhaps their most sensible scheme was to form a united German empire, with the Archduke Charles [29] as its head. The Archduke Ferdinand invaded the Duchy of Warsaw, and had he taken Thorn with its park of 100 cannon, Prussia was to join Austria. In Italy the Carbonari and Adelphes [30] only waited for the French troops to go north to meet the Austrians to spread revolt in Italy.

Of the former the head lodge was at Capua and its constitutions written in English, since England was aiding this *chouanerie religieuse* as a lever against Napoleon. England had an army of 40,000 men ready to embark in any direction—to Holland, Belgium, Naples, or Biscay,

---

29. This Archduke was the "international man" at this juncture. Louis Bonaparte speaks of a society at Saragossa, of which the object was to make the Archduke Charles king of Spain.

30. These Adelphes or Philadelphes were the socialists or educated anarchists of that day. They wished for the *statu quo* before Napoleon became supreme ruler. They had members in his army, and it seems quite probable that Bernadotte gave them passive support. General Oudet was their recognised head, and he died under suspicious circumstances after Wagram. The society was, unlike the Carbonari, anti-Catholic.

while the French troops in Portugal were being tampered with to receive Moreau as their leader, and to march with Spaniards and English for the Pyrenees. At Paris Talleyrand was in partial disgrace, but he and Fouché were still plotting—the latter, says Pelet, forwarding daily a copy of the private bulletin (prepared for Napoleon's eye alone) to the Bourbons. After Essling and the breaking of the Danube bridge, he hesitated between seizing supreme power himself or offering it to Bernadotte.

Up to the last—up to March 27th—the *Correspondence* proves that Napoleon had hoped that war would be averted through the influence of Russia. "All initiative," he declared, "rested on the heads of the court of Austria."

> Menaced on all sides; warned of the intentions of his enemies by their movements and by their intercepted correspondence; seeing from that moment hostilities imminent, he wishes to prove to France and Europe that all the wrongs are on their side, and awaits in his capital the news of an aggression that nothing justifies, nothing warrants. Vain prudence! Europe will accuse him of having been the instigator on every occasion, even in this.[31]

On April 8th the Austrians violated Bavarian territory, and during his supreme command for the next five days Berthier endangered the safety of the French empire in spite of the most elaborate and lucid instructions from Napoleon, which he failed to comprehend.

"Never," says Pelet, "was so much written, never so little done. Each of his letters (Berthier's) attests the great difference which existed between his own correspondence and that which was dictated to him." An ideal chief of staff, he utterly lacked the decision necessary for a commander-in-chief. The arrival of Napoleon changed in a moment the position of affairs. "The sudden apparition of the Emperor produced the effect of the head of Medusa, and paralysed the enemy."[32]

Within five days the Austrians were four times defeated, and Ratisbon, the *passe-partout* of Southern Germany and half-way house between Strasburg and Vienna, is once more in the hands of France and her allies. Pelet considers these operations as the finest which have been executed either in ancient or modern times, at any rate those of which the projects are authentically proved. He foretells that military

31. Pelet, vol. 1. 127.
32. Pelet, vol. 1. 282.

men from every country of Europe, but specially young Frenchmen, will religiously visit the fields of the Laber. They will visit, with Napoleon's *Correspondence* in their hands, "much more precious than every other commentary, the hills of Pfaffenhofen, the bridge of Landshut, and that of Eckmühl, the mill of Stangl, and the woods of Roking."

A few days later the Archduke Charles writes a letter to Napoleon, which is a fair type of those charming yet stately manners which made him at that moment the most popular man in Europe.

> "Sire," he writes, "your Majesty's arrival was announced to me by the thunder of artillery, without giving me time to compliment you thereon. Scarcely advised of your presence, I was made sensible of it by the losses which you have caused me. You have taken many of my men, Sire; my troops also have made some thousands of prisoners in places where you did not direct the operations. I propose to your Majesty to exchange them man for man, grade for grade, and if that offer is agreeable to you, please let me know your intentions for the place destined for the exchange. I feel flattered, sire, in fighting against the greatest captain of the age. I should be more happy if destiny had chosen me to procure for my country the benefit of a lasting peace. Whichsoever they be, the events of war or the approach of peace, I beg your Majesty to believe that my desires always carry me to meet you, and that I hold myself equally honoured in finding the sword, or the olive branch, in the hand of your Majesty."

No. 1.

Donauwerth.—On the same day Napoleon writes almost an identical letter to Cambacérès, adding, however, the news that the Tyrolese are in full revolt.

On April 20th he placed himself at the head of the Wurtembergers and Bavarians at Abensburg. He made a stirring speech (No. 15,099 of *Correspondence*), and Lejeune tells us that the Prince Royal of Bavaria translated into German one sentence after another as the Emperor spoke, and officers repeated the translations throughout the ranks.

On April 24th is issued from Ratisbon his proclamation to the army:—

> Soldiers, you have justified my expectations. You have made up for your number by your bravery. You have gloriously marked the difference between the soldiers of Caesar and the armed

cohorts of Xerxes. In a few days we have triumphed in the pitched battles of Thann, Abensberg, and Eckmühl, and in the combats of Peising, Landshut, and Ratisbon. A hundred cannon, forty flags, fifty thousand prisoners.... Before a month we shall be at Vienna.

It was within three weeks! He was specially proud of Eckmühl, and we are probably indebted to a remark of Pasquier for his chief but never divulged reason.

A noteworthy fact in connection with this battle was that the triumphant army was composed principally of Bavarians and Wurtembergers. Under his direction, these allies were as greatly to be feared as the French themselves.

At St. Helena was written:

The battle of Abensberg, the manoeuvres of Landshut, and the battle of Eckmühl were the most brilliant and the most skilful manoeuvres of Napoleon.

Eckmühl ended with a fine exhibition of a "white arm" *mêlée* by moonlight, in which the French proved the superiority of their double *cuirasses* over the breastplates of the Austrians. Pelet gives this useful abstract of the Campaign of Five Days:—

April 19th.—Union of the French army whilst fighting the Archduke, whose base is already menaced.

April 20th.—Napoleon, at Abensburg and on the banks of the Laber, breaks the Austrian line, totally separating the centre from the left, which he causes to be turned by Massena.

April 21st.—He destroys their left wing at Landshut, and captures the magazines, artillery, and train, as well as the communications of the enemy's grand army, fixing definitely his own line of operations, which he already directs on Vienna.

April 22nd.—He descends the Laber to Eckmiihl, gives the last blow to the Archduke's army, of which the remnant takes refuge in Ratisbon.

April 23rd.—He takes that strong place, and forces the Archduke to take refuge in the mountains of Bohemia.

No. 2.

May 6th. On May 1st Napoleon was still at Braunau, waiting for news from Davoust. Travelling by night at his usual speed he reached

Lambach at noon on May 2nd, and Wels on the 3rd. The next morning he heard Massena's cannon at Ebersberg, but reaches the field at the fall of night—too late to save the heavy cost of Massena's frontal attack. The French lost at least 1500 killed and wounded; the Austrians (under Hiller) the same number killed and 7000 prisoners. Pelet defends Massena, and quotes the bulletin of May 4th (omitted from the *Correspondence*): "It is one of the finest feats of arms of which history can preserve the memory! The traveller will stop and say, ' It is here, it is here, in these superb positions, that an army of 35,000 Austrians was routed by two French divisions'"(Pelet, 2. 225). Lejeune, and most writers, blame Massena, referring to the Emperor's letter of May 1st in Pelet's Appendix (vol. 2.), but not in the *Correspondence*.

Between April 17th and May 6th there is no letter to Josephine preserved, but plenty to Eugène, and all severe—not so much for incapacity as for not keeping the Emperor advised of what was really happening. On May 6th he had received no news for over a week.

The ball that touched me—*i.e.* at Ratisbon. This was the second time Napoleon had been wounded in battle—the first time by an English bayonet at Toulon. On the present occasion (April 23rd) Méneval seems to be the best authority: "Napoleon was seated on a spot from which he could see the attack on the town of Ratisbon. He was beating the ground with his riding-whip,[33] when a bullet, supposed to have been fired from a Tyrolean carbine, struck him on the big toe (Marbot says 'right ankle,' which is correct). The news of his wound spread rapidly[34] from file to file, and he was forced to mount on horseback to show himself to his troops. Although his boot had not been cut the contusion was a very painful one," and in the first house he went to for a moment's rest, he fainted.

The next day, however, he saw the wounded and reviewed his troops as usual, and Lejeune has preserved a highly characteristic story, somewhat similar to an experience of the Great Frederick's: When he had reached the seventh or eighth sergeant the Emperor noticed a handsome young fellow with fine but stern-looking eyes and of resolute and martial bearing, who made his musket ring again as he presented arms. 'How many wounds?' inquired the Emperor.

"'Thirty,' replied the sergeant.

"'I am not asking you your age,' said the Emperor graciously; 'I am asking how many wounds you have received.'

---

33. "Gaily asking his staff to breakfast with him" (Pelet).
34. Lejeune says "some hours afterwards."

"Raising his voice, the sergeant again replied with the one word, 'Thirty.'

"Annoyed at this reply, the Emperor turned to the colonel and said, 'The man does not understand; he thinks I am asking about his age.'

"'He understands well enough, sire,' was the reply; 'he has been wounded thirty times.'

"'What!' exclaimed the Emperor, 'you have been wounded so often and have not got the cross!'

"The sergeant looked down at his chest, and seeing that the strap of his cartridge-pouch hid his decoration, he raised it so as to show the cross. He said to the Emperor, with great earnestness, 'Yes, I've got one; but I've merited a dozen!'

"The Emperor, who was always pleased to meet spirited fellows such as this, pronounced the sacramental words, 'I make you an officer!'

"'That's right, Emperor,' said the new sub-lieutenant as he proudly drew himself up; 'you couldn't have done better!'"

No. 3.

Almost an exact duplicate of this letter goes on to Paris to Cambacérès, as also of No. 4. The moment the Emperor had heard that the Archduke had left Budweiss and was going by the circuitous route *via* Krems to Vienna, he left Enns (May 7th) and reached Moelk the same evening. Seeing a camp of the enemy on the other side of the river he sends Marbot with a sergeant and six picked men to kidnap a few Austrians during the night. The foray is successful, and three are brought before Napoleon, one weeping bitterly. The Emperor asked the reason, and found it was because he had charge of his master's girdle, and would be thought to have robbed him. The Emperor had him set free and ferried across the river, saying, "We must honour and aid virtue wherever it shows itself."

The next day he started for Saint-Polten (already evacuated by Hiller). On his way he saw the ruins of Dirnstein Castle, where Richard Coeur de Lion had been imprisoned. The Emperor's comments were interesting, but are now hackneyed, and are in most histories and memoirs—the parent source being Pelet (vol. 2 246).

No. 4.

Schoenbrunn, situated a mile from Vienna, across the little river of that name. Constant thus describes it:

Built in 1754 by the Empress Marie Thérèse, Schoenbrunn had

an admirable position; its architecture, if defective and irregular, was yet of a majestic, imposing type. To reach it one has to cross the bridge across the little river Vienna. Four stone sphinxes ornament this bridge, which is very large and well built. Facing the bridge there is a handsome gate opening on to a large courtyard, spacious enough for seven or eight thousand men to manoeuvre in. The courtyard is in the form of a quadrangle surrounded by covered galleries and ornamented with two large basins, in which are marble statues. On both sides of the gateway are two huge obelisks of pink stone surmounted by gilt eagles.

In German, Schoenbrunn means 'fair spring,' and the name is derived from a fresh and sparkling spring which is situated in the park. It wells forth from a little mound on which a tiny grotto has been built, carved within so as to resemble stalactites. Inside the grotto is a recumbent *naiad* holding a horn, from which the water falls down into a marble basin. In summer this little nook is deliciously cool.

The interior of the palace merits nothing but praise. The furniture is sumptuous, and in taste both original and distinguished. The Emperor's bedroom (the only place in the whole edifice where there was a chimney) was upholstered in Chinese lacquer-wood of great antiquity, yet the painting and gilding were still quite fresh. The study adjoining was decorated in a like way. All these apartments, except the bedroom, were heated in winter by immense stoves, which sadly spoilt the effect of the other furniture. Between the study and the bedroom there was a strange apparatus called a 'flying chair,' a sort of mechanical seat, which had been constructed for the Empress Marie Thérèse, and which served to transport her from one floor to another, so that she was not obliged to go up and down the staircase like everyone else. The machine was worked in the same way as at theatres, by cords, pulleys, and a counter-weight.

The Emperor drank a glassful from the beautiful spring, Schoen Brunn, every morning. Napoleon found the people of Vienna less favourable to the French than in 1805; and Count Rapp told him "the people were everywhere tired of us and of our victories." "He did not like these sort of reflections."

May 12th.—On May 13th is dated the *seventh* bulletin of the army of Germany, but none of the Bulletins 2 to 6 are in the *Correspondence*.

It states that on the 10th he is before Vienna; the Archduke Maximilian refuses to surrender; on the 11th, at 9 p.m., the bombardment commences, and by daybreak the city capitulated, and the Archduke fled. In his proclamation Napoleon blamed him and the house of Austria for the bombardment.

> While fleeing from the city, their *adieux* to the inhabitants have been murder and arson; like Medea, they have with their own hands slain their children.

The Viennese had sworn to emulate their ancestors in 1683, and the heroes of Saragossa. But Alison (than whom none can do the "big bow-wow "style better) has a thoughtful comment on what really occurred. "All history demonstrates that there is one stage of civilisation when the inhabitants of a metropolis are capable of such a sacrifice in defence of their country, and only one; and that when passed, it is never recovered. The event has proved that the Russians, in 1812, were in the state of progress when such a heroic act was possible, but that the inhabitants of Vienna and Paris had passed it. Most certainly the citizens of London would never have buried themselves under the ruins of the Bank, the Treasury, or Leadenhall Street before capitulating to Napoleon." 1870 and the siege of Paris modify this judgment; but the Prussian bombardment came only at the last, and barely reached the centre of the city.

No. 5.

Ebersdorf.—Written five days after the murderous battle of Essling. Montgaillard, whose temper and judgment, as Alison remarks, are not equal to his talents, cannot resist a covert sneer (writing under the Bourbons) at Napoleon's generalship on this occasion, although he adds a veneer by reminding us that Caesar was defeated at Dyrrachium, Turenne at Marienthal, Eugène at Denain, Frederick the Great at Kolin. The crossing of the river was one which none but a victorious army, with another[35] about to join it, could afford to risk, but which having effected, the French had to make the best of. As Napoleon said in his tenth bulletin:

> The passage of a river like the Danube, in front of an enemy knowing perfectly the localities, and having the inhabitants on its side, is one of the greatest operations of war which it is possible to conceive.

---

35. Eugène's.

The Danube hereabouts is a thousand yards broad, and thirty feet deep. But the rising of its water fourteen feet in three days was what no one had expected. At Ebersdorf the first branch of the Danube was 500 yards across to an islet, thence 340 yards across the main current to Lobau, the vast island three miles broad and nearly three miles long, separated from the farther bank by another 150 yards of Danube. Bertrand had made excellent bridges, but on the 22nd the main one was carried away by a floating mill.

Eugène . . . has completely performed the task.—At the commencement of the campaign the Viceroy was taken unprepared. The Archduke John, exactly his own age (twenty-seven), was burning with hatred of France. Eugène had the impudence, with far inferior forces, to attack him at Sacile on April 16th, but was repulsed with a loss (including prisoners) of 6000 men. It is now necessary to retire, and the Archduke follows him leisurely, almost within sight of Verona. By the end of April the news of Eckmühl has reached both armies, and by May 1st the Austrians are in full retreat.

As usual, Napoleon has already divined their altered plan of campaign, and writes from Braunau on this very day:

I doubt not that the enemy may have retired before you; it is necessary to pursue him with activity, whilst coming to join me as soon as possible *via* Carinthia. The junction with my army will probably take place beyond Bruck. It is probable I shall be at Vienna by the 10th to the 15th of May.

It is the successful performance of this task of joining him and of driving back the enemy to which Napoleon alludes in the letter. The Viceroy had been reproved for fighting at Sacile without his cavalry, for his precipitous retreat on Verona; and only two days earlier the Emperor had told him that if affairs went worse he was to send for the King of Naples (Murat) to take command:

I am no longer grieved at the blunders you have committed, but because you do not write to me, and give me no chance of advising you, and even of regulating my own affairs here conformably.

On May 8th Eugène defeats the Austrians on the Piave, and the Archduke John loses nearly 10,000 men and 15 cannon. Harassed in their retreat, they regain their own territory on May 14th—the day after the capitulation of Vienna. Henceforward Eugène with part of the army, and Macdonald with the rest, force their way past all difficulties, so that when the junction with the Grand Army occurs at Bruck, Napoleon sends (May 27th) the following proclamation:

> Soldiers of the army of Italy, you have gloriously attained the goal that I marked out for you. . . . Surprised by a perfidious enemy before your columns were united, you had to retreat to the Adige. But when you received the order to advance, you were on the memorable fields of Arcola, and there you swore on the manes of our heroes to triumph. You have kept your word at the battle of the Piave, at the combats of San-Daniel, Tarvis, and Goritz; you have taken by assault the forts of Malborghetto, of Prediel, and made the enemy's divisions, entrenched in Prewald and Laybach, surrender. You had not then passed the Drave, and already 25,000 prisoners, 60 cannon, and 10 flags signalised your valour.

This is the proclamation alluded to in this letter to Josephine.

No. 6.

May 29th.—The date is wrong; it should be May 19th or 24th, probably the latter. It sets at rest the vexed question how the Danube bridge was broken, and seems to confirm Marbot's version of a floating mill on fire, purposely sent down by an Austrian officer of *Jägers*, who won the rare order of Maria Theresa thereby—for performing *more* than his duty. Bertrand gained his Emperor's lifelong admiration by his expedients at this time. Everything had to be utilised—anchors for the boat bridges were made by filling fishermen's baskets with bullets; and a naval contingent of 1200 bluejackets from Antwerp proved invaluable.

No. 7.

I have ordered the two princes to re-enter France.—After so critical a battle as the battle of Essling the Emperor's first thoughts were concerning his succession—had he been killed or captured. He was therefore seriously annoyed that the heir-apparent and his younger brother had both been taken out of the country without his permission. He therefore writes the Queen of Holland on May 28th from Ebersdorf:

> My daughter, I am seriously annoyed that you have left France without my permission, and especially that you have taken my nephews out of it. Since you are at Baden stay there, but an hour after receiving the present letter send my two nephews back to Strasburg to be near the Empress—they ought never to go out of France. It is the first time I have had reason to be

annoyed with you, but you should not dispose of my nephews without my permission, you should realise what a bad effect it will have. Since the waters at Baden are doing you good you can stay there a few days, but, I repeat, lose not a moment in sending my nephews back to Strasburg. If the Empress is going to the waters at Plombières they may accompany her there, but they must never pass the bridge of Strasburg.—Your affectionate father,   Napoleon.

This letter passed through the hands of Josephine at Strasburg, who was so unhappy at not having heard from her husband that she opened it, and writes to Hortense on June 1st when forwarding the letter:

I advise you to write to him immediately that you have anticipated his intentions, and that your children are with me: that you have only had them a few days in order to see them, and to give them a change of air. The page who is announced in Méneval's letter has not yet arrived. I hope he will bring me a letter from the Emperor, and that at least he will not be as vexed with me for your being at Baden. Your children have arrived in excellent health.

The Duke of Montebello, who died this morning.—The same day he writes to *La Maréchale* as follows:—

Ma Cousine, The Marshal died this morning of the wounds that he received on the field of honour. My sorrow equals yours. I lose the most distinguished general in my whole army, my comrade-in-arms for sixteen years, he whom I looked upon as my best friend. His family and children will always have a special claim on my protection. It is to give you this assurance that I wished to write you this letter, for I feel that nothing can alleviate the righteous sorrow that you will experience.

The following year he bestowed the highest honour on the *Maréchale* that she could receive.

Thus everything ends. The fourteenth bulletin says that the end was caused by a pernicious fever, and in spite of Dr. Franck, one of the best physicians in Europe. "Thus ends one of the most distinguished soldiers France ever possessed."[36] He had received thirteen wounds. The death of Lannes, and the whole of the Essling period, is best told by Marbot. The loss of Lannes was a more serious one to Napoleon

---

36. "What a loss for France and for me," groaned Napoleon, as he left his dead friend.

than the whole 20,000 men lost in this battle. The master himself has told us that "*in war men are nothing, a man is everything.*" They could be replaced: Lannes never.

Like Kléber and Desaix, he stood on a higher platform than the older Marshals—except Massena, who had serious drawbacks, and who was the only one of Napoleon's best generals that Wellington met in the Peninsula. Lannes had always the ear of the Emperor, and always told him facts, not flattery. His life had been specially crowded the last few weeks. Rebuked by Napoleon for tardiness in supporting Massena at Ebersberg, his life was saved by Napoleon himself when he was thrown from his horse into the flooded Danube; and finally, on the field of Essling, he had under his orders Bessières, the man who had a dozen years before prevented his engagement to Caroline Bonaparte by tittle-tattling to Napoleon.

No. 9.

Eugène won a battle.—The remnant of the Archduke John's army, together with Hungarian levies, in all 31,000 men, hold the entrenched camp and banks of the Raab. Eugène defeats it, with a loss of 6000 men, of whom 3700 were prisoners. Napoleon, in commemoration of the anniversary of Marengo (and Friedland) calls it the little granddaughter of Marengo.

No. 11.

The curtain of the war's final act was rung up in the twenty-fourth bulletin.

At length there exists no longer the Danube for the French army; General Count Bertrand has completed works which excite astonishment and inspire admiration. For 800 yards over the most rapid river in the world he has, in a fortnight, constructed a bridge of sixteen arches where three carriages can pass abreast.

Wagram is, according to Pelet, the masterpiece of *tactical* battles, while the five days' campaign (Thann to Ratisbon) was one long *strategic* battle. Nevertheless, respecting Wagram, had the Archduke John, with his 40,000 men, turned up, as the Archduke had more right to expect than Wellington had to expect Blucher, Waterloo might have been antedated six years.

Lasalle was a prime favourite of Napoleon, for his sure eye and active bearing. His capture of Stettin with two regiments of hussars was

259

specially noteworthy. Like Lannes he had a strong premonition of his death. Marbot tells a story of how Napoleon gave him 200,000 *francs* to get married with. A week later the Emperor asked, "When is the wedding?"

"As soon as I have got some money to furnish with, sire."

"Why, I gave you 200,000 *francs* to furnish with last week! What have you done with them?"

"Paid my debts with half, and lost the other half at cards."

Such an admission would have ruined any other general. The Emperor laughed, and merely giving a sharp tug at Lasalle's moustache, ordered Duroc to give him another 200,000.

I am sunburnt, and, as he writes Cambacérès the same day, tired out, having been sixty out of the previous seventy-two hours in the saddle.

No. 12.

Wolkersdorf.—On July 8th he writes General Clarke:

> I have the headquarters lately occupied by the craven Francis II., who contented himself with watching the whole affair from the top of a tower, ten miles from the scene of battle.

On this day also he dictated his twenty-fifth bulletin, of which the last portion is so skilfully utilised in the last scene of Act 5. in *L'Aiglon*. One concluding sentence is all that can here be quoted:

> Such is the recital of the battle of Wagram, a decisive and ever illustrious battle, where three to four hundred thousand men, twelve to fifteen hundred guns, fought for great stakes on a field of battle, studied, meditated on, and fortified by the enemy for many months.

A surfeit of bile.—His usual source of relief after extra work or worry. In this case both. Bernadotte had behaved so badly at Wagram, that Napoleon sent him to Paris with the stern rebuke, "A bungler like you is no good to me." But as usual his anger against an old comrade is short-lived, and he gives General Clarke permission to send Bernadotte to command at Antwerp against the English.

No. 16.

My affairs follow my wishes.—In Austria, possibly, but not elsewhere. Prussia was seething with conspiracy, Russia with ill-concealed hatred, the English had just landed in Belgium, and Wellesley had just won Talavera. Souk was apparently no longer trustworthy, Bernadotte a conceited boaster, who had to be publicly snubbed (see The Order of the Day, August 5th, No. 15,614). Clarke and Cambacérès are so slow that Napoleon writes them (August 10th) "not to let the English come and take you in bed." Fouché shows more energy than everyone else put together, calls out National Guards, and sends them off to meet the northern invasion. The Minister of the Interior, M. Cretet, had just died, and the Emperor had wisely put Fouché, the most competent man available, into his place for the time being.

No. 17.

August 21st.—The list of birthday honours (August 15th) had been a fairly long one, Berthier becoming Prince of Wagram, Massena of Essling, Davoust of Eckmühl. Marshals Oudinot and Macdonald, Generals Clarke, Reynier, Gaudin and Champagny, as also M. Maret, became Dukes. Marmont had already, says Savary, been made delirious with the joy of possessing a baton.

No. 18.

Comedians.—Napoleon found relaxation more after his own heart in conversing with the savants of Germany, including the great mechanic Mäelzel, with whose automaton chess-player he played a game. Constant gives a highly-coloured picture of the sequel:

> The automaton was seated before a chess-board, and the Emperor, taking a chair opposite the figure, said laughingly, 'Now, my friend, we'll have a game.' The automaton, bowing, made signs for the Emperor to begin. After two or three moves the Emperor made a wrong one on purpose; the automaton bowed and replaced the piece on the board. His Majesty cheated again, when the automaton bowed again, but this time took the pawn.
>
> 'Quite right,' said His Majesty, as he promptly cheated for the third time. The automaton then shook its head, and with one sweep of its hand knocked all the chessmen down.

Women . . . not having been presented.—One woman, however, the mistress of Lord Paget, was quite willing to be presented at a late hour and to murder him at the same time—at least so says Constant.

No. 19.

All this is very suspicious.—For perfectly natural reasons Caesar's wife was now above suspicion, but Caesar himself was not so. Madame Walewski had been more than a month at Schoenbrunn, and on

May 4th, 1810, Napoleon has a second son born, who fifty years later helped to edit his father's *Correspondence*.

No. 20.

Krems.—He left here to review Davoust's corps on the field of Austerlitz. Afterwards all the generals dined with him, and the Emperor said, "This is the second time I come upon the field of Austerlitz; shall I come to it a third time?"

"Sire," replied one, "from what we see every day none dare wager that you will not!"

It was this suppressed hatred that probably determined the Emperor to dismantle the fortifications of Vienna, an act that intensified the hatred of the Viennese more than his allowing the poor people to help themselves to wood for the winter in the imperial forests had mollified them.

My health has never been better.—His reason for this remark is found in his letter to Cambacérès of the same date, "They have spread in Paris the rumour that I was ill, I know not why; I was never better." The reason of the rumour was that Corvisart had been sent for to Vienna, as there had been an outbreak of dysentery among the troops. This was kept a profound secret from France, and Napoleon even allowed Josephine to think that Corvisart had attended him (see Letter 22).

No. 23.

October 14th—Two days before, Stabs, the young Tugendbundist and an admirer of Joan of Arc, had attempted to assassinate Napoleon on parade with a carving-knife. The Emperor's letter to Fouché of the 12th October gives the most succinct account:—

A youth of seventeen, son of a Lutheran minister of Erfurt, sought to approach me on parade today. He was arrested by the officers, and as the little man's agitation had been noticed, suspicion was aroused; he was searched, and a dagger found upon him. I had him brought before me, and the little wretch, who seemed to me fairly well educated, told me that he wished to assassinate me to deliver Austria from the presence of the French. I could distinguish in him neither religious nor political fanaticism. He did not appear to know exactly who or what Brutus was. The fever of excitement he was in prevented our knowing more. He will be examined when he has cooled down and fasted. It is possible that it will come to nothing. He will be arraigned before a military commission.

I wished to inform you of this circumstance in order that it may not be made out more important than it appears to be. I hope it will not leak out; if it does, we shall have to represent the fellow as a madman. If it is not spoken of at all, keep it to yourself. The whole affair made no disturbance at the parade; I myself saw nothing of it.

P.S.—I repeat once more, and you understand clearly, that there is to be no discussion of this occurrence.

Count Rapp saved the Emperor's life on this occasion, and he, Savary, and Constant, all give detailed accounts. Their narratives are a remarkable object-lesson of the carelessness of the average contemporary spectator in recording dates. Savary gives vaguely the end of September, Constant October 13th, and Count Rapp October 23rd. In the present case the date of this otherwise trivial incident is important, for careless historians assert that it influenced Napoleon in concluding peace. In any case it would have taken twenty such occurrences to affect Napoleon one hairbreadth, and in the present instance his letter of October 10th to the Russian Emperor proves that the Peace was already settled—all but the signing.

No. 24.

Stuttgard.—General Rapp describes this journey as follows:

Peace was ratified. We left Nymphenburg and arrived at Stuttgard. Napoleon was received in a style of magnificence, and was lodged in the palace together with his suite. The King was laying out a spacious garden, and men who had been condemned to the galleys were employed to labour in it. The Emperor asked the King who the men were who worked in chains; he replied that they were for the most part rebels who had been taken in his new possessions. We set out on the following day. On the way Napoleon alluded to the unfortunate wretches whom he had seen at Stuttgard. 'The King of Würtemberg,'said he, 'is a very harsh man; but he is very faithful. Of all the sovereigns in Europe he possesses the greatest share of understanding.'

We stopped for an hour at Rastadt, where the Princess of Baden and Princess Stephanie had arrived for the purpose of paying their respects to the Emperor. The Grand Duke and Duchess accompanied him as far as Strasburg. On his arrival in that city he received despatches which again excited his displeasure against the Faubourg St. Germain. We proceeded to Fontainebleau; no preparations had been made for the Emperor's reception; there was not even a guard on duty.

This was on October 26th, at 10 a.m. Méneval asserts that Napoleon's subsequent bad temper was feigned. In any case, the meeting that moment so impatiently awaited—was a very bad *quart d'heure* for Josephine, accentuated doubtless by Fouché's report of bad conduct on the part of the ladies of St. Germain.

SERIES M

No. 1.

According to the *Correspondence of Napoleon I.*, No. 16,058, the date of this letter is December 17th. It seems, however, possible that it is the letter written immediately after his arrival at Trianon, referred to by Méneval, who was, in fact, responsible for it. Thiers, working from unpublished memoirs of Hortense and Cambacérès, gives a most interesting account of the family council, held at 9 p.m. on Friday, December 15th, at the Tuileries. Constant also describes the scene, but gives the Empress credit for showing the most self-command of those chiefly interested. The next day, 11 a.m., Count Lacépède introduced the resolutions of the family council to the Senatus-Consultus. [37] "It is today that, more than ever before, the Emperor has proved that he wishes to reign only to serve his subjects, and that the Empress has merited that posterity should associate her name with that of Napoleon."

He pointed out that thirteen of Napoleon's predecessors had broken the bonds of matrimony in order to fulfil better those of sovereign, and that among these were the most admired and beloved of French monarchs—Charlemagne, Philip Augustus, Louis XII. and Henry IV. This speech and the Decrees (carried by 76 votes to 7) are found in the *Moniteur* of December 17th, which Napoleon considers sufficiently authentic to send to his brother Joseph as a full account of what occurred, and with no further comment of his own but that it was the step which he thought it his duty to take. The Decrees of the

---

37. By here subordinating himself to the Senate, the Emperor was preparing a rod for his own back hereafter. 38. This clause gives considerable trouble to Lacépède and Regnauld. They cannot even find a precedent whether, if they met, Josephine or Marie Louise would take precedence of the other.

Committee of the Senate were:—

(1) The marriage contracted between the Emperor Napoleon and the Empress Josephine is dissolved. (2) The Empress Josephine will retain the titles and rank of a crowned Empress-Queen. [38] (3) Her jointure is fixed at an annual revenue of £80,000 from the public treasury. [39] (4) Every provision which may be made by the Emperor in favour of the Empress Josephine, out of the funds of the Civil List, shall be obligatory on his successors.

They added separate addresses to the Emperor and Empress, and that to the latter seems worthy of quotation:—

Your Imperial and Royal Majesty is about to make for France the greatest of sacrifices; history will preserve the memory of it forever. The august spouse of the greatest of monarchs cannot be united to his immortal glory by more heroic devotion. For long, Madame, the French people has revered your virtues; it holds dear that loving kindness which inspires your every word, as it directs your every action; it will admire your sublime devotion; it will award for ever to your Majesty, Empress and Queen, the homage of gratitude, respect, and love.

From a letter of Eugène's to his wife, quoted by Aubenas, it appears that he, with his mother, arrived at Malmaison on Saturday evening,[40] December 16th, and that it never ceased raining all the next day, which added to the general depression, in spite of, or because of, Eugène's bad puns. On the evening of the 16th Napoleon was at Trianon, writing letters, and we cannot think that if the Emperor had been to Malmaison on the Sunday,[41] Eugène would have included this without comment in the "some visits "they had received. The Emperor, as we see from the next letter, paid Josephine a visit on the Monday.

No. 2.

The date of this is Tuesday, December 19th, while No. 3 is Wednes-

---

39. In addition to this, Napoleon gives her £40,000 a year from his privy purse, but keeps most of it back for the first two years to pay her 120 creditors. (For interesting details see Masson, *Josephine Repudiée*.)

40. Which agrees with Madame d'Avrillon, who says they left the Tuileries at 2.30. Méneval says Napoleon left for Trianon a few hours later. Savary writes erroneously that they left the following morning.

41. M. Masson seems to indicate a visit on December 16th, but does not give his authority (*Josephine Repudiée*, 114)

day the 20th.

Savary, always unpopular with the Court ladies, has now nothing but kind words for Josephine.

> She quitted the Court, but the Court did not quit her; it had always loved her, for never had anyone been so kind. . . . She never injured anyone in the time of her power; she protected even her enemies—(*such as Fouché at this juncture.*)

And Lucien earlier:

> During her stay at Malmaison, the highroad from Paris to this *château* was only one long procession, in spite of the bad weather; every one considered it a duty to present themselves at least once a week.

Later, Marie Louise became jealous of this, and poor Josephine had to go to the *château* of Navarre, and finally to leave France.

Queen of Naples.—For some reason Napoleon had not wanted this sister at Paris this winter, and had written her to this effect from Schoenbrunn on October 15th:

> If you were not so far off, and the season so advanced, I would have asked Murat to spend two months in Paris. But you cannot be there before December, which is a horrible season, especially for a Neapolitan.[42]

But sister Caroline, "with the head of a Cromwell on the shoulders of a pretty woman," was not easy to lead; and her husband had in consequence to bear the full weight of the Emperor's displeasure. Murat's finances were in disorder, and Napoleon wrote Champagny on December 30th to tell Murat plainly that if the borrowed money was not returned to France, it would be taken by main force. [43]

The hunt.—In pouring rain, in the forest of St. Germain.

No. 4.

Thursday, December 21st, is the date.

The weather is very damp.—Making Malmaison as unhealthy as its very name warranted, and rendering more difficult the task which Madame de Rémusat had set herself of resting Josephine mentally by tiring her physically. This typical toady—Napoleon's Eavesdropper Extraordinary—had arrived at Malmaison on December 18th. She writes on the Friday (December 22nd), beseeching her husband to advise the Emperor to moderate the tone of his letters, especially this

---

42. *Correspondence of Napoleon I.*, No. 15,952.
43. *New Letters of Napoleon*, 1898.

one (Thursday, December 21st), which had upset Josephine frightfully. Surely a more harmless letter was never penned.

But it is the Rémusat all over; she lives in a chronic atmosphere of suspicion that all her letters are read by the Emperor, and therefore, like Stevenson's nursery rhymes, they are always written with "one eye on the grown-up person"[44] on the grown-up person *par excellence* of France and the century. The opening of letters by the government was doubtless a blemish, which, however, Napoleon tried to neutralise by entrusting the Post Office to his wife's relative, Lavalette, a man whose ever-kind heart prevented this necessary espionage degenerating into unnecessary interference with individual rights.

No. 5.

Date probably Sunday, December 24th.

King of Bavaria.—Eugène had gone to Meaux to meet his father-in-law, who had put off the "dog's humour" which he had shown since the 16th.

No. 6.

Josephine had gone by special invitation to dine at the little Trianon with Napoleon on Christmas Day, and Madame d'Avrillon says she had a very happy day there. "On her return she told me how kind the Emperor had been to her, that he had kept her all the evening, saying the kindest things to her."

Aubenas says, "The repast was eaten in silence and gloom," but does not give his authority. Eugène, moreover, confirms Madame d'Avrillon in his letter to his wife of December 26th:

> My dear Auguste, the Emperor came on Sunday to see the Empress. Yesterday she went to Trianon to see him, and stayed to dinner. The Emperor was very kind and amiable to her, and she seemed to be much better. Everything points to the Empress being more happy in her new position, and we also.

On this Christmas Day Napoleon had his last meal with Josephine.

No. 7.

Tuileries.—His return from Trianon to this, his official residence, made the divorce more apparent to everyone.

---

44. Canon Ainger's comparison.

No. 8.

A house vacant in Paris.—This seems a hint for Josephine. She wishes to come to Paris, to the Elysée, and to try a little diplomacy of her own in favour of the Austrian match, and she sends secretly to Madame de Metternich—whose husband was absent. Eugène more officially is approaching Prince Schwartzenberg, the ambassador. Josephine, like Talleyrand, wished to heal the schism with Rome by an Austrian alliance; while Cambaceres, foreseeing a war with the power not allied by marriage, would have preferred the Russian match.

No. 9.

Thursday, January 4th.

Hortense.—Louis had tried to obtain a divorce. Cambacérès was ordered on December 22nd to summon a family council (*New Letters of Napoleon I.*, No. 234); but the wish of the King was refused (verbally, says Louis in his *Historical Documents of Holland*), whereupon he refused to agree to Josephine's divorce, but had to give way, and was present at what he calls the farewell festival given by the city of Paris to the Empress Josephine on January 1st. The ecclesiastical divorce was pronounced on January 12th.

No. 10.

January 5th. He duly visits Josephine the next day.

No. 11.

January 7th is the date.

What charms your society has.—Her repertoire of small talk and scandal. He had also lost in her his Agenda, his Journal of Paris. Still the visits are growing rarer. This long kind letter was doubtless intended to be specially so, for two days later the clergy of Paris pronounced the annulment of her marriage. This was far worse than the pronouncement by the Senate in December, as it meant to her that she and Napoleon had never been properly married at all. The Emperor, who hated divorces, and especially *divorcées*, had found great difficulty in breaking down the barriers he had helped to build, for which purpose he had to be subordinated to his own Senate, *the Pope to his own bishops.*

Seven of them allowed the annulment of the marriage of 1804 on account of (1) its secrecy, (2) the insufficiency of consent of the contracting parties, and (3) the absence of the local parish priest at the ceremony. The last reason was merely a technical one; but with respect to the first two it is only fair to admit that Napoleon had undoubtedly, and perhaps for the only time in his life, been completely "rushed," *i.e.* by the Pope and Josephine. The coronation ceremony was waiting, and the Pope, secretly solicited by Josephine, insisted on a religious marriage first and foremost. The Pope suffered forthwith, but the other bill of costs was not exacted till five years after date.

No. 12.

Wednesday, January 12th.

King of Westphalia.—Madame Durand (Napoleon and Marie Louise) says that, forced to abandon his wife (the beautiful and energetic Miss Paterson) and child, Jerome "had vowed he would never have any relations with a wife who had been thus forced upon him." For three years he lavished his attentions upon almost all the beauties of the Westphalian court. The queen, an eye-witness of this conduct, bore it with mild and forbearing dignity; she seemed to see and hear nothing; in short, her demeanour was perfect. The king, touched by her goodness, weary of his conquests, and repentant of his behaviour, was only anxious for an opportunity of altering the state of things. Happily the propitious moment presented itself. The right wing of the palace of Cassel, in which the queen's apartments were situated, took fire; alarmed by the screams of her women the queen awoke and sprang out of her bed, to be caught in the arms of the king and carried to a place of safety. From that time forth the royal couple were united and happy.

No. 13.

Saturday, January 13th.

Sensible.—This was now possible after a month's mourning. In the early days, according to Madame Rémusat, her mind often wandered, But Napoleon himself encouraged the Court to visit her, and the road to Malmaison was soon a crowded one.

As the days passed, however, life became sadly monotonous. Reading palled on Josephine, as did whist and the daily feeding of her golden pheasants and guinea-fowls. Remained "Patience!" Was it the "General" she played or the "Emperor," or did she find distraction in the "Demon"?

No. 14

D'Audenarde.—Napoleon's handsome equerry, whom Mile. d'Avrillon calls "*un homme superbe.*" His mother was Josephine's favourite *dame du palais*. Madame Lalaing, Viscountess d'Audenarde, *née*

Peyrac, was one of the old *régime* who had been ruined by the Revolution.

No. 16.

Tuesday, January 23rd.

On January 21st a Privy Council was summoned to approve of Marie Louise as their "choice of a consort, who may give an heir to the throne" (Thiers). Cambacérès, Fouché, and Murat wished for the Russian princess; Lebrun, Cardinal Fesch, and King Louis for a Saxon one; but Talleyrand, Champagny, Maret, Berthier, Fontanes were for Austria.

No. 17.

Sunday, January 28th.

No. 18.

Josephine had heard she was to be banished from Paris, and so had asked to come to the Elysée to prove the truth or otherwise of the rumour.

L'Elysée.—St. Amand gives the following interesting *précis*:

Built by the Count d'Evreux in 1718, it had belonged in succession to the Marchioness de Pompadour, to the financier Beaujon, a Croesus of the eighteenth century, and to the Duchesse de Bourbon. Having, under the Revolution, become national property, it had been hired by the caterers of public entertainments, who gave it the name of L'Elysée.

In 1803 it became the property of Murat, who, becoming King of Naples, ceded it to Napoleon in 1808.

Here Napoleon signed his second abdication, here resided Alexander I. in 1815, and here Josephine's grandson effected the *Coup d'Etat* (1851). When the Senatus-Consultus fixed the revenue of Josephine, Napoleon not only gave her whatever rights he had in Malmaison, *viz.*, at least 90 *per cent*, of the total cost, but the palace of the Elysée, its gardens and dependencies, with the furniture then in use.

The latter residence was, however, for her life only.

No. 19.

February 3rd is the date.

L'Elysée.—After the first receptions the place is far worse than Malmaison. Schwartzenberg, Talleyrand, the Princess Pauline, Berthier, even her old friend Cambacérès are giving balls,[45] while the Emperor goes nearly every night to a theatre. The carriages pass by the Elysée, but do not stop. "It is as if the palace were in quarantine, with the yellow flag floating."

No. 20.

Bessières' country-house.—M. Masson says Grignon, but unless this house is called after the *château* of that name in Provence, he must be mistaken.

No. 21.

Rambouillet.—He had taken the Court with him, and was there from February 19th to the 23rd, the date of this letter. While there he had been in the best of humours. On his return he finds it necessary to write his future wife and to her father—and to pen a legible letter to the latter gives him far more trouble than winning a battle against the Austrians, if not assisted by General Danube.

Adieu.—Sick and weary, Josephine returns to Malmaison, Friday, March 9th, and even this is not long to be hers, for the new Empress is almost already on her way. The marriage at Vienna took place on March 11th, with her uncle Charles,[46] the hero of Essling, for Napoleon's proxy; on the 13th she leaves Vienna, and on the 23rd reaches Strasbourg. On the 27th she meets Napoleon at Compiègne, spends three days with him in the *château* there, and arrives at St. Cloud on April 1st, where the civil marriage is renewed, followed by the triumphal entry into Paris, and the religious ceremony on April 2nd. This day Josephine reaches the *château* of Navarre.

SERIES N

Navarre, on the site of an old dwelling of Rollo the Sea-King, was built by Jeanne of France, Queen of Navarre, Countess of Evreux. At the time of the Revolution it belonged to the Dukes of Bouillon, and was confiscated. In February 1810, Napoleon determined to purchase it, and on March 10th instructed his secretary of state, Maret, to confer the Duchy of Navarre, purchased by letters patent, on Josephine and

---

45. See Baron Lejeune for an interesting account of a chess quadrille at a dance given by the Italian Minister, Marescalchi.

46. On this occasion Baron Lejeune sees the Archduke Charles, and remarks: "There was nothing in his quiet face with its grave and gentle expression, or in his simple, modest, unassuming manner, to denote the mighty man of war; but no one who met his eyes could doubt him to be a genius."

her heirs male. The old square building was, however, utterly unfit to be inhabited: not a window would shut, there was neither paper nor tapestry, all the wainscoting was rotten, draughts and damp everywhere, and no heating apparatus.[47]

What solace to know its beautiful situation, its capabilities? No wonder if her household, banished to such a place, sixty-five miles from the "capital of capitals," should rebel, and secessions headed by Madame Ney become for a time general. Whist and piquet soon grow stale in such a house and with such surroundings, and even *trictrac* with the old bishop of Evreux becomes tedious. Eugène as usual brings sunshine in his path, and helps to dispel the gloom caused by the idle gossip imported from Paris that Josephine is not to return to Malmaison, and the like.

No. 1.

This was Josephine's second letter, says D'Avrillon, the first being answered *vivâ voce* by Eugène.

To Malmaison.—Napoleon had promised Josephine permission to return to Malmaison, and would not recant: his new wife was, however, very jealous of Josephine, and very much hurt at her presence at Malmaison. Napoleon managed to be away from Paris for six weeks after Josephine's arrival at Malmaison.

No. 1A.

It is written in a bad style.—M. Masson, however, is loud in its praises, and adds, "*Voilà donc le protocol du tutoiement*" re-established between them in spite of the second marriage, and their correspondence re-established on the old terms.

No. 2.

This letter seems to have been taken by Eugène to Paris, and thence forwarded to the Emperor with a letter from that Prince in which he enumerates Josephine's suggestions and wishes—(1) that she will not go to Aix-la-Chapelle if other waters are suggested by Corvisart; (2) that after stopping a few days at Malmaison she will go in June for three months to the baths, and afterwards to the south of France; visit Rome, Florence, and Naples *incognito*, spend the winter at Milan, and return to Malmaison and Navarre in the spring of 1811; (3) that in

---

47. "This gloomy and forsaken *château*," says St. Amand, "whose only attraction was the half-forgotten memory of its vanished splendours, was a fit image of the woman who came to seek sanctuary there."

her absence Navarre shall be made habitable, for which fresh funds are required; (4) that Josephine wishes her cousins the Taschers to marry, one a relative of King Joseph, the other the Princess Amelie de la Leyen, niece of the Prince Primate. To this Napoleon replies from Compiègne, April 26th, that the De Leyen match with Louis Tascher may take place,[48] but that he will not interest himself in the other (Henry) Tascher, who is giddy-headed and bad-tempered.

> I consent to whatever the Empress does, but I will not confer any mark of my regard on a person who has behaved ill to me. I am very glad that the Empress likes Navarre. I am giving orders to have £12,000 which I owe her for 1810, and £12,000 for 1811 advanced to her. She will then have only the £80,000 from the public treasury to come in. . . . She is free to go to whatever spa she cares for, and even to return to Paris afterwards.

He thinks, however, she would be happier in new scenes which they had never visited together, as they had Aix-la-Chapelle. If, however, the last are the best she may go to them, for "what I desire above all is that she may keep calm, and not allow herself to be excited by the gossip of Paris." This letter goes far to soothe the poor *châtelaine* of Navarre.

No. 2A.

Two letters.—The other, now missing, may have some reference to the pictures to which he refers in his letter to Fouché the next day.

> Is it true that engravings are being published with the title of Josephine Beauharnais nee La Pagerie? If this is true, have the prints seized, and let the engravers be punished.—(*New Letters*, No. 253).

No. 3.

Probably written from Boulogne about the 25th. His northern tour with Marie Louise had been very similar to one taken in 1804, but his *entourage* found the new bride very cold and callous compared to Josephine. Leaving Paris on April 29th Napoleon's *Correspondence* till June is dated Laeken (April 30th); Antwerp (May 3rd); Bois-le-Duc; Middleburg, Gand, Bruges, Ostend (May 20th); Lille, Boulogne, Dieppe, Le Havre, Rouen (May 31st). He takes the Empress in a canal barge from Brussels to Malines and himself descends the subterranean

---

48. He endows the husband with £4000 a year, and the title of Count Tascher.

vault of the Escaut-Oise Canal, between St. Quentin and Cambrai. He is at St. Cloud on June 2nd.

Josephine has felt his wanderings less, as she has the future Emperor, her favourite grandson, with her, the little Oui-Oui, as she calls him, and for whom the damp spring weather of Holland was dangerous. She was also at Malmaison from the middle of May to June 18th. The original collection of Letters (Didot Frères, 1833) heads the letter correctly to the Empress Josephine at *Malmaison,* but the *Correspondence,* published by order of Napoleon III., gives it erroneously, to the Empress Josephine, *at the Château of Navarre* (No. 16,537).

I will come to see you.—He comes for two hours on June 13th, and makes himself thoroughly agreeable. Poor Josephine is light-headed with joy all the evening after. The meeting of the two Empresses is, however, indefinitely postponed, and Josephine had now no further reason to delay her departure. Leaving her little grandson Louis behind, she travels under the name of the Countess d'Arberg, and she is accompanied by Madame d'Audenarde and Mile, de Mackau, who left the Princess Stephanie to come to Navarre. M. Masson notes that Madame de Rémusat needs the Aix waters, and will rejoin Josephine (within a week), under pretext of service, and thus obtain her cure gratuitously. They go *via* Lyons and Geneva to Aix-les-Bains. M. Masson, who has recently made a careful and complete study of this period, describes the daily round.

> Josephine, on getting out of bed, takes conscientiously her baths and douches, then, as usual, lies down again until *déjeuner,* 11 a.m., for which the whole of the little Court are assembled at *The Palace*—wherever she lives, and however squalid the dwelling-place, her abode always bears this name. Afterwards she and her women-folk ply their interminable tapestry, while the latest novel or play (sent by Barbier from Paris) is read aloud. And so the day passes till five, when they dress for dinner at six; after dinner a ride. At nine the Empress's friends assemble in her room, Mile, de Mackau sings; at eleven everyone goes to bed.

This programme, however, varies with the weather. Here is St. Amand's version (*Dernierès Années de l'Impératrice Joséphine,* p. 237):

> A little reading in the morning, an airing (*le promenade*) afterwards, dinner at eight on account of the heat, games afterwards, and some little music; so passed existence.

No. 4.

July 8th.—On July 5th, driving along the Chambéry road, Josephine met the courier with a letter from Eugène describing the terrible fire at Prince Schwartzenberg's ball, where the Princess de la Leyen, mother of young Taschre's bride-elect, was burnt. It is noteworthy that the Emperor makes no allusion to the conflagration. As, however, this is the first letter since the end of May, others may have been lost or destroyed.

You will have seen Eugène—i.e. on his way to Milan, who arrived at Aix on July 10th. He had just been made heir to the Grand Duchy of Frankfort—a broad hint to him and to Europe that Italy would be eventually united to France under Napoleon's dynasty. This was the nadir of the Beauharnais family—*Josephine repudiée*, Hortense unqueened and unwed,[49] and Eugène's expectations dissipated, and all within a few short months. Eugène had left his wife ill at Geneva, whither Josephine goes to visit her the next day, duly reporting her visit to Napoleon in her letter of July 14th (see No. 5). Geneva was always the home of the disaffected, and so the Empress had to be specially tactful, and the De Rémusat reports:

> She speaks of the Emperor as of a brother, of the new Empress as the one who will give children to France, and if the rumours of the latter's condition be correct, I am certain she will be delighted about it.

That unfortunate daughter is coming to France—i.e. to reside when she is not at St. Leu (given to her by Napoleon) or at the waters. On the present occasion she has been at Plombières a month or more. On July 10th Napoleon instructs the Countess de Boubers to bring the Grand Duke of Berg to Paris, "whom he awaits with impatience." (*Brotonne*, 625).

No. 5.

The conduct of the King of Holland has worried me.—This was in March, and by May the crisis was still more acute and Napoleon's patience exhausted. On May 20th he writes:

> Before all things be a Frenchman and the Emperor's brother, and then you may be sure you are in the path of the true interests of Holland. Good sense and policy are necessary to the government of states, not sour unhealthy bile.

---

49. "*Une épouse sans époux, et une reine sans royaume*"—St. Amand.

And three days later:

Write me no more of your customary twaddle; three years now it has been going on, and every instant proves its falsehood! This is the last letter I shall ever write you in my life.

Louis at one time determined on war, and rather than surrender Amsterdam, to cut the dykes. The Emperor hears of this, summons his brother, and practically imprisons him until he countermands the defence of Amsterdam.

On July 1st Louis abdicated and fled to Toeplitz in Bohemia. Napoleon is terribly grieved at the conduct of his brother, who would never realise that the effective Continental blockade was Napoleon's last sheet-anchor to force peace upon England.

No. 6.

To die in a lake—*i.e.* the Lake of Bourget, shut in by the Dent du Chat, where a white squall had nearly capsized the sailing boat. Josephine had been on July 26th to visit the abbey Haute-Combe, place of sepulture of the Princes of Savoy, and the storm had overtaken her on the return voyage.

No. 8.

Paris, this Friday.—A very valuable note of M. Masson (*Josephine Repudiée*, 198) enables us to fix this letter at its correct date. He says: "It has to do with the exile of Madame de la T—— (*viz.*, the Princess Louis de la Trémoille), which takes place on September 28th, 1810, and this 28th September is also a Friday: there is also the question of Mile, de Mackau being made a baroness" (and this lady had not joined the Court of Josephine till May 1810); "lastly, the B—— mentioned therein can only be Barante, the Prefect, whose dismissal (from Geneva) almost coincides with this letter." It may be added that the La Tremoille family was one of the oldest in France, allied with the Condés, and consequently with the Bourbons. Barante's fault had been connivance at the letters and conduct of Madame de Staël.

No. 9.

The only suitable places . . . are either Milan or Navarre.—Milan had been her own suggestion conveyed by Eugène, but Napoleon, two months later, had told her she could spend the winter in France, and in spite of danger signals ("inspired by diplomacy rather than devotion"[50]) from Madame de Rémusat (in her fulsome and tedious

---

50. Aubenas,

"despatch" sent from Paris in September, and probably inspired by the Emperor himself) she manages to get to Navarre, and even to spend the first fortnight of November at Malmaison. Before leaving Switzerland Josephine refuses to risk an interview with Madame de Staël.

> In the first book she publishes she will not fail to report our conversation, and heaven knows how many things she will make me say that I have never even thought of.

No. 10.

In spite of the heading Josephine was at Malmaison on this day, and Napoleon writes Cambacérès:

> My cousin, the Empress Josephine not leaving for Navarre till Monday or Tuesday, I wish you to pay her a visit. You will let me know on your return how you find her.—(*Brotonne*, 721).

The real reason is to hasten her departure, and she gets to Navarre November 22nd (Thursday).

The Empress progresses satisfactorily.—Napoleon writes to this effect to her father, the Emperor of Austria, on the same day:

> The Empress is very well. . . . It is impossible that the wife for whom I am indebted to you should be more perfect. Moreover, I beg your Majesty to rest assured that she and I are equally attached to you.

Series O

No. 1.

The New Year.—On this occasion, instead of her usual gifts (*étrennes*) she organised a lottery of jewels, of which Madame Ducrest gives a full account. Needless to say, Josephine worked the oracle so that everyone got a suitable gift—including the old Bishop (see next note).

More women than men.—The Bishop of Evreux (Mgr. Bourlier) was the most welcome guest. He amused Josephine, and although eighty years of age, could play *trictrac* and talk well on any subject. Madame de Rémusat wrote her husband concerning him, "We understand each other very well, he and I."

Keep well.—At Navarre Josephine lost her headaches, and put on flesh.

No. 2.

There is a full account of the birth of the King of Rome in Napoleon's letter to the Emperor of Austria on March 20 (No. 17,496).

The letter of this date to Josephine is missing, but is referred to by D'Avrillon. It began, "My dear Josephine, I have a son. I am *au comble de bonheur.*"

Eugène.—Josephine much appreciated this allusion. "Is it possible," she said, "for anyone to be kinder than the Emperor, and more anxious to mitigate whatever might be painful for me at the present moment, if I loved him less sincerely? This association of my son with his own is well worthy of him who, when he likes, is the most fascinating of all men." She gave a costly ring to the page who brought the letter.

On the previous day Eugène had arrived at Navarre,—sent by the Emperor.

> You are going to see your mother, Eugène; tell her I am sure that she will rejoice more than any one at my happiness. I should have already written to her if I had not been absorbed by the pleasure of watching my boy. The moments I snatch from his side are only for matters of urgent necessity. This event, I shall acquit myself of the most pleasant of them all by writing to Josephine.

No. 4.

Written in November 1811.

As fat as a good Normandy farmeress.—Madame d'Abrantès, who saw her about this time, writes:

> I observed that Josephine had grown very stout[51] since the time of my departure for Spain. This change was at once for the better and the worse. It imparted a more youthful appearance to her face; but her slender and elegant figure, which had been one of her principal attractions, had entirely disappeared. She had now decided *embonpoint,* and her figure had assumed that matronly air which we find in the statues of Agrippina, Cornelia, &c. Still, however, she looked uncommonly well, and she wore a dress which became her admirably. Her judicious taste in these matters contributed to make her appear young much longer than she otherwise would. The best proof of the admirable taste of Josephine is the marked absence of elegance shown by Marie Louise, though both Empresses employed the same milliners and dressmakers, and Marie Louise had a large sum allotted for the expenses of her toilet.

51. Mlle. d'Avrillon says that during the Swiss voyage Josephine found it desirable, for the first time, to "wear whalebone in her corsets,"

St. Amand says that 1811 was for Josephine a happy year, compared to those which followed.

Series P

No. 1.

Written from Königsberg (M. Masson, in *Josephine Repudiée*, says Dantzig; but on June 11th Napoleon writes to Eugène, "I shall be at Königsberg tomorrow," where his correspondence is dated from henceforward). A day or two later he writes the King of Rome's governess that he trusts to hear soon that the fifteen months old child has cut his first four teeth.

No. 2.

Gumbinnen, June 20th.—From this place and on this date goes forth the first bulletin of the *Grande Armée*. It gives a *résumé* of the causes of the war, dating from the end of 1810, when English influence again gained ascendency.

On July 29th he writes Hortense from Witepsk to congratulate her on her eldest son's recovery from an illness. A week later he writes his librarian for some amusing novels—new ones for choice, or old ones that he has not read—or good memoirs.

Josephine meanwhile has permission to go to Italy. Owing to her grandson's illness she defers starting till July 16th. Through frightful weather she reaches Milan *via* Geneva on July 28th, and has a splendid reception. On the 29th she writes to Hortense: "I have found the three letters from Eugène, the last one dated the 13th; his health is excellent. He still pursues the Russians, without being able to overtake them. It is generally hoped the campaign may be a short one. May that hope be realised! "Two days later she announces the birth of Eugène's daughter Amelia, afterwards Empress of Brazil.

Towards the end of August Josephine goes to Aix and meets the Queen of Spain with her sister Desirée Bernadotte, the former "kind and amiable as usual," the latter "very gracious to me"—rather a new experience. From Aix she goes to Prégny-la-Tour, on the Lake of Geneva, and shocks the good people in various ways, says M. Masson, especially by innuendoes against Napoleon; and he adds, "if one traces back to their source the worst calumnies against the morals of the Emperor, it is Josephine that one encounters there." She gets to Malmaison October 24th. Soon after his return from Moscow Napoleon pays her a visit, and about this time she begins to see the King of Rome, whose mother has always thought more of her daily music and drawing lessons than of whether she was making her son happy or not,

1812 closed in gloom, but 1813 was in itself terribly ominous to so superstitious a woman as Josephine. Thirteen is always unlucky, and moreover the numbers of 1813 add up to 13; also the doom-dealing year began on a Friday. Everyone felt the hour approaching. As Napoleon said at St. Helena:

> The star grew pale; I felt the reins slipping from my hand, and I could do no more. A thunderbolt could alone have saved us, and every day, by some new fatality or other, our chances diminished. Sinister designs began to creep in among us; fatigue and discouragement had won over the majority; my lieutenants became lax, clumsy, careless, and consequently unfortunate; they were no longer the men of the commencement of the Revolution, nor even of the time of my good fortune. The chief generals were sick of the war; I had gorged them too much with my high esteem, with too many honours and too much wealth. They had drunk from the cup of pleasure, and wished to enjoy peace at any price. *The sacred fire was quenched.*

Up to August Fortune had smiled again upon her favourite. With conscripts for infantry and without cavalry he had won Lutzen, Bautzen, and Dresden; and even so late as September Byron was writing that "bar epilepsy and the elements he would back Napoleon against the field." But treachery and incompetence had undermined the Empire, and Leipsic (that battle of giants, where 110,000 soldiers were killed and wounded) made final success hopeless. In 1814 his brothers Lucien and Louis rallied to him, and Hortense was for the only time proud of her husband. She thinks if he had shown less suspicion and she less pride they might have been happy after all. "My husband is a good Frenchman ... he is an honest man."

Meanwhile, Talleyrand is watching to guide the *coup de grâce*. Napoleon makes a dash for Lorraine to gather his garrisons and cut off the enemy's supplies. The Allies hesitate and are about to follow him, as per the rules of war. Talleyrand, the only man who could ever divine Napoleon, sends them the message, "You can do everything, and you dare nothing; dare therefore *once!*" Hortense is the only *man* left in Paris, and in vain she tries to keep Marie Louise, whose presence would have stimulated the Parisians to hold the Allies at bay. It is in vain. Unlike Prussia or Austria who fought for months, or Spain who fought for years, after their capitals were taken:

Like Nineveh, Carthage, Babylon and Rome,
France yields to the conqueror, vanquished at home.

After Marmont's betrayal Napoleon attempts suicide, and when he believes death imminent sends a last message to Josephine by Caulaincourt, "You will tell Josephine that my thoughts were of her before life departed."

It was on Monday, May 23rd, that Josephine's illness commenced, after receiving at dinner the King of Prussia and his sons (one afterwards Wilhelm der Greise, first Emperor of Germany). Whether the sore throat which killed her was a quinsy or diphtheria[52] is difficult to prove, but the latter seems the more probable. Corvisart, who was himself ill and unable to attend, told Napoleon that she died of grief and worry. Before leaving for the Waterloo campaign Napoleon visited Malmaison, and there, as Lord Rosebery reminds us, allowed his only oblique reproach to Marie Louise to escape him: "Poor Josephine. Her death, of which the news took me by surprise at Elba, was one of the most acute griefs of that fatal year, 1814. She had her failings, of course; *but she, at any rate, would never have abandoned me*"

---

52. The same question may be asked respecting the death of Montaigne.

Appendix

(1)

A Reputed Poem by Napoleon I.

Le Chien, Le Lapin, et Le Chasseur.
Fable.—Composée a l'âge de 13 ans, par Napoleon I.
César, chien d'arrât renommé,
Mais trop enflé de son mérite,
Tennait arrêté dans son gîte
Un malheureux lapin de peur inanime.
"Rends-toi! "lui cria-t-il, d'une voix de tonerre
Qui fit au loin trembler les peuplades des bois.
"Je suis César, connu par ses exploits,
Et dont le nom remplit toute la terre."
A ce grand nom, Jeannot Lapin,
Recommandant a Dieu son âme pénitente,
Demande d'une voix tremblante:
"Trés-sérénissime mâtin,
Si je me rends quel sera mon destin?"
"Tu mourras." "Je mourrai!" dit la bête innocente.
"Et si je fuis?" "Ton trépas est certain."
"Quoi!" reprit l'animal qui se nourrit de thym,
"Des deux côtés je dois perdre la vie!
Que votre auguste seigneurie
Veuille me pardonner, puisqu'il me faut mourir,
Si j'ose tenter de m'enfuir."
Il dit, et fuit en héros de garenne.
Caton 1'aurait blamé; je dis qu'il n'eut pas tort.
Car le chasseur le voit à peine

Qu'il l'ajuste, le tire—et le chien tombe mort
Que dirait de ceci notre bon La Fontaine?
Aide-toi, le ciel t'aidera.
J'approuve fort cette méthode-là.

(2)
GENEALOGY OF THE BONAPARTE FAMILY

Many more or less fictitious genealogies of the Bonapartes have been published, some going back to mythical times. The first reliable record, however, seems to be that of a certain Bonaparte of Sarzana, in Northern Italy, an imperial notary, who was living towards the end of the thirteenth century, and from whom both the Corsican and the Trevisan or Florentine Bonapartes claim their origin. From him in direct line was descended Francois de Sarzana, who was sent to Corsica in 1509 to fight for the Republic of Genoa. His son Gabriel, having sold his patrimony in Italy, settled in Ajaccio, where he bore the honourable title of Messire, and where, being left a widower, he assumed the tonsure and died Canon of the cathedral.

From him an unbroken line of Bonapartes, all of whom in turn were elected to the dignity of Elder of Ajaccio, brings us to Charles Bonaparte Napoleon, father of the Emperor.

(3)
REPUTED LETTERS OF NAPOLEON TO JOSEPHINE. TAKEN
FROM THE *MEMOIRS* OF MADAME DUCREST.

The author asked the advice of Monsieur Frédéric Masson about these Letters, to which he at once received the courteous reply, "*Il faut absolument rejeter les Lettres publiées par Regnault Varin[1] et reproduites par Georgette Ducrest; pas une n'est authentique.*" No one who has read much of Napoleon's correspondence can in fact believe for a moment in their authenticity. They are interesting, however, as showing the sort of stuff which went to form our grandfathers' fallacies about the relations of Napoleon and Josephine. Madame Ducrest occasionally played and sang for Josephine after the divorce. Her father was a nephew of Madame de Genlis. Madame Ducrest married a musical composer, M. Bochsa, the then celebrated author of *Dansomanie* and *Noces de Gamache*.

---

1. *Memoires et Correspondance de l'Imperatrice Joséphine, par J. B. J. Innocert Philadelphe Regnault Varin*. Paris, 1820, 8°. This book is not in the British Museum Catalogue.

He afterwards deserted her, and her voice having completely failed, she was compelled to write her *Memoirs* to earn sustenance thereby. Of these *Memoirs* M. Masson has said [2] that:

in the midst of apocryphal documents, uncontroverted anecdotes, impossible situations, are yet to be found some firsthand personal observations.

No. 1.—1796

My first laurel, my love, must be for my country; my second shall be for you. While beating Alvinzi I thought of France; when I had defeated him I thought of you. Your son will present to you a standard which he received from Colonel Morbach, whom he made prisoner with his own hands. Our Eugène, you see, is worthy of his father; and I trust you do not think me an unworthy successor of the great and unfortunate general, under whom I should have been proud to learn to conquer. I embrace you.   Bonaparte.

No. 2.—1804.

To General Bonaparte.

I have read over your letter, my dear, perhaps for the tenth time, and I must confess that the astonishment it caused me has given way only to feelings of regret and alarm. You wish to raise up the throne of France, and that, not for the purpose of seating upon it those whom the Revolution overthrew, but to place yourself upon it. You say, how enterprising, how grand and, above all, useful is this design; but I should say, how many obstacles oppose its execution, what sacrifices will its accomplishment demand, and when realised, how incalculable will be its results? But let us suppose that your object were already attained, would you stop at the foundation of the new empire? That new creation, being opposed by neighbouring states, would stir up war with them and perhaps entail their ruin. Their neighbours, in their turn, will not behold it without alarm or without endeavouring to gratify their revenge by checking it. And at home, how much envy and dissatisfaction will arise; how many plots must be put down, how many conspiracies punished! Kings will despise you as an upstart, subjects will hate you as an usurper, and your equals will denounce you as a tyrant.

2. *Josephine Impératrice et Reine*, Paris, 1899.

None will understand the necessity of your elevation; all will attribute it to ambition or pride. You will not want for slaves to crouch beneath your authority until, seconded by some more formidable power, they rise up to oppose you; happy will it be if poison or the poignard! ... But how can a wife, a friend dwell on these dreadful anticipations!

This brings my thoughts back to myself, about whom I should care but little were my personal interests alone concerned. But will not the throne inspire you with the wish to contract new alliances? Will you not seek to support your power by new family connections? Alas! whatever those connections may be, will they compensate for those which were first knit by corresponding fitness, and which affection promised to perpetuate? My thoughts linger on the picture which fear—may I say love, traces in the future. Your ambitious project has excited my alarm; console me by the assurance of your moderation.

No. 3.—December 1809.

To the Emperor.

My forebodings are realised! You have just pronounced the word which separates us forever; the rest is nothing more than mere formality. Such, then, is the result, I shall not say of so many sacrifices (they were light to me, since they had you for their object), but of an unbounded friendship on my part and of the most solemn oaths on yours! It would be a consolation for me if the state which you allege as your motive were to repay my sacrifice by justifying your conduct! But that public consideration which you urge as the ground for deserting me is a mere pretence on your part. Your mistaken ambition has ever been, and will continue to be, the guide of all your actions, a guide which has led you to conquests and to the assumption of a crown, and is now driving you on to disasters and to the brink of a precipice.

You speak of the necessity of contracting an alliance, of giving an heir to your empire, of founding a dynasty! But with whom are you about to form an alliance? with the natural enemy of France, that artful house of Austria, whose detestation of our country has its rise in its innate feelings, in its system, in the laws of necessity. Do you believe that this hatred, of which she has given us such abundant proof, more particularly for the last fifty years, has not been transferred by her from the kingdom of France to the French empire? That the children of Maria Theresa, that skilful sovereign, who purchased from Madame de Pompadour the fatal treaty of 1756, which you never mention without shuddering; do you imagine, I repeat, that her posterity, when inheriting her power, has not also inherited her spirit? I am merely repeating what you have so often said to me; but at that time your ambition was satisfied with humbling a power which you now find it convenient to restore to its former rank. Believe me, as long as you shall exercise a sway over Europe, that power will be submissive to you; but beware of reverses of fortune.

As to the necessity of an heir, I must speak out, at the risk of appearing in the character of a mother prejudiced in favour of her son; ought I, in fact, to be silent when I consider the interests of one who is my only delight, and upon whom alone you had built all your hopes? That adoption of the 12th of January 1806 was then another political falsehood! Nevertheless the talents, the virtues of my Eugène are no illusion. How often have you not spoken in his praise? I may say more; you thought it right to reward him by the gift of a throne, and have repeatedly said that he was deserving of greater favours. Well, then! France has frequently re-echoed these praises; but you are now indifferent to the wishes of France.

I say nothing to you at present of the person who is destined to succeed me, and you do not expect that I should make any allusion to this subject. You might suspect the feelings which dictated my language; nevertheless, you can never doubt of the sincerity of my wishes for your happiness; may it at least afford me some consolation for my sufferings. Great indeed will be that happiness if it should ever bear any proportion to them!

No. 4.
Part of a Letter Said to be Dated Brienne, 1814.

... On revisiting this spot, where I passed my youthful days, and contrasting the peaceful condition I then enjoyed with the state of terror and agitation to which my mind is now a prey, often have I addressed myself in these words: 'I have sought death in numberless engagements; I can no longer dread its approach; I should now hail it as a boon ... nevertheless, I could still wish to see Josephine once more!

No. 5.
To the Empress Josephine, at Malmaison.

Fontainebleau, 16th April 1814.

My dear Josephine,—I wrote to you on the 8th instant (it was on a Friday). You have perhaps not received my letter; fighting was still going on; it is possible that it may have been stopped on its way. The communications must now be re-established. My determination is taken; I have no doubt of this note coming to your hands.

I do not repeat what I have already told you. I then complained of my situation; I now rejoice at it. My mind and attention are relieved from an enormous weight; my downfall is great, but it is at least said to be productive of good.

In my retreat I intend to substitute the pen for the sword. The history of my reign will gratify the cravings of curiosity. Hitherto, I have only been seen in profile; I will now show myself in full to the world. What facts have I not to disclose! how many men are incorrectly estimated! I have heaped favours upon a countless number of wretches; what have they latterly done for me?

They have all betrayed me, one and all, save and except the excellent Eugène, so worthy of you and of me. May he ever enjoy happiness under a sovereign fully competent to appreciate the feelings of nature and of honour!

Adieu, my dear Josephine; follow my example and be resigned. Never dismiss from your recollection one who has never forgotten, and never will forget you! Farewell, Josephine.

Napoleon.

P. S.—I expect to hear from you when I shall have reached the island of Elba. I am far from being in good health.

LEONAUR

ALSO FROM LEONAUR
AVAILABLE IN SOFTCOVER OR HARDCOVER WITH DUST JACKET

THE FALL OF THE MOGHUL EMPIRE OF HINDUSTAN *by H. G. Keene*—By the beginning of the nineteenth century, as British and Indian armies under Lake and Wellesley dominated the scene, a little over half a century of conflict brought the Moghul Empire to its knees.

LADY SALE'S AFGHANISTAN *by Florentia Sale*—An Indomitable Victorian Lady's Account of the Retreat from Kabul During the First Afghan War.

THE CAMPAIGN OF MAGENTA AND SOLFERINO 1859 *by Harold Carmichael Wylly*—The Decisive Conflict for the Unification of Italy.

FRENCH'S CAVALRY CAMPAIGN *by J. G. Maydon*—A Special Correspondent's View of British Army Mounted Troops During the Boer War.

CAVALRY AT WATERLOO *by Sir Evelyn Wood*—British Mounted Troops During the Campaign of 1815.

THE SUBALTERN *by George Robert Gleig*—The Experiences of an Officer of the 85th Light Infantry During the Peninsular War.

NAPOLEON AT BAY, 1814 *by F. Loraine Petre*—The Campaigns to the Fall of the First Empire.

NAPOLEON AND THE CAMPAIGN OF 1806 *by Colonel Vachée*—The Napoleonic Method of Organisation and Command to the Battles of Jena & Auerstädt.

THE COMPLETE ADVENTURES IN THE CONNAUGHT RANGERS *by William Grattan*—The 88th Regiment during the Napoleonic Wars by a Serving Officer.

BUGLER AND OFFICER OF THE RIFLES *by William Green & Harry Smith*—With the 95th (Rifles) during the Peninsular & Waterloo Campaigns of the Napoleonic Wars.

NAPOLEONIC WAR STORIES *by Sir Arthur Quiller-Couch*—Tales of soldiers, spies, battles & sieges from the Peninsular & Waterloo campaingns.

CAPTAIN OF THE 95TH (RIFLES) *by Jonathan Leach*—An officer of Wellington's sharpshooters during the Peninsular, South of France and Waterloo campaigns of the Napoleonic wars.

RIFLEMAN COSTELLO *by Edward Costello*—The adventures of a soldier of the 95th (Rifles) in the Peninsular & Waterloo Campaigns of the Napoleonic wars.

LEONAUR

ALSO FROM LEONAUR
AVAILABLE IN SOFTCOVER OR HARDCOVER WITH DUST JACKET

OFFICERS & GENTLEMEN *by Peter Hawker & William Graham*—Two Accounts of British Officers During the Peninsula War: Officer of Light Dragoons by Peter Hawker & Campaign in Portugal and Spain by William Graham .

THE WALCHEREN EXPEDITION *by Anonymous*—The Experiences of a British Officer of the 81st Regt. During the Campaign in the Low Countries of 1809.

LADIES OF WATERLOO *by Charlotte A. Eaton, Magdalene de Lancey & Juana Smith*—The Experiences of Three Women During the Campaign of 1815: Waterloo Days by Charlotte A. Eaton, A Week at Waterloo by Magdalene de Lancey & Juana's Story by Juana Smith.

JOURNAL OF AN OFFICER IN THE KING'S GERMAN LEGION *by John Frederick Hering*—Recollections of Campaigning During the Napoleonic Wars.

JOURNAL OF AN ARMY SURGEON IN THE PENINSULAR WAR *by Charles Boutflower*—The Recollections of a British Army Medical Man on Campaign During the Napoleonic Wars.

ON CAMPAIGN WITH MOORE AND WELLINGTON *by Anthony Hamilton*—The Experiences of a Soldier of the 43rd Regiment During the Peninsular War.

THE ROAD TO AUSTERLITZ *by R. G. Burton*—Napoleon's Campaign of 1805.

SOLDIERS OF NAPOLEON *by A. J. Doisy De Villargennes & Arthur Chuquet*—The Experiences of the Men of the French First Empire: Under the Eagles by A. J. Doisy De Villargennes & Voices of 1812 by Arthur Chuquet .

INVASION OF FRANCE, 1814 *by F. W. O. Maycock*—The Final Battles of the Napoleonic First Empire.

LEIPZIG—A CONFLICT OF TITANS *by Frederic Shoberl*—A Personal Experience of the 'Battle of the Nations' During the Napoleonic Wars, October 14th-19th, 1813.

SLASHERS *by Charles Cadell*—The Campaigns of the 28th Regiment of Foot During the Napoleonic Wars by a Serving Officer.

BATTLE IMPERIAL *by Charles William Vane*—The Campaigns in Germany & France for the Defeat of Napoleon 1813-1814.

SWIFT & BOLD *by Gibbes Rigaud*—The 60th Rifles During the Peninsula War.

LEONAUR

ALSO FROM LEONAUR
AVAILABLE IN SOFTCOVER OR HARDCOVER WITH DUST JACKET

THE RELUCTANT REBEL *by William G. Stevenson*—A young Kentuckian's experiences in the Confederate Infantry & Cavalry during the American Civil War..

BOOTS AND SADDLES *by Elizabeth B. Custer*—The experiences of General Custer's Wife on the Western Plains.

FANNIE BEERS' CIVIL WAR *by Fannie A. Beers*—A Confederate Lady's Experiences of Nursing During the Campaigns & Battles of the American Civil War.

LADY SALE'S AFGHANISTAN *by Florentia Sale*—An Indomitable Victorian Lady's Account of the Retreat from Kabul During the First Afghan War.

THE TWO WARS OF MRS DUBERLY *by Frances Isabella Duberly*—An Intrepid Victorian Lady's Experience of the Crimea and Indian Mutiny.

THE REBELLIOUS DUCHESS *by Paul F. S. Dermoncourt*—The Adventures of the Duchess of Berri and Her Attempt to Overthrow French Monarchy.

LADIES OF WATERLOO *by Charlotte A. Eaton, Magdalene de Lancey & Juana Smith*—The Experiences of Three Women During the Campaign of 1815: Waterloo Days by Charlotte A. Eaton, A Week at Waterloo by Magdalene de Lancey & Juana's Story by Juana Smith.

TWO YEARS BEFORE THE MAST *by Richard Henry Dana. Jr.*—The account of one young man's experiences serving on board a sailing brig—the Penelope—bound for California, between the years1834-36.

A SAILOR OF KING GEORGE *by Frederick Hoffman*—From Midshipman to Captain—Recollections of War at Sea in the Napoleonic Age 1793-1815.

LORDS OF THE SEA *by A. T. Mahan*—Great Captains of the Royal Navy During the Age of Sail.

COGGESHALL'S VOYAGES: VOLUME 1 *by George Coggeshall*—The Recollections of an American Schooner Captain.

COGGESHALL'S VOYAGES: VOLUME 2 *by George Coggeshall*—The Recollections of an American Schooner Captain.

TWILIGHT OF EMPIRE *by Sir Thomas Ussher & Sir George Cockburn*—Two accounts of Napoleon's Journeys in Exile to Elba and St. Helena: Narrative of Events by Sir Thomas Ussher & Napoleon's Last Voyage: Extract of a diary by Sir George Cockburn.